# AWAKENING:
## THE RISE
## OF WESTERN
## CIVILIZATION

## Part One of the
## *March of the Titans*
## Quadrilogy

## By Arthur Kemp

Ostara Publications

Awakening: The Emergence of Western Civilization

Part One of the *March of the Titans* Quadrilogy

Previously published as chapters 1 to 19 of
March of the Titans: A History of the White Race

Revised, expanded and updated
January 2009

ISBN 978-0-557-05049-9

This book was designed and produced by

Ostara Publications
P.O. Box 671
Burlington
Iowa, 52601-0671
United States of America

http://www.white-history.com
Email: ostara@white-history.com

Cover images: Main picture: Bust of Queen Nefertiti, 1325 BC. Inset images, from top to bottom: Lapus Lazuli blue eyed statue, Tell Asmos, Sumeria, circa 3000 BC; Persian soldier, Susa, circa 500 BC; Detail from mosaic at Pella, northern Greece, circa 380 BC; "Profile of a Woman" Etruscan, fourth century BC; Silver coin with Hannibal's face, struck at Carthage, circa 220 BC; Augustus Octavian, Roman emperor circa 10 AD.

# CONTENTS

# Foreword to the 2009 Edition

When this manuscript was completed in its first draft some ten years ago, I had no idea that a decade later I would see it being republished for the eighth time, and still going strong. This does not include the internet version, which has been online since 1999 as well.

The idea of breaking this book up into four volumes for its tenth anniversary is to make it more portable. Complaints about the previous editions were that it was so bulky that either reading it, or just carrying it around, was impractical. I hope that this new edition solves those issues.

The manuscript has also been considerably revised, edited, and expanded. I have acquired a number of new photographs, and either pared away or replaced others. The sequential order of the chapters has remained the same, with one exception: the prologue now combines the basic explanation of race as a taxonomic concept and discusses the rise and fall of civilizations, as opposed to previous editions which saw it buried in chapter nine.

Finally, I must thank my wife Jeannine from the bottom of my heart for all her work, encouragement, and whose idea it was to create the four volume set in the first place. She is also my editor-in-chief and has worked tirelessly in this regard. I cannot think what I would have done without her.

Arthur Kemp,
22 January 2009, Chester, UK

# Foreword to the 1999 edition

The idea for writing this book came from a perusal of the history section of the Jagger Library at the University of Cape Town, South Africa, in 1983. While undertaking some unrelated research, I chanced upon a book dealing with the history of the Chinese people.

Intrigued, I investigated further in that section of the library. I found rows of books dealing with the history of the Japanese, the black race, the Incas, Aztecs, the Australian Aborigines, the Arabs, the Native Americans, the Polynesians—in fact there was a history of every people and every race on earth—except, much to my surprise, the white race.

This lack of a history of the white people of the world has persisted to this day: and it is to correct this imbalance that this book has been written. As it is a history of a defined race, not of any particular country, its narrative follows several continents and centuries, not limiting itself to any one geographical region.

I have always felt that the point of studying history is not the memorizing of some dates and facts, but rather the search for and discovery of the forces causing the results we see before our eyes as historical events.

History lost its value through the efforts of academics producing lists of meaningless dates and names, expecting everyone else to be as interested in their lists as they are.

The proper study of history is in reality a tremendously exciting field of endeavour—the exploits and tribulations detailed in this book will hopefully convince sceptics of this!

More importantly, history does indeed contain lessons—sobering ones, with massive implications. As this book will show, it raises issues which confronted past civilizations and which confront modern society—how we answer them will determine if our society will survive or vanish like those of old.

Arthur Kemp
14 September 1998, Oxford, UK

# The March of the Titans Quadrilogy:

**Volume One:** *Awakening: The Rise of Western Civilization*

From Stonehenge to Sulla, this first volume deals with the emergence of Western Civilization from the Late Paleolithic Era to the fall of the Western Roman Empire. It includes Sumeria, Egypt, classical Greece and Rome, the First Great Race War of Attila the Hun.

**Volume Two:** *Europa: The Making of the Nation States*

Starting out with the end of the Eastern Roman Empire, this volume deals with the creation of each individual nation on the European Continent. It includes the Viking era and five Great Race Wars: the Crusades, the Buglar and Avar invasions, Genghis Khan, and the Ottoman holocaust.

**Volume Three:** *Manifest Destiny: European Expansion across the Globe*

Starting with the impact of the Dark Ages, the Renaissance, and the Reformation, this volume deals with the colonization of the world by Europe. Includes the founding of America, and the two Great Race Wars fought there.

**Volume Four:** *Twilight: The Impending Death of the West*

Starting with the western origin of the Industrial Revolution, this volume deals with the fratricidal World Wars I and II, the rise and fall of Communism, and the mass Third World immigration wave which now threatens to engulf and finally wipe out Western Civilization.

All available from www.white-history.com

## *Some Important Facts*

**Crucial to the understanding of the theme of this book and its related volumes is an understanding of the concepts of race, ethnicity, and culture.**

### *Race, Ethnicity, and Culture*

A race is defined as a group of individuals sharing common genetic attributes which determine that group's physical appearance and, more controversially, their cognitive abilities. Ethnicity is defined as the creation of groups by individuals (most often within racial groups but also possible across racial divides) of certain common traditions, languages, art forms, attitudes, and other means of expression.

A culture is the name given to the physical manifestations created by ethnic groups—the actual language, art forms, religion, social order, and achievements of a particular ethnic group. In practical terms then, it is possible to talk of a white race; of a Scottish ethnicity, and a Scottish culture. The last two—ethnicity and culture—are directly dependent upon each other, and flow from each other in a symbiotic relationship. This book deals primarily with white racial history, and flowing from that, white ethnic groups and cultures.

### *The White Race—Three Subgroups*

What exactly is meant by the white race? Essentially there are three main subgroups with two further divisions of note. The three major subgroups are known to academics as Nordic, Alpine, and Mediterranean.

Although these names have come about mainly as a result of the geographic areas these subgroups have been associated with in the Christian era (Nordics in northern Europe, Alpines in central Europe and Mediterraneans in southern Europe), it is incorrect to believe that these groups always occupied these regions.

The three main subgroups have played a role in events in almost every geographical region where the white race as a group has appeared. Of these three original groups, only two are existent in any large number today: the Nordics and the Alpines. The original Mediterraneans of ancient history are not to be confused with those people loosely termed "Mediterranean" today. The original white Mediterranean component has been largely dissipated into two distinct groups: those who have absorbed Alpine or Nordic white subracial elements; and those who have absorbed North African or other nonwhite racial elements.

To illustrate the concept of these three main subgroups: although there is a broadly termed "black race" in existence, there are major subgroups amongst that racial group. The Congo basin Pygmy and the ultra tall Masai tribesmen of Kenya are two good examples of subgroups within the black racial group.

A subgroup, therefore, is a branch of a particular race which exhibits slightly different physical characteristics but still shares enough of a common genetic inheritance with other subgroups to be included in a broad racial category. This is known as the concept of genetic commonality, and is the basis of all racial categories.

### Nordic—Tall, Slim, Light Eyes, and Hair

The Nordic racial subgroup, which is still largely in existence today, is characterized by light colored hair and eyes, a tall slim build, and a distinctive "long" (that is, thin and extended) skull shape.

### Alpine—'Solid' Body, Round Head, Brown Eyes

The Alpine racial subgroup, which also still exists in a large measure today, is characterized by brown hair and eyes, a short, more "solid" body build and a distinctive "round" (that is, almost, but not quite, circular) skull shape.

### Mediterranean—Mixture of Body Types

The original Mediterranean racial subgroup no longer exists today. It was the first of the three white racial subgroups to disappear from the earth, submerged into the gene pools of surrounding races.

The Mediterranean subgroup was predominantly (but not totally) characterized by dark hair and eye color, slim (Nordic), or solid (Alpine) build and either long or round skull shapes. It is worth stating again, as it is of great significance in more ways than one, that there are very few of these original Mediterranean racial types left in the world today. They were known as the "Old Europeans" and inhabited large parts of Europe, the Middle East, and Egypt at the dawn of history. These

## THE WHITE RACE: THE THREE MAIN SUBGROUPS

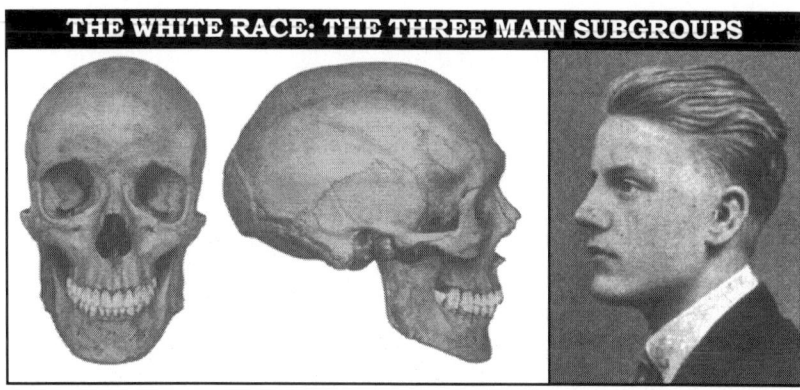

*Nordic—The skull of a member of the Nordic white subrace, viewed from the front and the side. The "long" nature of the facial structure is clearly visible. Alongside is a classic Nordic male from Sweden.*

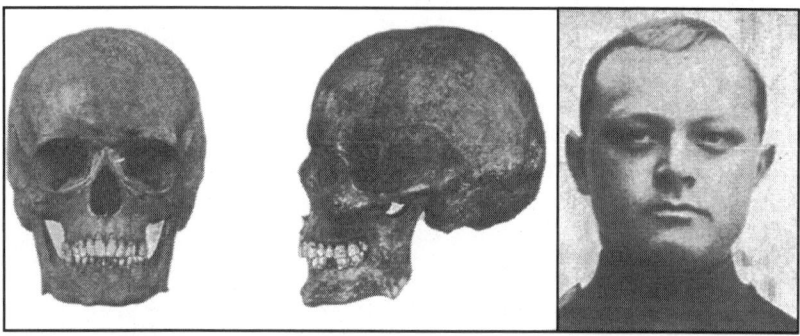

*Alpine—The skull of a member of the Alpine white subrace, viewed from the front and the side. The "shorter" facial structure is apparent. Alongside is a classic Alpine male from southern Germany.*

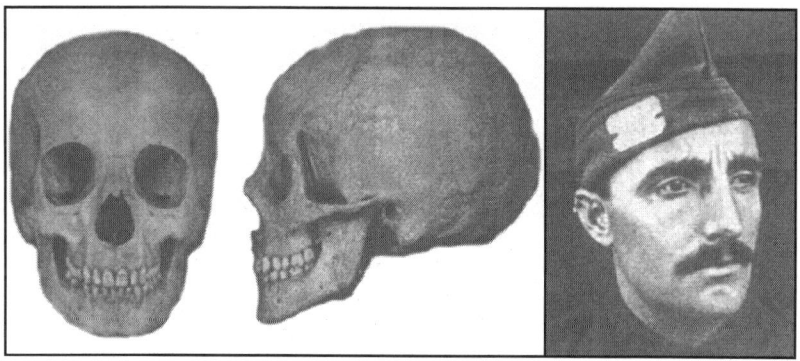

*Mediterranean—A skull of a member of the Mediterranean white subrace, viewed from the front and side. Alongside, a WWI Welsh soldier—as close an example of a Mediterranean as can be found in modern times.*

Mediterranean types bear almost no resemblance to the present day inhabitants of the Mediterranean basin.

The original Old Europeans have been absorbed almost completely into either the Nordic/Alpine stock in Europe, or the African/Semitic/Asian stock of North Africa, and the Middle East.

There are two places in Europe where occasional glimpses of this original Mediterranean racial subgroup can still be seen: the Celtic fringes of Britain (most notably in Wales and Devonshire) and in the Basque territory of Spain. In these regions there exists a short, dark strain—remnants of the original inhabitants of Europe.

Pure examples of this Mediterranean type are rare, as they have for the largest degree had some Nordic or Alpine admixture over the years. Unfortunately there has also been some admixture from North Africa. Nonetheless, it is still possible today to talk of "Mediterranean" whites even though they do not identically represent those of antiquity.

### Other Subgroups—Dinarics and East Baltics

Two other white racial subgroups exist (Dinarics and East Baltics). These types differ slightly in skull shape and body dimensions from the three main groups outlined above, but they share a great number of physical characteristics such as hair and eye color.

As with the Alpines and Mediterraneans, there has been a great deal of mixing with the three main subgroups. They are found in large numbers in present day Eastern Europe. A very small percentage of these two subgroups also display the physical characteristics resulting from mixing with the waves of Asiatic invaders who penetrated Europe from the east during the course of history.

### Whites Defined by Genetic Commonality

For the purposes of this book, an ethnic or cultural group is defined as part of the white race as long as it shares enough of a common genetic inheritance with the broader racial group. When an ethnic group loses this genetic commonality it is then formally excluded from the white racial category.

### Tracking Race

How is race tracked in civilization? How is it determined whether the populations of certain societies or civilizations belonged to

## USING DNA TO TRACK RACE IN HISTORY

*Research carried out by L.L. Cavalli-Sforza and two colleagues, P. Menozzi and A. Piazzia, in their work* The History and Geography of Human Genes *(1994), has revealed an astonishing 2,288 genetic point difference between whites and black Africans.*

*The research found that the English differ from the Danes, Germans, and French by a mere 21–25 points of genetic distance, whereas they differ from North American Indians by 947 points, from black Africans by 2,288 points, and from Mbuti Pygmies by 2,373 points.*

*Cavalli-Sforza also used Mitochondrial DNA (mtDNA—transferred through the maternal line) to divide the world up into seven distinct races, classifying whites as part of the "Caucasoid" group for his study.*

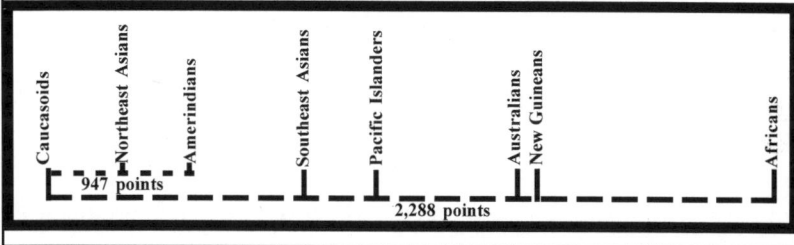

specific races? The answer to this is simple. Race in history is tracked in four ways: paleoserology, art forms, language, and the science of genetics. This last test has only come into its own in the last ten years of the twentieth century, but has proven to be a major aid in tracking racial history.

### Paleoserology Reveals Racial Types

Paleoserology is the study of skeletal remains. As different racial groups have different physical characteristics, it is a relatively simple matter to determine the racial makeup of the inhabitants of a particular region by studying the contents of grave sites. This skill is often used by modern police pathologists to identify the race of corpses. This science has proven equally useful in historical diggings where the examination of burial sites has created an understanding of the racial makeup of ancient peoples.

### Race Appears in Art Forms

Art forms (whether conventional pictures, illustrations on pottery, or even statues) also provide significant indicators of the racial makeup of contemporary inhabitants. The ancient civilizations in particular—of all racial group—reflected themselves in their art forms (often because

## CULTURAL ARTIFACTS REFLECT RACIAL TYPES

*Tracking race in history: race depicted in art forms. Early civilizations very often depicted images of their own racial types in their works of art, based on the reality that their own types were the most common (or only) human models with which they had to work. A comparison of (from left to right) Olmec art, 400 BC; African art, circa 1400 AD; Japanese art, 1000 AD; and Greek art, 340 BC, reflects this principle well. The study of art forms is a reliable indicator of the racial type of the communities in which the art works were created.*

 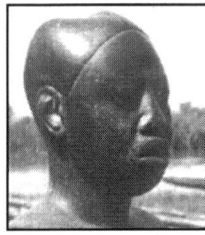 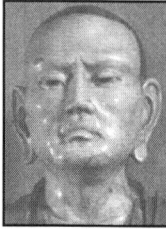 

their own racial types were the only human models from which they had to work). In this way, for example, early Chinese art depicted principally Chinese people; Incan and Aztec art depicted only Incan or Aztec people, and so on.

In all societies, original art forms which portrayed people closely followed contemporary physical appearances. This principle is well illustrated in the four art forms portrayed above.

### Genetics Reveals Racial Past

All human beings have three sorts of genes: mitochondrial DNA, which is inherited through the female line; Y-Chromosomes which are inherited through the male line, and autosomal DNA, which is inherited from both sexes. The study of genetics has served to confirm the accuracy of many historical accounts of racial movements, and is particularly useful in showing cause and effect in the rise and fall of civilizations, as demonstrated in this book.

### Language Reflects Racial Similarities

The study of language is another important clue to the dispersion of peoples. Commonalities in language forms leave clearly identifiable "fingerprints" in cultures. Similar words, phrases, or language forms are a clear indication of a single origin for civilizations, due to the fact that the people in those civilizations would at some stage have had a common origin. In this way the route of a culture (and hence a people) can be traced by following a language.

## An Objective Defintion of Civilization

For the purposes of this book, civilization will be taken to mean the entire ambit of social/cultural manifestations which are characteristic to any particular nation or racial group. In this way the accusation of subjectivity can be avoided. Civilization, in the broadest sense of the word, includes all social manifestations, from social interactions to language, art forms, science, technology, customs, and culture.

It is therefore possible to talk of a Japanese civilization, an American Indian (Amerind) civilization, a Polynesian civilization, an Australian Aboriginal civilization, a black civilization and a white civilization, without being subjective about any of them.

## The Question Posed by Rise and Fall

When reviewing the historical development of all nations, quite often mention is made of a "rise and fall" of a particular civilization. This poses a major question: Why have some civilizations lasted a thousand years or more, while others rise and collapse within a few hundred? Why is it, for example, that nations such as Japan, Sweden, and England—all nations with limited natural resources—could have progressive active cultures for more than one thousand years; whereas mighty civilizations such as Classical Rome, Greece, or Persia, amongst others, collapse after only a few centuries?

Politically correct historians blame the rise and fall of the great nations of the past on politics, economics, morals, lawlessness, debt, environment, and a host of other superficial reasons.

However, Japan, England, and Sweden have gone through similar crises scores of times, without those countries falling into decay. It is obvious that there must be some other factor at work—something much more fundamental than just variations in politics, morals, lawlessness, or any of the other hundreds

| English | German |
|---------|--------|
| brother | bruder |
| mother | mutter |
| father | vater |

| Latin | Greek |
|-------|-------|
| frater | bhrater |
| mater | meter |
| pater | pater |

| Old Persian | Sanskrit |
|-------------|----------|
| brater | bhrater |
| matar | matar |
| pitar | pitar |

**Russian/Ukrainian (non-Cyrillic spelling.)**
Brat (pronounces as "Braht")
Mater (or just Maht with soft "t")
Batya (pronounces as "Bahtya")

7

of reasons that historians have manufactured in their attempts to explain the collapse of civilizations.

### Each Society Unique to Each People

Herein lies the key to understanding the rise and fall of all civilizations. In any given territory, the people making up the society in that territory create a culture which is unique to themselves.

A society or civilization is only a reflection of the population of that particular territory. For example, the Chinese civilization is a product of the Chinese people, and is a reflection of the makeup of the population living in China. The Chinese civilization is unique to the Chinese people; they made it and it reflects their values and norms.

As the Chinese people made the Chinese civilization, it logically follows that the Chinese culture would disappear if the Chinese people were to disappear. Presently the overwhelming majority of Chinese people live in China, creating the Chinese civilization in that land. If, however, Australian Aborigines had to immigrate into China in their millions, and the Chinese population had to dramatically reduce in number, then in a few years the character of Chinese civilization would change—to reflect the new inhabitants of that territory.

In other words, the society or civilization of that territory would then reflect the fact that the majority of inhabitants were now Aborigines rather than Chinese people. If China had to fill up with Aborigines, this would mean the end of Chinese civilization. Aborigines would create a new civilization which would reflect themselves, and not that of the Chinese people.

That this should happen is perfectly logical. It has nothing to do with which culture is more advanced, or any notions of superiority or inferiority. It is merely a reflection of the fact that a civilization is a product of the nature of the people making up the population in the territory.

### A Theoretical Example: No Chinese People Means No Chinese Civilization

To go back to the Chinese example: If all Chinese people on earth had to disappear tomorrow, then fairly obviously, Chinese civilization and culture would disappear with them. It is this startlingly obvious principle which determines the creation and dissolution of civilizations—once the people who create a certain society or civilization disappear, then that society or civilization will disappear with them. If the vanished population is replaced by different peoples, then a new society or culture is created which reflects the culture and civilization of the new inhabitants of that region.

## *A Practical Example: Arrival of Whites Changed American Civilization*

There are numerous examples of this process at work. One which will be familiar to all is the shift which occurred in North America. On that continent, the Amerind (American Indian) people lived for thousands of years, creating a civilization which dominated that continent. In other words, the civilization and culture which dominated North America reflected the fact that the Amerind people lived and formed the majority population there.

After 1500 AD that continent filled up with white immigrants from Europe. These white immigrants displaced the Amerinds by squeezing them out of possession of North America.

The great shift in North American civilization then occurred. Whereas the Amerind culture had dominated for thousands of years, within a couple hundred years the dominant civilization on that continent had become white European. This shift reflected the fact that the majority of inhabitants of North America were white Europeans—and the Amerind civilization, for all practical purposes, disappeared. The Amerind civilization in North America "fell" because the population of North America changed.

### *Racial Shift Paramount*

This effect—the displacement of peoples and the subsequent disappearance of their civilization—has direct implications in racial terms. The rise and fall of any particular civilization can be traced, not by the economics, politics, morals, etc., of a particular civilization, but rather by the actual racial presence of the people themselves.

If the society which has produced a particular civilization stays intact as a racially homogeneous unit, then that civilization remains active. If, however, the society within any particular given area changes its racial makeup—through invasion, immigration, or any decline in numbers—then the civilization which that society has produced will disappear with them, to be replaced by a new civilization reflecting the new inhabitants of that territory.

### *Disappearance of Whites Led to the Collapse of Their Civilizations*

Originally created by Proto-Nordics, Alpines, and Mediterraneans, and then influenced by waves of Indo-European invaders, the white civilizations in the Middle East all flourished, producing the wonders of the ancient world.

These regions were either invaded or otherwise occupied (through the use of laborers, immigration, or in rare cases, by conquest) by nonwhite nations of varying races. When the original white peoples who created those civilizations vanished or became an insignificant minority (through death and absorption into other races), their civilizations "fell" in exactly the same way that the Amerind civilization in North America "fell."

### *500 BC—First Turning Point*

It was around the year 500 BC that the first great turning point in white history was reached. This was the decline of the first great white civilizations in the Middle East and their subsequent replacement by nations and peoples of a substantially different racial makeup.

Up until this time the development of the white race's territorial expansion was such that they were a majority in Europe and all of Russia west of the Urals. They formed a significant component of the population of the Middle East and their rule extended into the Indus River Valley in Northern India.

### *India—Origin of the Caste System*

In India, for example, the Indo-Aryan population was diminished by four factors:
• A large nonwhite (Indian) immigration northward to do work offered by the society set up by the conquering Indo-Aryans;
• A high natural reproduction level amongst the nonwhite immigrants;
• The level of racial mixing amongst Aryans and the Indians, which, by creating a new mixed ethnic identity, also changed the racial makeup of the inhabitants of the region; and
• A decline in the birth rate amongst the Aryans.

In India, the invading Indo-Aryans established a strict segregation system to keep themselves separate from the local dark skinned native population. This system was so strict that it has lasted to this day and has become known as the caste system.

## EGYPT: DIFFERENT PEOPLE, DIFFERENT CIVILIZATION

### How a Changing Population Changes the Nature of a Civilization.

**1350 BC**

**100 AD**

*Egypt: Same country, different people. Above left: The white pharaoh, Queen Nefertiti, circa 1350 BC; Above right: The effects of racial mixing are clearly to be seen on the face of this coffin portrait of a Roman lady in Hawara, Egypt, 100 AD; Right: The mixed race Egyptian, Anwar Sadat, president of Egypt in the twentieth century. Nefertiti ruled over an advanced civilization; Sadat ruled over a third world country. The reason for the difference in cultures between Nefertiti's Egypt and Sadat's Egypt was that the Egyptian people had changed.*

**1970 AD**

11

However, even the strictest segregation (and Aryan laws prescribing punishments such as death for miscegenation) did not prevent the majority population from eventually swallowing up the ruling Aryans until the situation has been reached today where only a very few high caste Brahmin Indians could still pass as Europeans.

Exactly the same thing happened in Central Asia, Egypt, Sumeria, and to a lesser degree, modern Turkey. Slowly but surely, as these civilizations relied more and more on others to do their work for them, or were physically conquered by other races, their population makeup became darker and darker.

### Miscegenation with Nonwhite Slaves Caused Egyptian Decline

From the time of the Old Kingdom, the original white Egyptians had been using Nubians, blacks, and Semites (or Arabs) to work on many of their building projects or as general slaves.

At various stages the pharaohs also employed Nubian mercenaries, and ultimately Nubia and Sudan were physically occupied and incorporated into the Egyptian empire. Although the buildings of ancient Egypt are very impressive—many having survived through to the present day, their construction was dependent on the Egyptian ability to organize an unprecedented mass of human labor.

Under the direction of a scribe and architect, thousands of slaves and regiments of soldiers labored for decades to create the great buildings, using only levers, sleds, and massive ramps of earth. It is impossible to think that such massive use of slave and foreign labor would not have left some mark on the population of the land. Interbreeding took place, and this, combined with the natural growth and reproduction patterns of the slaves and laborers, meant that in a relatively short time they comprised a significant section of the population.

Several attempts were made to prevent large numbers of Nubians from settling in Egypt. One of the first recorded racial separation laws was inscribed on a stone on the banks of the southern Nile which forbade Nubians from proceeding north of that point. Nonetheless, the continuous use of Nubians for labor eventually led to the establishment of a large resident nonwhite population in Egypt, with their numbers being augmented by natural reproduction and continued immigration.

The region was also occupied for two hundred years by the Semitic Hyksos, who intermarried with the local population, and this was followed by other Semitic/Arabic immigration, fueled by the long existing black settlement on the southernmost reaches of the Nile River.

Once again the factors which led to the extinction of the Aryans in India came into play in Egypt: a resident nonwhite population to do the labor, a natural increase in nonwhite numbers, physical integration, and a decline in the original white birthrate.

All these factors compounded to produce an Egyptian population makeup of today that is very different from the men and women who founded Egypt and designed the pyramids.

As the population makeup shifted, so the cultural manifestations, or civilization, of that region changed to the point where the present day population of the Middle East is not by any stretch of the imagination classifiable as white. This explains why the present inhabitants of Egypt are not the same people who designed the pyramids. The Egyptians of today are a completely different people, racially and culturally, living amongst the ruins of another race's civilization.

### Identical Reasons for Decline in Middle East

The decline and eventual extinction of the white population in the Middle East marked the end of the original civilizations in those regions. In all the Middle Eastern countries the Semitic (Arabic) and black populations grew as they were used as labor by the ruling whites. In the case of Sumer, the white rulers were physically displaced by military conquest at the hands of Semitic invaders.

This process continued until almost all remains of the original whites in the greater region were assimilated into the darker populations. Only the occasional appearance of light colored hair or eyes amongst today's Iraqis, Iranians, Syrians, and Palestinians serve as reminders of the original rulers of these territories.

### Lesson—Role of Racially Foreign Labor in the Decline of a Civilization

The lesson is clear: a civilization will remain intact as long as its creating race remains in existence. This applies to all races equally— white, black, Mongolian or any other. As long as a civilization's founding race maintains its territorial integrity and does not use large numbers of any other alien race to do its labor, that civilization will remain in existence.

If a civilization allows large numbers of racial aliens into its midst (most often as laborers) and then integrates with those newcomers, that civilization will change to reflect the new racial makeup of the population.

## BLACK SLAVES IN EGYPT AND GREECE

*Evidence of black slaves in Egyptian and Grecian society. Left: This Eighteenth dynasty (1567–1320 BC) Egyptian kohl (eye paint) pot is carried by a young black Nubian slave girl. Below center and right: Two Greek vases, dating from the fifth century BC, show the racial types of two slaves: a Semite and a black.*

Any civilization—be it white, black, Asian, or Aboriginal—stands or falls by the homogeneity of its population, and nothing else. As soon as a society loses its homogeneity, the nature of that society changes. This simple fact, often ignored by historians, provides the key to understanding the rise and fall of all civilizations, irrespective of race.

### History Is a Function of Race

The early white civilizations in Greece and Rome also fell to this process. The last great Grecian leader, Pericles, actually enacted a law in the year 451 BC limiting citizenship of the state according to racial descent. However, some four hundred years later this law was changed as the population shifts had become more and more evident. Certain Roman leaders tried to turn back the racial clock, but their efforts were in vain.

The sheer vastness of the Roman Empire meant that all sorts of races were included in its borders, and this brew ultimately led to the dissolution of the original Roman population.

Those who occupy a territory determine the nature of the society in that territory. This is an immutable law of nature. It is the iron rule upon which all of human endeavor is built—that history is a function of race.

## *The Rise and Fall of Civilizations Explained*

■   Each and every society and culture is the sum and unique product of the people making up that society;

■   For example: The Chinese civilization is the product of the Chinese people, the Australian Aboriginal culture is the product of the Aboriginal people, and white society is the product of white people;

■   This has nothing to do with subjective notions of superiority or inferiority;

■   If the people in a society change their racial makeup, it is therefore logical that the culture of that society will change to reflect this shift in society;

■   This is what is called the "rise and fall" of civilizations—where one culture gets replaced by a different culture;

■   The cause of this replacement of cultures is the replacement of the people in that society;

■   In this way, the American Indian culture "fell" because they were replaced by whites as the dominant race on the North American continent;

■   Civilizations do not then "fall"—they are merely replaced by another culture, which is the product of the new population;

**A civilization "rises and falls" by its racial homogeneity and nothing else. As long as it maintains its racial homogeneity, it will last—if it loses its racial homogeneity, and changes its racial makeup, it will "fall" or be replaced by a new culture.**

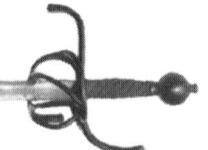

# CHAPTER ONE

# The First White Racial Types

**It is often argued that climatic influence is the cause of physical racial differences. This is, however, not borne out by the historical facts. For example, the argument is often heard that the white race has its color because it originated in the cold north, and that the black race has its color because it originated in the hot south.**

Apart from the obvious geographical impossibility of this conjecture (because many of the white race's greatest achievements were made in a hot climate—the Middle East and Egypt), this argument does not explain why members of the Mongoloid races (Chinese, Japanese, and others) have their distinctive racial characteristics. How did the climate of Asia create the distinctive eye shape and skull structure by which Mongoloid races are known?

The reality is that physical characteristics are genetically determined at the moment of conception, and there is absolutely no evidence to indicate that living in a cold or a hot climate changes the genetic makeup of a group of people. If a large group of Chinese people moved to Norway, and lived there for any length of time, all the while remaining (marriage and children wise) within their racial group, would anyone seriously suggest that they would "evolve" into blue-eyed blond people over any period of time?

The same argument can be used in reverse. Who would seriously contend that if whites moved to China (and remained within their own genetic community, not interbreeding with the local population), they would become Mongoloid in physical appearance after any length of time? People may

*Right: A representation of Australopithecus— a Homo erectus type, based on archaeological and fossil evidence. There is no clear evidence linking any Homo erectus type with the modern white racial type, or even with the Neanderthal racial type.*

grow a little taller, or live a little longer with better nutrition or medical services, but this is merely an extension of the genetic potential of those people, rather than a change in the genes themselves. Climate, then, can never change the gene pool of a people.

### Genes Change through Mixing

The only way a gene pool can be changed is if enough members of that gene pool physically mix—physically integrate and have offspring—with a gene pool outside of that original group. This is the only way in which genes can "change." History is full of examples where this has happened, where original racial groups have integrated with other previously separate racial groups to produce new groups which overall have different physical and even cognitive characteristics from both the original parent groups.

### Environment and Achievement

Another popular modern myth is that some racial groups developed faster than others because of the accident of their geographic location. This is known collectively as the environmental theory of development: because some races were "lucky" enough to live around fertile river basins, or had access to certain types of domesticated animals or edible plants, they then developed faster than other racial groups elsewhere in the world.

This worldview attempts to explain the huge technological gap which existed between the white Europeans and the black Africans, Native Americans (Amerinds), Asians, and Australian Aborigines at the time of white exploration and colonization of the world.

While it is not the purpose of this book to delve into what are, after all, subjective notions of superiority and inferiority (what is regarded as superior by some can be regarded as inferior by another), the issue of the technological gap between the races needs addressing, if only because it played such a huge role in the history of the white race's interaction with the other races of the world.

The "environmental" theory as expounded by modern sociologists is destroyed by two main examples: Egypt, and a comparison between the indigenous cultures of Equatorial Africa and Central America.

In Egypt, as will be shown, the black and white races shared an identical geographic location along the banks of the Nile River—yet the ancient white Egyptians produced a civilization which is still a marvel of world history, while the achievements of the black (Nubian) inhabitants of the same region were distinctly unremarkable in comparison.

If the "lucky environmental accident" were true, then there should not have been such a vast difference between the original white Egyptians and the black Nubians, since they shared an identical environment.

Often the argument is made that whites had an advantage because they had pack animals and horses while the native peoples did not—this argument ignores the fact that the white Egyptians did not have horses until long after the creation of many of their finest technological marvels. In fact, horses were introduced to Egypt by the Semitic Hyksos invasion which occurred hundreds of years after the first flowering of Egyptian civilization.

### *Disparity in Achievement—Same Environment*

It is of value to compare the achievements of the nonwhite Inca and Aztec Amerind peoples in Central and South America, lying just north and south of the equator, with that of the original heartland of the black race, also just north and south of the equator in Africa.

Due to the proximity to the equator, virtually identical environmental conditions prevailed (and still prevail) in Central America and Central Africa. Neither region had horses, and both had the challenges of the equatorial rain forest with which to deal.

Despite the similarity in environment, the Amerinds in Central America were able to build sophisticated buildings, establish written forms of communication, produce gold and precious metal working, and a host of other advances, while in Africa little progress beyond the Stone Age was made. The disparity between the nonwhite Amerinds and the nonwhite Africans cannot be explained by the "accident of geography."

Lastly, and most devastatingly, the "environment" argument falls flat when measured against the rise and fall of civilizations.

Why is it that Ancient Egypt at one stage led the world in culture and civilization, yet today is a backward third world country? If environment alone gave certain peoples a "permanent advantage" then it would surely follow that Egypt would today be one of the most advanced countries in the world. In reality it is, as any visitor to that land will testify, filled with misery, poverty, and backwardness—despite the "environment" being exactly the same as it was during the great age of the civilization which built the pyramids. The "environmental" theory does not, therefore, explain why Egypt, with exactly the same environmental conditions, lost its preeminence over the rest of the world.

### *Technological Ascendancy—Reasons*

What caused the technological gap? If environment did not cause it, the only other logical explanation must be that certain types of cultures, or civilizations, are the products of certain types of people—representative of the innate potential of any given group. While this is presently deemed a politically incorrect point of view, the facts of historical development support no other conclusion.

Another example: North America was for the greatest part colonized by white Europeans, and subsequently became the leading power in the modern world. South America, on the other hand, having far richer natural resources than North America, was never majority colonized by white Europeans and today has a majority mixed race population. This continent is classed as third, or at best, second world.

If environment were the only factor determining levels of achievement, South America should in theory be more advanced than North America, since it has far more "environmental advantages."

### *Homo Erectus and Neanderthals—Doubtful White Ancestors*

Archaeology and its allied science, paleoserology, have revealed that life forms in the general shape of humans (that is, two arms, two

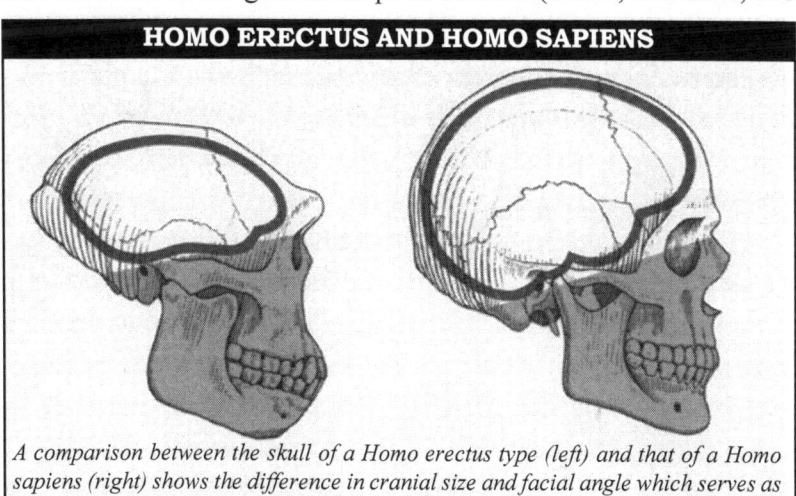

**HOMO ERECTUS AND HOMO SAPIENS**

*A comparison between the skull of a Homo erectus type (left) and that of a Homo sapiens (right) shows the difference in cranial size and facial angle which serves as an outstanding marker of the huge distance between the two racial types.*

legs, a torso, a head, and the ability to walk upright on the two legs) appeared in different places across the earth approximately two million years ago. These were the "Homo erectus" (or "upright man") racial types so favored by evolutionists as the "ancestors of man." These creatures have been found scattered throughout Europe, Africa, China, and Australia. It remains speculative to say with any certainty that modern man is descended from any of these Homo erectus racial types.

The time of the Homo erectus types is known as the Paleolithic Age, and is deemed to have come to an end coinciding with the appearance of a new racial type, Neanderthal man. Once again, however, there is no clearly established link to modern white racial types. The results of DNA tests carried out on Neanderthal remains by researchers at the University of Glasgow, U.K., and published in the journal *Nature,* in March 2000, proved conclusively that modern humans do not have Neanderthal ancestors in their family tree, and are thus completely unrelated.

### Cro-Magnon—First White Racial Type

The first modern white racial type emerged between approximately 40,000 BC and 15,000 BC in differing parts of Europe and the Middle East. This time period is known as the Late Paleolithic period, also known generically as the Stone Age. This first racial type is known as Cro-Magnon man—after a site in the Dordogne region of France where the first skeletal remains were found. Cro-Magnon man

**CRO-MAGNON MAN—FIRST WHITE RACIAL TYPE**

Above left and center: *The well-preserved skull of a complete example of Cro-Magnon man, discovered in the Cheddar Gorge in England. The skeleton was originally dated at between 40,000 and 30,000 years old, but recent research indicates that it may be only 9,000 years old.* Above right: *A reconstruction bust of Cro-Magnon man, made by the famous anthropologist, M. P. Coon. It is from Cro-Magnon man that recorded white history begins.*

## NEANDERTHAL MAN

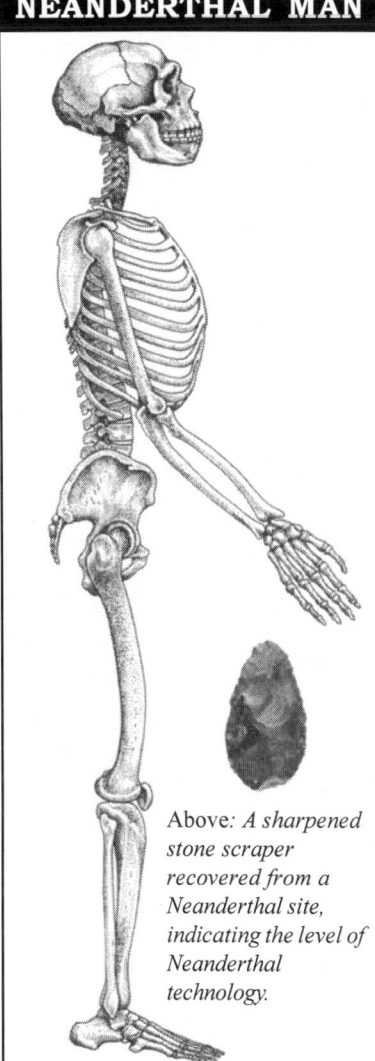

Above: *A sharpened stone scraper recovered from a Neanderthal site, indicating the level of Neanderthal technology.*

*A reconstruction of Neanderthal man based on skeletal remains. Known in common parlance as the "cave man;" this race is no relation at all to the early or modern white racial type, as can clearly be seen by a comparison with the early white racial type on the opposite page. Of particular interest is the prognathic jawline, or jutting out dentition, and the cranial shape.*

## CRO-MAGNON MAN

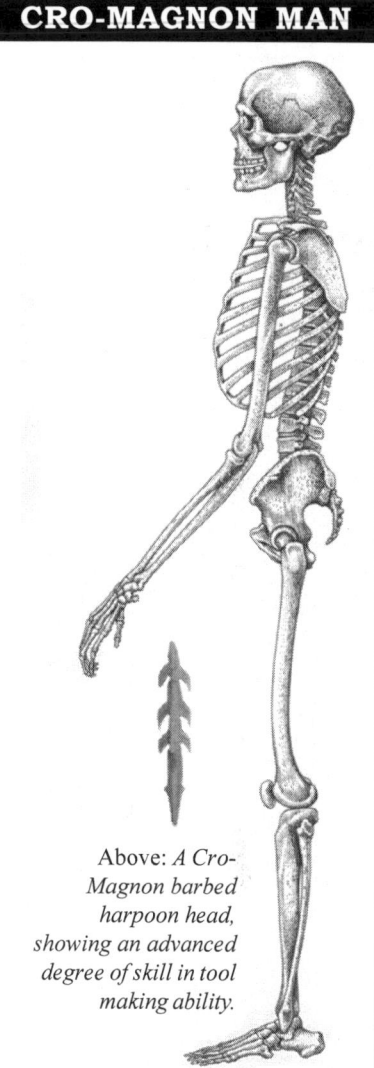

Above: *A Cro-Magnon barbed harpoon head, showing an advanced degree of skill in tool making ability.*

*A reconstruction of the first white racial type, also called Cro-Magnon man. The skeleton differs only very slightly in skull length from modern day Nordic subracial types.*

*In isolated parts of Europe it is still possible to find living examples of this particular racial type. The difference in cranial shape, size, rib structure, and forearm shape, with the Neanderthal type, opposite, is apparent.*

21

is the first biped life form with whom modern whites can clearly claim a direct genetic affinity.

White racial history therefore begins around the year 35,000 BC—and so it is with the Late Paleolithic period that the story in this book really begins.

# CHAPTER TWO

## *The First Stirrings—The Late Paleolithic Age*

**The first racial types identifiable as similar to modern whites first appeared in parts of Europe, southern Russia, and the Middle East during the time period 30,000 BC to 15,000 BC, following the end of the last great Ice Age around the year 40,000 BC.**

The new arrivals were known as Homo sapiens (or "wise man") in order to differentiate them from the other life forms known as Homo erectus and Neanderthal man.

These first racial types occurred in two main physical forms: the original Mediterraneans ("Old Europeans") who had dark hair and dark eyes, and the Proto Nordic or Cro-Magnon racial type—tall, with light hair and light eyes. In certain isolated areas in Europe—centered in Scandinavia—it is possible even today to find perfect living examples of this Proto Nordic racial type, differing only slightly in height from modern day Nordics.

This Proto-Nordic race's physical remains are plentiful as they wandered far and wide. They lived in a broad band spanning from Spain right across Europe all the way to Asia, where skeletal remains have also been found.

### *Nordic Types Comprise Ruling Elite*

The Mediterranean and Proto-Nordic types often inhabited the same geographic

**EARLY ART WILLENDORF 30000 BC**

*An example of some of the earliest art: The Woman from Willendorf, present day Austria, dating from 30,000 BC.*

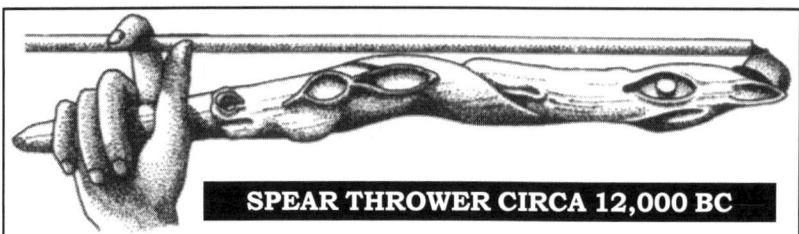

**SPEAR THROWER CIRCA 12,000 BC**

*The first advance over a spear or dagger: a spear thrower circa 12,000 BC, Late Paleolithic period. The spear thrower was utilized as an accelerator for a spear.*

areas—particularly so in the Middle East, but also extending to western Europe and the Balkans. A certain amount of mixing took place, but as the Mediterranean types were in the overwhelming majority, the incidence of Nordic characteristics amongst these first whites was relatively low, with most Nordic types comprising the ruling elite of these peoples.

This time period, circa 25,000 BC, is known as the Late Paleolithic era and was marked by two main characteristics—the hunter-gatherer stage of early white existence, and the extinction of Neanderthal man (through conflict with the new arrivals).

### Hunter Gatherers—Bow and Arrow 9000 BC

The Proto-Nordics of the Late Paleolithic age wandered from area to area, sometimes following new lands opened up by the retreating last ice sheets, but never settling for long, often driven on by the elements and the need for food and shelter. As a result of the transient nature of these people, they generally traveled in family groups, usually varying between five and twenty individuals. Small numbers of livestock and hunting provided their main means of sustenance.

While no great buildings or fixed structures remain from this period, smaller day-to-day artifacts are relatively plentiful. Excavations across Europe and Russia have shown that these early whites had fire, paint, stone blades, and the ability to fashion animal bones into weapons and tools. Sewing needles were also developed during this period.

### 27,000 BC—Introduction of Musical Instruments and Use of Coal and Ceramics

Musical instruments also made their appearance—at sites in southern France, flutes dating back 27,000 years have been found. Coal was also first used as a fuel at about this time. The southern parts of Europe would have been the primary point of contact between the northern Proto-Nordics and the Mediterranean types.

These early whites also developed fired ceramics. Statuettes and other fired objects dating from approximately 26,000 BC have been found in the present day Czech Republic.

Two significant weapons were also developed at this time which marked a great improvement on the spear: the spear thrower (an instrument made of bone which gave the thrower greater leverage and thus greater speed and distance) which made its appearance around 12,000 BC, and the bow and arrow which first made its appearance around 9,000 BC. It was this period which produced, across Europe, a number of voluptuous female figure forms which have become known as "primitive Venuses." It is speculated that these figurines were fertility symbols.

### Azilian Art—First Writing? 7000 BC

**SUNGIR, RUSSIA 27,000 BC— BEADS AND MATERIAL**

*One of the most remarkable finds from the Upper Paleolithic era is this clothed adult white male, discovered in Sungir, Russia, buried some 25,000 years ago. This was the type of person who created the first known inklings of white civilization of the present interglacial period starting approximately 40,000 BC. The intricacy of the bead work and material with which the corpse was buried is evidence that white Upper Paleolithic man was at this stage already fairly advanced—compared to Africa where woven material was introduced as recently as five hundred years ago.*

Perhaps the greatest difficulty in studying people of the Late Paleolithic age is that they left no written records of their achievements— only paintings on rock walls. One of the best preserved examples is also the most intriguing—the rock paintings found in the caves of Mas d'Azil in southern France. Here stones were found with what appears to be writing on them, although they have never been deciphered. If it is

## 7,000 BC - AZILIAN EARLIEST WRITING?

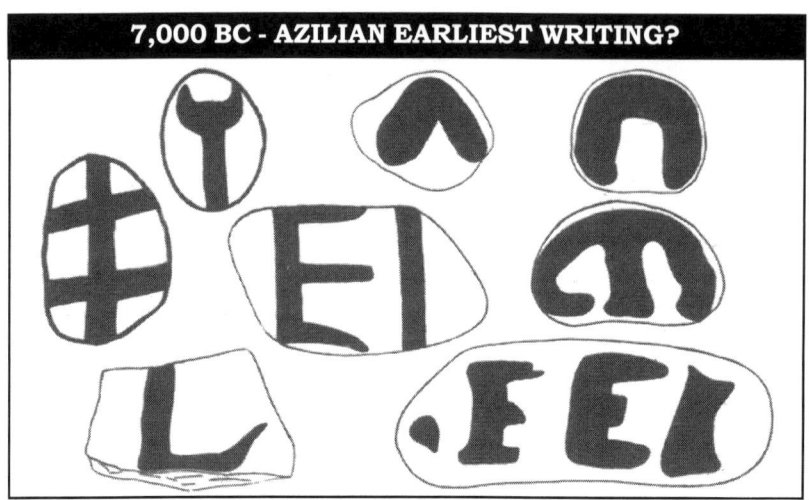

indeed writing, then it might be the first and oldest form of written communication in the world.

### *Earliest Houses—Circa 30,000 BC*

The earliest remains of buildings date from the time of the hunters of the Late Paleolithic period who inhabited the areas now known as the Czech and Slovak Republics and southern Russia. To withstand the cold weather, Late Paleolithic hunter groups made clothes from sewn skins—traces of which have survived in sites in the Czech and Slovak Republics.

Mammoths—elephantine creatures now extinct—were hunted during this period and houses were constructed out of mammoth ribs (which were used as roof supports). There are also traces of Late Paleolithic people having used the limestone caves of western Europe as shelters. All in all, Late Paleolithic life must have been bare, hard, and cruel.

The transient nature of society at this time was the primary cause of the lack of any great fixed settlements. This would be a development that would come with the establishment of agriculture, a feature of the time period after 10,000 BC.

Around this time, the Alpine subgroup appeared: possibly as a result of mixing between the Proto-Nordic and Mediterranean types (this is, however, speculation). These three groups: Proto-Nordics, original Mediterraneans, and Alpines, settled large parts of Europe and the Middle East, a situation which remained stable until the entire continent was subjected to invasions by Nordic tribes—called the Indo-European

## TOOL DEVELOPMENT MARKS APPEARANCE OF HOMO SAPIENS

**MAGDALENIAN** 15,000

**AZILIAN** 10,500

**SOLUTRIAN** 20,000

**PERIGORDIAN** 30,000

**AURIGNACIAN** 40,000

**MOUSTERIAN** 45,000

**ACHEULIAN** 75,000–150,000

**OLDOWAN** 500,000 + Years Ago

## DRILLED NECKLACES, CZECHOSLOVAKIA 20,000 BC

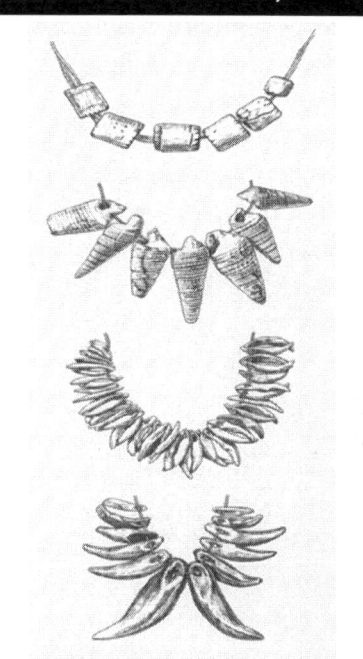

*The technical ability of early whites is demonstrated with the intricacy of these four necklaces, all dating from approximately 20,000 BC which were found in Upper Paleolithic sites in the Czech Republic. The cylindrical beads of the top necklace were carved from the tusk of a mammoth. Next is a string of snail shells. The bottom two necklaces are made up of the teeth of predators: wolves, foxes, and bears. All items have had holes drilled in them, which is a remarkable feat for such an early time period.*

Left: *Archaeological research has mapped the development of tools: here the different types of tools and their age periods are shown. Note the massive jump in tool shape and technological ability coinciding with the arrival of the first white racial type, Cro-Magnon man, simultaneous with the so-called "Aurignacian" period (named after the site in France where the tools where discovered).*

## HOUSES, ART AND ARTIFACTS—LATE PALEOLITHIC ERA

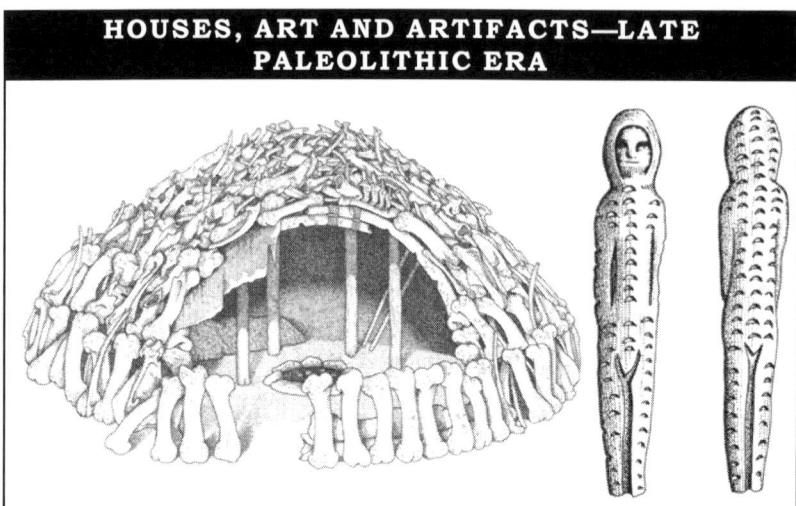

Above left: *The first houses were constructed out of mammoth bones and hide. This reconstruction is based on evidence found in southern Russia, dated between 30,000 and 20,000 BC.* Above right: *A carved ivory piece found at Buret, Siberia, circa 20,000 BC, shows how the early white hunters clothed themselves in cold climates: the man wears a single hooded coat made from skins, with the fur turned to the outside.*

peoples, which started around 5000 BC. The Indo-Europeans, the original European groups, and the Alpines together form the basis of the white race which today inhabits Europe.

These three white subgroups eventually combined to dominate territory which stretched from Britain to the Ural Mountains; from Scandinavia to North Africa and the Middle East.

With the advent of time, the Middle East was to become a maelstrom of races, with waves of settling whites, Arabics, Semites, and even Mongoloids at one time or another dominating the region and establishing their own cultures and civilizations.

The present day inhabitants of the Middle East are the product of many thousands of years of mixing between all these groups, and traces of each can be seen in their physiognomy.

### STATUETTE 22,000 BC FRANCE

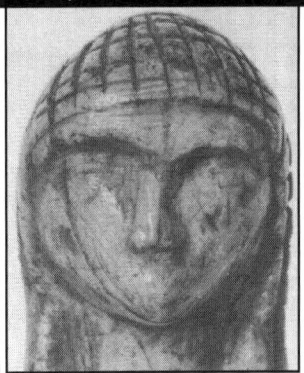

Above: *A small ivory head of a female figure with delicately carved features and stylized long hair, found at Brassempouy in France—circa 22,000 BC. This piece is notable as racial characteristics are identifiable in the face.*

# CHAPTER THREE

## Vast Temples and First Cities—
## The Neolithic Age

**As the climate improved with the recession of the last great ice age, Late Paleolithic man gradually became more settled and stayed in favorable spots.**

These first fixed settlements led to a shift from a food gathering society to a food cultivating society, and the appearance of crops and the domestication of animals became features of their way of life. This change in culture is called the Neolithic Age.

A regular and continuous food supply created by the establishment of farming meant that bigger populations could live in settled, more secure areas, and this marked the first time that the luxury of non-food producing professions within society became possible.

This shift from hunter-gatherer to settled agriculturalism occurred in fits and starts all over white-occupied Europe and the Middle

## WORLD'S FIRST WRITING

*Top left: Undeciphered writing found on tablets at Glozel, central France, dating from around 1500 BC.*
*Top right: Writing from Jemdet Nasr, Sumeria, Middle East, dated at around 3000 BC;*
*Right: Undeciphered writing on the Tartaria tablet, found in Tartaria, Romania, and dated at 4500 BC. All three writing forms contain many similarities, and note the swastika on the Glozel tablet; it's a letter of the original Indo-European written language.*

East. The earliest farming sites in northern Europe are to be found in Ireland, dating from approximately the same time as the cultivation of crops in the Mesopotamian River Valley. As a general rule, the first Neolithic settlements can be said to have been established around 10,000 BC, and the cultivation of edible plants and the domestication of animals was commonplace all over Europe and the Middle East by 5000 BC.

### Europe and the Middle East—Equally Advanced Around 5000 BC

The existence of an original civilization on the continent of Europe which predated the civilizations in the Middle East, has to a large degree been ignored by traditional history writers, particularly those who wrote during the dominant Christian era in Europe.

This was largely because of a biblical Judeo-Christian bias which held that all civilization started in the Middle East (the biblical Old Testament deals exclusively with events in the Middle East, and conventional wisdom during the Age of the Church held that the Garden of Eden was in that region).

This is not an accurate reflection of the facts, as in many parts of Europe relatively advanced societies were in existence either before or simultaneously with the Mesopotamian or Egyptian civilizations. While it is most certainly true that the great cities and states in the Middle East were towering achievements, it is incorrect to regard them as the only flowering of civilization in the world at that time.

There are many huge buildings (called megaliths), early Neolithic settlements, artifacts, burial sites, and even a form of writing, which show that the inhabitants of Europe were advanced in the evolution of their societies and culture. This Old European civilization lasted for approximately three thousand years, and then fell before waves of new invaders, the Indo-European tribes sweeping in from the area we now know as Russia.

### White Mediterraneans and Proto-Nordics Populate Middle East

This is not to say that the original Old European inhabitants—mainly Mediterranean racial types with a minority of Proto-Nordics—were of a different race than the inhabitants of the Middle East at that time. Indeed, the first civilizations in the Mesopotamian River Valley (in present day Iraq) were also created by white Mediterranean and Proto-Nordic racial types, as can be seen by the large number of surviving artifacts and images dating from this period in early white history.

## INGENIOUS MEGALITH BUILDING TECHNIQUES

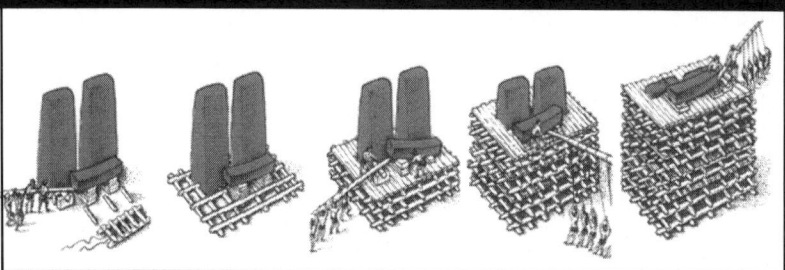

*Building megaliths was no easy task. Pulling one of the massive stones erect was in itself a marathon effort, and then raising the equally huge lintels onto the top of other stones required a great deal of planning and foresight. Exactly how the early whites did it is still a puzzle to archaeologists. These illustrations of how the stones were raised and of how a lintel was placed are the most commonly accepted theories of how these superhuman feats were achieved.*

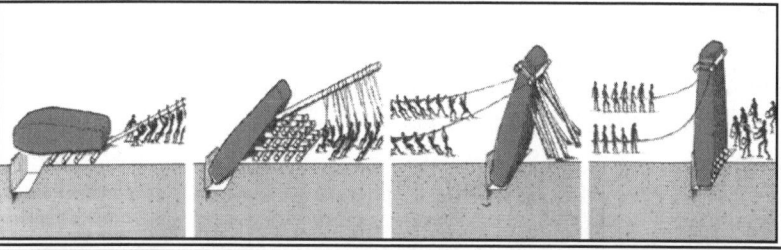

**The "Et Oriente Lux" or "All light comes from the East" dogma held that all progress and civilization came from the Middle East. With accurate dating methods and intensified archaeological research, it has now been shown that advanced civilizations flourished in Europe, sometimes thousands of years before similar technological advances were made in the Middle East.**

## FIFTY THOUSAND MEGALITH SITES IN EUROPE REVEAL EXTENSIVE STONE AGE CIVILIZATION

Left: *Intricately carved walls on a Megalith tomb dating from before 3000 BC in Brittany, France. There are over fifty thousand such sites in Europe—the often ignored*

*proof of a flourishing culture thousands of years old.*
*Right: A Megalith temple, Malta, circa 3000 BC.*
*This island in the Mediterranean contains a massive Neolithic temple complex of great complexity which included enclosed circular halls.*

## Europe—Organized Farming and Copper

Cereal grain farms were established in central Europe by 8000 BC (almost simultaneous with the Mesopotamian "Fertile Crescent" River Valley crop cultivation) with some of the best preserved farming settlements in France and Britain positively dated as existing prior to 4000 BC.

Significantly, copper working had been established in the Balkans by 5000 BC—some two thousand years before it was produced in the Mesopotamian River Valley. In Neolithic Europe, where wood was abundant, rectangular timber houses were constructed. Some had two rooms and even gabled roofs. Remains found in Switzerland dating from around 5000 BC show that on soft, swampy ground the builders were able to erect houses by first laying down wooden foundations or by using piles driven deep into the ground.

By 5000 BC, white Neolithic settlements had taken the form of established villages, towns, and in a few cases, even cities, scattered throughout Europe and western and southern Russia. These early Neolithic farmers cultivated cereals, and kept domesticated animals such as pigs, cattle, and dogs.

Farms were established across the European continent, with some of the best preserved sites being found in Ireland. Their tools and hunting weapons were mostly made of flint, and their houses of timber. Clothes were made of leather, and there is also evidence of weaving. Other small implements were made of antler and bone, and they have left many examples of fairly sophisticated pottery.

## Burial Mounds Expose Racial Makeup

The leaders of this early white society were buried according to religious rituals which are now lost, but the physical graves are a good source of knowledge about their society as a whole. Important leaders were buried in specially constructed narrow mounds called barrows. The existence of these grave sites—and a number of chance discoveries of less important graves—has served as a valuable indicator of the racial makeup of these early Europeans.

The general rule is that the further north, the more dominant Nordic or Proto-Nordic, while in places like Britain and central Europe there were a significant number of Alpine and Mediterranean racial types.

## Old European Linear Script 4000 BC—Basis for Runes

These original continental European inhabitants had also developed a form of writing—called Old European linear script—around 4000 BC.

The exact origins of this language are lost (there is evidence that some or all of it may have come from Indo-European or Nordic invaders who penetrated Europe from their bases in southern Russia around this time), but it most likely laid the basis for sharp angular writing known as runes.

### Fired Pottery and Gold Working in the Balkans

Hand fired pottery was produced in the Balkans around 6500 BC. Cities of more than one thousand inhabitants—huge by the standards of the time—had been established by approximately 5000 BC. There are copper mine shafts—some twenty meters deep—still existing in the Balkans which date from before 4000 BC.

Gold worked jewelry discovered in the Balkans predates the gold working skills of the Egyptians by at least 1,600 years. By 2500 BC, copper working had spread all over continental Europe, with

### JOINTS—IN STONE

*The huge megalithic monuments of Neolithic times were not simply piles of stones thrown on top of each other. The stones used at Stonehenge, England, were cut on site and used an ingenious ball and joint system to lock into place. The ball can still be clearly seen on the top of the upright stone to the right, and below, how the locks worked.*

*The ability to create such structures from solid stone shows that these white people were intellectually adept, and not the 'savage barbarians' so often maliciously portrayed in the popular media.*

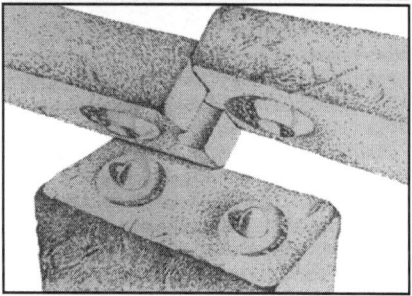

archaeological evidence showing extensive trade between settlements in England, France, Holland, and into central Europe.

### Critical Development—Iron Working 1000 BC

The introduction of iron working into western and northern Europe around 1000 BC—from central Europe and the Middle East—ushered in a new era, and it is from approximately this time that the early west Europeans started building hilltop forts, which later evolved into castles. These hilltop forts are scattered all over Europe, and some remained in use as forts right until the time of early Christianity, approximately 1,600 years later.

### Megaliths—Formidable Achievements

In many parts of Europe, the longest lasting remnants of this era are the megaliths (large stones) which may have had some religious or recreational purpose. Massive blocks of stone, and sometimes wood, were moved great distances and erected in chosen areas throughout Europe: from Britain right across the Continent, some even as far as the Black Sea in southern Russia—a stupendous achievement.

The most famous of these megalith sites is Stonehenge in Wiltshire, England, which was built in stages, the first part being erected between 3500 BC and 3000 BC. To put this in perspective, the first stage of Stonehenge was built about one thousand years before the great Egyptian pyramids were built.

**STONEHENGE, ENGLAND—BEGUN BEFORE THE EGYPTIAN PYRAMIDS**

*A masterpiece of Stone Age engineering—Stonehenge, England, circa 4000–1000 BC, Neolithic Period. The circular upright stones have become worldwide icons of Neolithic culture, and are possibly the best preserved ruins of their kind, despite damage inflicted over the course of thousands of years by souvenir hunters and uncaring locals.*

The last part of Stonehenge was built around the year 1000 BC—hundreds of years before even the Greek and Roman civilizations.

Neolithic farmers in Europe created a number of other impressive structures which predate Stonehenge. One of the earliest is situated quite close to Stonehenge, called Robin Hood's Ball, and consists of what appears to be circular foundations for either a large hall, or a number of buildings, and a grave site (judging by the human remains found in surrounding ditches). This structure dates from the very early Neolithic time, around 4000 BC, and indicates the establishment of set social structures at this early stage of European history.

### *Burial Chambers and Tombs All Over Europe*

Often overlooked as historical evidence for the technological ability of the Neolithic settlements are the burial chambers and tombs which are scattered over large parts of Europe.

Some of the oldest megalithic chamber tombs have been radiocarbon dated at 6000 BC—some 3,500 years older than the famous Egyptian pyramids.

## WORLD'S FIRST STEP PYRAMID ENGLAND 2660 BC

*One of the oldest pyramids in the world is to be found near the present day town of Marlborough, in Wiltshire, Britain. Called Silbury Hill, it is the largest prehistoric mound anywhere in Europe, standing nearly 131 feet (40 meters) high. It dates from around 2660 BC, preceding the great pyramids of Egypt. Although today covered with soil (as in the picture to the right), excavations have revealed a carefully constructed step pyramid under the silt (as shown in the illustration below). The exact purpose of the pyramid is unknown, but it forms part of the great Avebury stone ring complex, which includes a stone circle larger than Stonehenge and a series of round and long barrow tombs. The enormity of the building stands as a monument to the technical abilities of the whites of early Britain. These were no uncivilized barbarians who erected technically sophisticated structures before the great pyramids of Egypt were even built.*

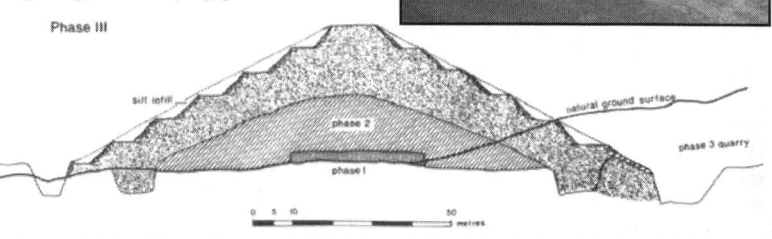

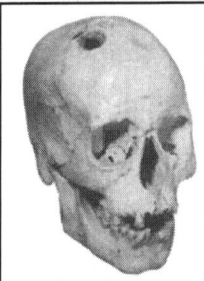

*A dolichocranic ("long" or usually Nordic) skull, recovered from ancient Jericho showing what is believed to be early skull surgery.*

There are four types of megaliths: the menhir, or monolith, which is a single standing stone often of great size; a group of menhirs set in a circle, as at Stonehenge in England; a row of menhirs such as those to be found at Carnac in France; and the burial chamber, or chamber tomb, sometimes called a dolmen.

The chamber tombs are the most common type of megalith, and more than fifty thousand examples have been found on the European continent. Some of these tombs' interiors were decorated with intricate stone carvings and geometrical patterns, making stunning viewing even thousands of years after they were created.

### Creation of World's Oldest Cities Circa 7000 BC

The growth of Neolithic settlements in Europe was matched by the growth of similar settlements in the Middle East. Once again the majority of the population were Mediterranean racial types accompanied by a significant number of Proto-Nordics who were very often tribal leaders (a tradition which was most pronounced in Egypt).

By 7000 BC, a town of mud brick houses and town walls had been built by Mediterraneans at the site now known as Jericho in Palestine.

In Anatolia, Turkey, remains of another major city, Catal Huyuk, have been excavated, dating from approximately 6200 BC. This city also possessed brick making facilities, as well as the already established cereal crop cultivations. By around 5000 BC, farming villages were established all over the Middle East.

At this time pottery made its appearance in large quantities throughout the areas of Neolithic settlement. In the Middle East, the original white racial types were eventually displaced and intermingled with massive waves of Semitic Arabs, along with imported Negroid slaves and eventually by Mongoloid invaders. It is from this mixture that the modern Egyptian and many other North Africans are descended.

### Old European Civilizations Founded

With the creation of fixed settlements and continuous, albeit slow, technological advances, it became inevitable that these communities

## CATAL HUYUK—ONE OF THE WORLD'S FIRST CITIES 6000 BC

*A reconstruction of one of the first cities in the world, Catal Huyuk, Anatolia, in present day Turkey. This city flourished from about 6250 BC to 5400 BC, and was partly excavated in 1961. The photo* below left, *shows the rectangular shape of the buildings: as there was no readily available stone to build defensive walls, the buildings were made to face inwards, with no windows on the outside. The only entrance to the city was through ladders leading onto the roofs of the outside buildings. The streetless city offered a high degree of protection from outside attackers. If the city were under attack, the outside ladders were withdrawn, and any would-be attacker was faced with a solid wall and no gate or other weak point. This city marked a revolution in Neolithic settlements. The people of Catal Huyuk were most likely farmers and cattle herders who needed to live closely to the broad plain stretching to the north of the city.*

would take their next great step: the creation of a system of literacy and law establishing a formal social contract between the individuals making up the communities. The creation of fixed settlements in Europe and the Middle East as a result of the farming revolution, known as the Neolithic Age, laid the basis for the next great leap in white civilization: the establishment of Old European civilizations in central Europe and in the Middle East.

# CHAPTER FOUR

# Laying the Foundations—The Old European Civilizations

**As the Neolithic revolution became more widespread and larger fixed settlements began to spring up, it was inevitable that these Old Europeans and Proto-Nordic types would start establishing formal societies. The Old European civilizations then came into being, laying much of the groundwork for the later development of classical Greece and Rome.**

Although these Old European civilizations were quite distinct from classical Greece and Rome, they are often mistakenly thought of as one and the same thing. The original, or Old European settlements, dominated huge areas of Europe and Russia, stretching from Italy right through to the Black Sea, including all of modern Austria, Hungary, Bulgaria, and part of the Ukraine.

The crucial difference is that the Old European civilizations were created by the original continental Europeans (Proto-Nordic, Alpine, and Mediterranean, with the latter two being in the majority) while the classical civilizations of Greece and Rome received their impetus from Indo-European or Nordic invasions which had started around 5000 BC.

The continental Old European civilizations in the Aegean were the Cretan civilization, centered at Knossos on the island of Crete; the city state of Troy situated adjacent to the Dardanelles in Asia Minor; certain smaller city states on the

**IMPOSING KNOSSOS PALACE 2000 BC**

*An idea of the enormity and sophistication of the Old European palace of Knossos, Crete, can be gained from this view of surviving pillars and stairs. Three floors high with thousands of rooms, the palace was a masterpiece of early architecture.*

*An image of three Old European, or Mediterranean, racial types, taken from a surviving fresco on the walls of the ruins of the palace at Knossos. The links between this ancient civilization and ancient Egypt are confirmed through surviving records and the fact that the artists at Knossos followed the Egyptian convention of painting males with red skins and females with white skins.*

Greek mainland; and the Etruscans in Italy. These city states were the first to fall before the great Indo-European invasions. Absorbed into the Indo-European peoples, the Old Europeans largely disappeared and this mix of white peoples laid the basis for the Mycenaean culture which replaced the Cretan civilization as the dominant force in the Aegean.

### *Crete—World's First Flushing Toilets*

The island of Crete, situated to the south of Greece, was home to the Cretan civilization, also known as the Minoan civilization (named after Minos, in legend the most powerful of the Cretan kings).

The original Mediterranean racial composition of this first Cretan civilization has been confirmed by the anatomists Bowdy Dawkins, W.L.H. Duckworth, and Felix von Lauschan, all of whom excavated and examined skeletal remains on Crete.

Their unanimous conclusion was that the Cretans were all members of the Mediterranean subrace (*Race,* John R. Baker, Oxford University Press, 1974, page 516). This skeletal evidence is backed up by the art forms left by the Cretans themselves, particularly in the depictions of social events which are still existent on the walls of the now ruined great Cretan palace at Knossos.

By the year 3000 BC, Crete had contact with the budding Egyptian civilization, and many Cretan religious customs and social habits were taken directly from Egypt. Being an island state, it would be fairly logical that the Cretans would possess well developed seafaring skills.

## KNOSSOS—MULTIFLOOR PALACE

*The sophisticated nature of the palace of Knossos on Crete is apparent from the fine staircases which can still be seen today—a magnificent example of Old European civilization at its height. The palace remains suffered earthquake damage and possible war damage after the Old European civilizations were toppled by Nordic Indo-European invaders. The vast palace, with its thousands of rooms, spawned the myth of the Minotaur, a half bull, half man creature in Greek mythology, and of the labyrinth or maze in which it lived.*

The Cretans were governed by a priest king who had his residence at Knossos. This palace was several stories high and was the ultimate in luxury at the time.

The city of Knossos itself appears to have been destroyed by an earthquake in 1400 BC—the result of the titanic volcanic eruption which destroyed the neighboring island civilization of Santorini. However, enough artifacts have survived to provide a clear picture of the racial types who inhabited the island.

Most of the walls were of painted plaster, decorated with elaborate frescoes, with the most famous being of a Cretan national sport, "bull jumping"—where brave athletes would grab a charging bull by the horns and somersault backwards over the length of the bull's body.

Minoan art provides fascinating insights into the nature of the society at the time—men and women dressed for the warm climate, with women bare breasted, and men beardless. Ancient Cretans followed the Egyptian artistic convention of painting males with red skins and females with white skins. Flowers, plants, sea creatures, and dolphins

## PALACE OF KNOSSOS, CRETE—WORLD'S OLDEST EXISTING THRONE 2000 BC

*Above: A reconstruction of the throne room of Minos in the palace of Knossos on Crete, and inset, the remarkably well preserved room as it may be viewed today. It is the oldest existing throne in the world, cut out of stone and built into the wall. The palace was constructed circa 2000 BC. Right: A fine depiction of a Minoan king, as shown on a fresco on the walls of the palace of Knossos on Crete.*

feature prominently in their art forms, indicating that their society was advanced and wealthy enough to concern itself beyond just basic survival activities.

One interesting original produced by the Cretan palace of Knossos was a running water sanitation system—the first "flushing" toilet in the world.

The exact date of the collapse of the Cretan civilization is unfortunately not recorded, but it stopped functioning as a cultural unit when the island was invaded by an Indo-European Nordic tribe, the Mycenaeans, around the year 1500 BC. The Cretans were thereafter physically absorbed into the Mycenaeans, and later became an integral part of the civilization of classical Greece.

In 1900, a British archaeologist, Sir Arthur Evans, rediscovered Knossos and found baked clay tablets with two types of writing dating from around 2000 BC. These are called Linear A and Linear B scripts which are possibly the oldest identifiable forms of European continental writing (if the "writing stones" found at the Caves of Mas d'Azil in France and the Tartaria Tablet from Romania are discounted).

Later research showed that the Linear B script was a form of Mycenaean writing (which has been deciphered), while the Linear A script was original Cretan (which has not been deciphered).

### City of Troy—First Built 3000 BC

Around the year 750 BC, two great epics, *The Iliad* and *The Odyssey,* were set down and attributed to the blind poet Homer. *The Iliad* describes the war between the Greek city states and the city of Troy, while *The Odyssey* tells of the adventures of an Ionian king, Odysseus, during his journey home after the war with Troy had ended.

For many years the city of Troy was thought to exist only in Homer's poems and was associated with the famous story of the wooden horse. (Greek soldiers supposedly infiltrated the city of Troy hidden in a trick wooden horse after having unsuccessfully besieged Troy for nearly ten years.) In 1870 an amateur archaeologist, Heinrich Schliemann, discovered the city of Troy. He unearthed a total of nine cities, all built on top of one another, indicating entire periods of history about which very little is known.

The earliest city on the site dates from about 3000 BC, and the various cities (called Troy I–IX) were destroyed in a series of earthquakes, fires, or wars, as recounted in Homer's poems. It is difficult to state for certain how much of the wooden horse story is true but it is likely to have some basis in fact as Troy and many Greek city states were at war with one another around the year 1200 BC.

The last Trojan city, number IX, appears to have been a Greek and later a Roman city known as Ilium. As with Crete, the date of the exact end of Troy has also been lost with the passage of time. By the time Troy had fallen, the great Indo-European invasions of the Greek mainland had begun, and it is possible that the city may at one stage have been destroyed during one of these invasions.

### The Etruscans—Origins North of the Alps

The Etruscans became one of the original Mediterranean and Proto-Nordic peoples living in the Italian peninsula before the Indo-European invaders reached that part of the world.

Originally called the Villanovans (after a place where they lived), the Etruscans penetrated Italy from somewhere north of the Alps. They apparently had close contact with some of the Old European civilizations around the Aegean Sea, as they adopted Greek characters for writing their language.

Villanovan grave sites have revealed a rich yield of impressive worked metal armor and personal artifacts, some dating from 1000 BC, the time when iron working first became widespread in Italy.

## LEGEND BECOMES REALITY: TROY REDISCOVERED

*Once thought only to exist in the imagination of the poet Homer, the city of Troy did, in fact, exist and was discovered by the German archaeologist Heinrich Schliemann in the late nineteenth century. Instead of finding one city, Schliemann discovered nine different cities, each built on top of the other. Very little is known about some of the earliest.* Left : *The main northeastern tower of the sixth city. Troy was originally founded by the Old European civilizations and was occupied by numerous powers during its history: hence the nine different layers. The wall at the very left of the picture dates from the city built by the Romans when they occupied Troy.*
Right: *A Trojan bowman, carved from marble. A figure on the east facade of the temple of Aphaia, in Aegina, Greece.*

With the advantage provided by iron weapons, the Etruscans quickly subdued other original Mediterranean peoples in Italy, and established a state running from the Po River Valley in the north to about a third of the way from the end of the Italian peninsula.

Their most notable achievement was the settlement of towns and concentrated urban areas, one of which was later to become the city state of Rome.

With the arrival of new invading Indo-European tribes—in this case the most important being the Latini—the Etruscans were absorbed into the new Roman state, with the last official Etruscan king being expelled from Rome in 509 BC.

After a few hundred years, the assimilation process between the Etruscans and the Indo-European Latini tribe (the Romans) had reached the point where the Romans offered the Etruscans full

**ETRUSCANS—FOUNDERS OF ROME**

*Original representations of the racial characteristics of the Etruscan peoples, who occupied the Italian peninsula before the arrival of the Indo-European Latini tribe. The Latini, who gave their name to the language they spoke, Latin, mixed with the Etruscans and from this combination came the Romans.*
*From left to right: "Profile of a Woman"—Etruscan, late fourth century BC. Wall painting, Tomb of Orcus, Tarquina; "Dancing woman and lyre player"—Etruscan, fifth century BC. Wall painting, Tomba del Triclinio, Tarquinia. (Note the Old European artistic tradition of painting the men red.) "Ritual Dance"—Etruscan, sixth century BC. Wall painting, Tomba delle Leonese, Tarquinia. Note the hair coloring, both Old European (Mediterranean) female on the left, and Nordic, or proto-Nordic, male, on the right.*

citizenship. By 100 BC, the Etruscans had been completely absorbed into the Roman Empire, which was in turn to dominate the known world.

In addition to the Old European civilizations on the European continent, the Mediterranean and Proto-Nordic subracial groups had by 4000 BC occupied much of what is today known as the Middle East—from Egypt through to the Fertile Crescent (the region between the Tigris and Euphrates Rivers).

These original Mediterraneans were responsible for many of the civilizations in that region. They were subject to almost constant invasion: either by waves of Nordic Indo-Europeans from the north, or by waves of invading Semites from the south. Sometimes these Old Europeans managed to defeat the invaders, but more often than not they were unable to resist. In this way they were gradually absorbed into the gene pools of their conquerors—these events are reviewed in another chapter.

### Ancient White Civilization in India Circa 2500 BC— The Indus River Valley

One of the most far-flung of the Old European settlements is to be found centered in modern day northern India. Known as the Harappan culture (after an excavated city, Harappa in modern Pakistan) or the

Indus Valley Civilization, it was unknown until 1927 when the first major excavations took place. The remains of settlements belonging to this culture have been found throughout the Indus River Valley in Pakistan, westward along the coast to the Iranian border, in India's northwestern states as far east as New Delhi, and on the Oxus River in northern Afghanistan.

The Old European—white Mediterranean—racial makeup of the people who created the Indus River Valley civilization has been proven by an examination of skulls and skeletal remains, undertaken by Col. R.B.S. Selwell and Dr. B.S. Guha of the Zoological Society of India, who both conclusively found that almost all were of the Mediterranean subrace (Chapter 11, in Marshall, J, *Mohenjo-Daro and the Indus Civilization*, 1931, London).

The first Old European settlement of the region was made around 2500 BC, when the white Mediterraneans probably arrived after trekking from the Tigris and Euphrates River Valley. They found darker natives in the region whom they easily subjected.

The Old European civilization lasted until the region was invaded by Indo-European Nordics around 1500 BC. The two major cities of the Indus Valley civilization were Mohenjo Daro, in the lower Sind, and Harappa in the Punjab. In many respects the cities of the Old European Indus Valley civilization were almost identical to that of other Old European civilizations, particularly that of Knossos on Crete. Even the layout of the cities, with their huge square buildings, is identical.

### Mohenjo-Daro—Forty Thousand Inhabitants

The major site in this region is the city of Mohenjo-Daro. The remains of this citadel—excavated between 1927 and 1930—bear a striking physical resemblance to the Old European settlements in early Mesopotamia and Crete.

At its peak, Mohenjo-Daro must have had over forty thousand inhabitants, a substantial amount for the time. The city was based on an advanced grid plan layout, with streets running in very clearly arranged city blocks.

One of the most astonishing aspects of the city was the sewerage system—the people of Mohenjo-Daro developed both public and private hygiene to a degree unmatched in many parts of the modern world. Each house, large or small, was provided with earthenware pipe fitted crossways into the walls which opened into a small individual gutter. This in turn, joined central covered sewers. At intervals there were decantation ditches where the main sewers joined. These were designed to collect the heaviest waste so that it would not obstruct the mains. The houses also all had baths—another innovation for the time—and the water for this purpose was supplied from the many wells throughout the city.

## THE INDUS RIVER VALLEY—ANCIENT WHITE CIVILIZATION IN INDIA

Right and below center: *Mohenjo-Daro, the center of the Old European Indus River Valley civilization. Excavated first in 1921, this white Mediterranean civilization was situated in the present day Sind and Punjab regions of India. It was settled by Old Europeans around 2500 BC who were possibly migrants from the Tigris/Euphrates River area. Mohenjo-Daro was the greatest city of this civilization and its ruins and water borne sewerage system can be seen to this day.* Below left: *A bust recovered from Mohenjo-Daro shows the racial type of the inhabitants of this civilization, which extended north to the borders of modern Afghanistan. These white Mediterraneans were absorbed into two sets of outsiders: nonwhite dark skinned locals and Indo-Aryan invaders who entered the region around 1500 BC. A study of the racial composition of the inhabitants of this region—taken from grave sites—confirms the great mix of racial types and the ultimate vanishing of the original Old Europeans into this new mixed population.*

All the Indus River Valley civilization towns had great building works and an orderly administration built upon an agricultural economy. Many of the houses were built on mud-brick platforms that protected the buildings from seasonal floods, and multiple story dwellings were common. Other structures included large buildings that may have been used for storing grain for private or government use.

The Old European inhabitants of The Indus River Valley also developed pictographic writing. A large number of clay seals bearing this language have been recovered, but sadly it has never been deciphered.

## *1500 BC: Old Europeans Absorbed into Dark Natives and Nordic Indo-European Invaders*

It is often suggested that the drying up of a major river in north India—the Hakra River—was the cause of the collapse of the Indus River Valley civilization. This is not the likely cause of the collapse of the entire culture as it was spread out further than just around one river.

The real reason for the disappearance of the people of the Indus River Valley is much simpler. Like all of the Old European civilizations, the Indus Valley Harappans were overwhelmed and integrated into other peoples, whether dark natives or the new white invaders, the Indo-European Aryans (as detailed in chapter 5).

In this way all the original white Mediterranean civilizations—from western Europe right through to northern India—were all but wiped out through racial assimilation.

# CHAPTER FIVE

# *Born of the Black Sea—The Indo-European Invasions*

**Many modern day whites are either direct or part descendants of a great wave of white peoples who swept into Europe from about 5500 BC till around 500 BC. These peoples, largely Nordic in terms of the white racial subgroups, had their original heartland in the region known today as central and southern Russia.**

Genetic studies of European populations which have emerged since the year 2000 have confirmed the Indo-European invasion, but have also shown that it was not as numerically overwhelming as previously thought. Its importance in cultural terms was unquestionably significant, sparking an upsurge in civilizations from China to Europe.

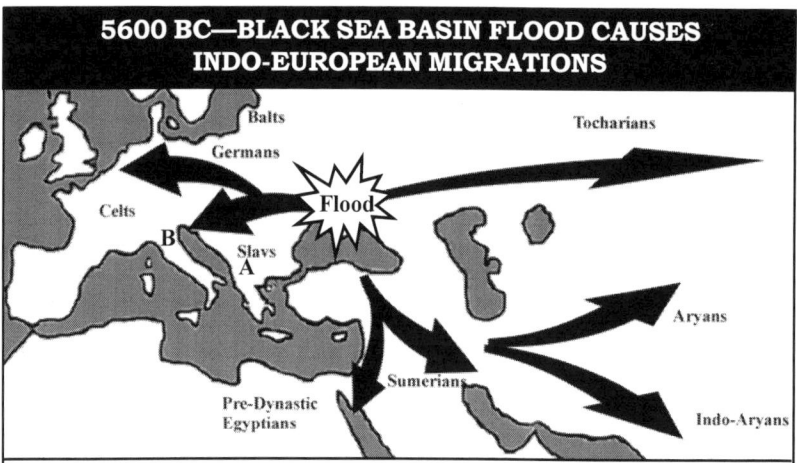

## 5600 BC—BLACK SEA BASIN FLOOD CAUSES INDO-EUROPEAN MIGRATIONS

*Meltwaters from the retreating ice sheets at the end of the Pleistocene caused the world's oceans to rise by almost 328 feet (100 meters). In 5600 BC, the risen waters of the Mediterranean Sea burst through the narrow neck of the Bosporus, inundating and destroying the civilization ringing the fertile Black Sea basin. It is this catastrophe which triggered the great Indo-European migrations and spawned the legend of the biblical flood. Leaving the Black Sea basin, the Nordic Indo-European peoples invaded Europe and Asia. Europe was settled by four main groups: the Celts, the Germans, the Balts, and the Slavs. Offshoots included the Mycenae (A) into Greece and the Latini (B) into Italy. In all of these regions, the invaders found the already present population of Old Europeans to be racially assimilable. In the south they settled pre-dynastic Egypt and the Middle East, penetrating India (the Indo-Aryans), Afghanistan (the Aryans), and China (the Tocharians).*

Research by Robert Ballard and *National Geographic* magazine has proven that the Black Sea basin was flooded from the Mediterranean around 5600 BC—and that this was the probable cause of the first great Indo-European movement. With the aid of the horse, the first Indo-Europeans moved in all directions, disrupting the slow but steady pace of development everywhere they went.

Large numbers settled in northern Europe, others moved off to the Middle East, and yet more ventured west, crossing into Britain and Spain.

### *Nordic "Battle Axe People"—Their Iron Making Advantage*

These Nordics moved slowly westward, invading and re-invading western Europe for a period of nearly six thousand years, finally resulting in the establishment of a new Nordic heartland in northern Europe.

Their great advantage over the already existing white Mediterranean and Proto-Nordic populations was that they brought with them the secret of iron working: this is why some became known as the "battle axe people."

From this heartland in northern Europe—the womb of nations (*vagina gentium,* as the Romans called the region)—successive waves of Indo-European invaders swept down over a period of centuries into all parts of Europe and into the Near East, conquering or displacing the peoples they found. These original tribes had stone buildings and worked bronze and copper.

How much of this metal working skill was passed south to the Middle Eastern civilizations remains a matter of debate. However, what is certain is that successive waves of Indo-European tribes started invading central and southern Europe in earnest about 2000 BC, which caused the Old European civilizations to topple.

These tribes occupied large regions of Turkey, Crete, Greece, and southern Europe and Italy and soon integrated with the largely Mediterranean populations of these areas, often providing the leadership elite of these territories.

Some migrated into the Far East—as far as China, where Nordic remains have been found in burial chambers. The Indo-European tribes were responsible for many of the world's principal civilizations: the Aryans in India, the Kassites, the Hittites, and the Persian, Mycenaean, Greek, Roman, Celtic, Teutonic, Slavic, and latter day western European cultures.

## The Indo-European Invasions—Europe

The largest Indo-European invasion of Europe was carried out by four main groups: Celts, Germans, Balts, and Slavs. These four major groups arrived in the European continent in waves from around 4000 BC up to as late as 500 BC. The great Indo-European invasions of Europe took place in four main waves, culminating in a series of subwaves. Each subwave was a smaller tribe from one of the four major migrations.

Leaving their ancestral homeland in the Caucasus, the Celts, Germans, Balts, and Slavs settled different regions of Europe, often giving their names to those areas. Subwaves of note included the Mycenae into Greece, and the Latini into Italy—which sparked off the great classical civilizations for which those lands became famous.

In all of these regions, the invaders found the already present population of Old Europeans to be largely racially assimilable. Hence the Latini mixed with the Etruscans in Italy, producing a Nordic/Mediterranean mix which typified the original Roman type. The same process occurred in Ireland, which is the cause of the "Irish look" varying between Nordic (blue eyed and blonde) and dark hair and dark eyes, or dark hair and light eyes.

The word Celt is derived from Keltoi, the name given to the invaders by the Greek writer Herodotus. To the Romans, the Celts were known as Galli, or Gauls, and in the British Isles as Britanni. Celtic tribes also invaded Greece and Italy.

In 390 BC Celts sacked Rome itself, and followed this up with a raid on the holy Greek site of Delphi in 279 BC. Although these Indo-European tribes used different names, they were all of common Nordic subracial stock. Their languages all stemmed from a single proto-Indo-European language, which formed at a time when all of their ancestors lived together in their original Indo-European heartland in modern day Russia.

The influx of a relatively large amount of new Nordic subgroups into Europe affected the racial makeup of the various regions in different ways, depending upon the nature of the already existing original European population. In areas where there was a sparse population, or where there were larger numbers of Proto-Nordics, the Indo-Europeans maintained to a greater degree their Nordic characteristics.

Where there was an already existing Proto-Nordic/Alpine/Mediterranean mix, the nordicism of the new arrivals was soon diluted. The least populated areas and the region with the fewest number of

Alpine/Mediterranean peoples were in northern and western Europe. These areas became a new Nordic heartland, a situation which remained unaltered until very recently.

By 600 BC, the Britanni Celts had occupied much of what is today known as western Europe—France, parts of the Low Countries (Belgium, Holland), Britain and Spain. The names Brittany (in France) and Britain are derived from this group. These Celts migrating westward

**PRE-ROMAN GERMANIC ROLLER BEARINGS— CIRCA 700–500 BC**

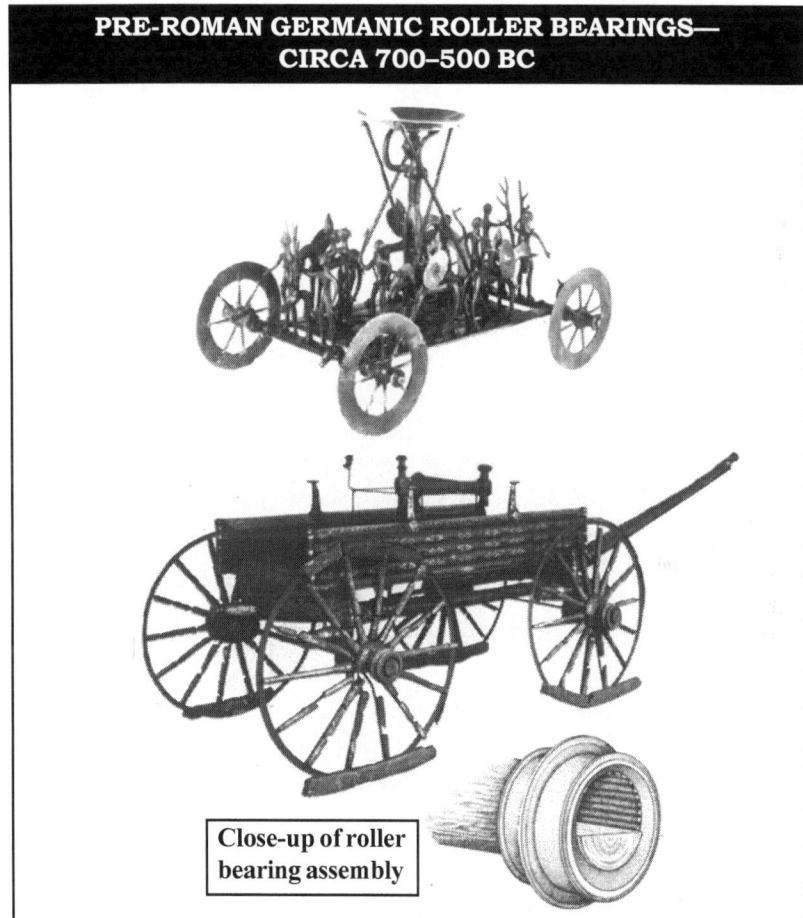

**Close-up of roller bearing assembly**

*Two wagons which illustrate the technical sophistication of pre-Roman Germans. Above: A finely cast bronze wagon complete with figures from Strettweg, Austria, 700 BC. Below: The Dejbjerg wagon, dated between 500 and 50 BC, on display at the National Museum, Copenhagen, Denmark. It contains an astonishingly sophisticated roller bearing system of wooden pins in a bronze brace, to facilitate the turning of the wheel on its axle. Such sophisticated technology shows that the pre-Roman Empire Celts, Germans, Balts, and Slavs were actually not "barbarians," but highly developed people capable of stunning technological feats.*

found the regions sparsely populated with an already quite mixed Proto-Nordic/Alpine/Mediterranean people. In most parts the Celts mixed easily with these groups, producing a wide range of subgroup racial types. This has led to the Celtic "look" varying between the typical short, brown eyed and haired "Celtic" Welshman, and the red haired blue eyed Scotsman also being called a "Celt." These western European Celts were later overrun by the descendants of other Indo-European tribes who had invaded Italy.

## The Germans and Balts in Central and Northern Europe

The Germani Indo-European tribes initially settled in what is today Denmark and southern Scandinavia around the year 4000 BC, but soon thereafter starting moving south, closer to central Europe, later giving their name to Germany. The Balts occupied the northern coast of the continent (giving their name to the Baltic Sea) and the Scandinavian countries (dominating them, with the notable exception of Finland, which has to this day retained a large part of its original Alpine/Mediterranean population makeup).

From 1800 to 400 BC, Celts in southern Germany and Austria developed two advanced metalworking cultures, named by archaeologists after the places where the most plentiful artifacts were found: Urnfield and Hallstatt in Upper Austria. They introduced the use of iron for tools and weapons, and the skills developed in these cultures spread throughout Europe.

In Central Europe the Germans also established themselves in a wide belt running from eastern France through to Poland and south into the Balkans. It is presumed that advance parties of Germans could also have been responsible for the wave of Indo-European peoples called the Latini, who penetrated Italy around this time.

## The Celts Invade Southern Europe

A tribe of Indo-Europeans called the Latini penetrated as far south as Italy, taking control of that peninsula and mixing with the existing original European populations creating what was later to become the world's greatest empire—Rome. The Latini gave their name to the language they carried with them, Latin. In an act of irony, Roman military power was to later overwhelm their distant Indo-European cousins, the Celts in France and Britain, but was in turn to be overrun by the descendants of the Indo-European Germans.

The Latini were not the only Celts to move down the Italian peninsula. Around 400 BC another tribe of Celts invaded northern Italy, drove out an Etruscan settlement, and founded the city of Milan. In 390 BC, a Celtic army succeeded in invading the city of Rome, and only left once the Romans had paid them a ransom in gold.

In southern France and Spain, the Celts met and mixed with a well established Mediterranean population, losing much of their original Nordic physiology because of the far greater number of Mediterraneans present in that region.

Spain would later be occupied by Arabic Islamic armies during the first thousand years AD. Intermingling with the Arabic conquerors produced many people in Spain who are actually Celtic/Mediterranean/Arabic mixes, displaying less of the physical characteristics of their

**BLOND NORDICS IN GREECE:
MOSAIC AT PELLA, FOURTH CENTURY BC**

*The influence of Indo-European Nordic racial types (even the pubic hair of the figures is blond colored) on the Balkans is clear from this floor mosaic at the Macedonian capital of Pella, just northwest of Salonika in northern Greece, circa fourth century BC.*

original Indo-European ancestors. There are still many examples of original Celtic and Mediterranean peoples in Spain to this day.

### *Mycenae—The First Indo-European Invaders in Greece*

The Greek mainland, which was occupied by original Old European Mediterranean types, fell before an invasion of Indo-Europeans called the Mycenae. They flourished on a part of the Greek mainland known as the Peloponnesus, around 1900 BC. There is evidence that the Mycenae had contact with another invading Indo-European tribe, the Hittites, as indications of trading activity exists between these two groups.

On the Greek mainland, many towns emerged at this time, and Mycenaean colonies were established on the coast of Turkey, and even as far as Syria. Mycenaeans are regarded as the forerunners of the classic Greek civilization. They left a magnificent city at Mycenae, whose most famous inhabitant was the king Agamemnon. Mycenae was sacked and destroyed in 1100 BC by an invasion of another Indo-European tribe, the Dorics.

The descendants of the Dorics were known as the Spartans and the Corinthians, two peoples later to feature dramatically in Greek history. The destruction of Mycenae caused many Mycenaeans to flee the Peloponnesus, and a sizable number went to the east coast of today's Turkey. This coastal settlement became known as Ionia, and the Ionian civilization retained the rich legacy of Mycenae and also added elements of Lydian culture. The civilization that was later to rise to great heights in Athens was born in Ionia.

### *The Dorics—Founders of Greece, 1100 BC*

Starting about 1100 BC, a new wave of Indo-Europeans invaded Greece from the north: the Dorics. The period from the time of the Dorian invasion to about 750 BC, is known for the introduction of iron working to the Grecian peninsula.

The time of the Dorian Age is known to historians as the Homeric Age, because little is known about it except from the writings of the poet Homer, in his epics *The Iliad* and *The Odyssey*.

Homeric man was warlike, brave, and desirous of hardship. By all accounts it seems that he had all three attributes in abundance. The economies of the time were subsistence agricultural systems with tribal kings and advisors drawn from noble families.

It was at about this time that the city state was started. Each city had an elevated fortified site, known as its acropolis—where the city's important inhabitants could take refuge or gather to worship their gods. In time the place directly below the acropolis developed a residential and trading area known as the asty.

The asty and the acropolis combined under one central jurisdictive rule, and this unit became known as the polis. The very word politics is derived from this Greek word.

### *The Slavs—From the Cauldron of Conflict*

The Slavs were the one migratory group who settled the closest to the ancestral Indo-European homelands in southern Russia. The land they settled—today known as the Ukraine and Byelorussia ("White" Russia)—was ideal for cereal farming and this encouraged the settlers

**SLAVIC FUNERAL WITH VIKING-STYLE BOAT**

*This idealized painting is of a Slav funeral pyre for one of their chieftains around the year 900 AD. In common with many Indo-Europeans, the Slavs traditionally cremated their important dead along with all their possessions. Where burial was chosen over cremation, it was also common to bury all the chief's artifacts with the corpse. This painting was made based on a description provided by a visitor to southern Russia. It is significant that the painting contains a Viking style boat—an indication that the original Slavs were of identical racial and cultural stock to the Indo-Europeans who settled in Scandinavia and became Vikings.*

to turn to agriculture rather than war or conquest. By 1000 BC, they had started to move westward, occupying territory around the Vistula River, in present day Poland.

Around 700 BC, the whole region was conquered by yet another Indo-European tribe, the Scythians, who appeared from the south (where another branch of that tribe had penetrated into Asia Minor and the Middle East).

By 200 BC, the Scythians had mastered much of the area, easily outfighting the agricultural Slavic farmers. However, by 100 BC another Indo-European invader, a tribe called the Sarmatians, had replaced the Scythians as masters of the Slavic lands, and the last of the Scythian peoples were absorbed into the new Indo-European conquerors, the two groups being almost racially identical. By 600 AD, another tribe of Indo-Europeans, the Goths, swept down from northern Europe and conquered the Sarmatians, taking possession of the lands in eastern Europe.

This repeated conquering and reconquering by peoples who were all essentially of the same stock—Indo-European—created the mix known as the Slavs. Originally then, the Slavs were a virtually pure Indo-European people. Later, a small number of the Slavic population mixed with Mongoloid conquerors, creating a number of mixed-race peoples, who quite incorrectly have come to be regarded as "Slavic." They are nothing of the sort, and true Slavs are as European as any other subgroup, despite much early twentieth century propaganda, from German nationalists in particular, to the contrary.

Probably because of their proximity to the ancient homeland in southern Russia, the tribes who eventually formed the Slavs retained the cultural traits of their ancestors the longest. The Indo-European sun worship religion persisted right into the twelfth century amongst the Slavs, and principal amongst their gods was a hammer wielding deity who rode in a chariot—obviously sharing a common mythological ancestry with the Scandinavian god, Thor.

As the Roman Empire began to unravel at the seams, the Slavs started moving westwards, first penetrating into the Balkan Peninsula, and then into central Europe.

By 650 AD the Slavs had seized the coastline along the Adriatic Sea opposite Italy (today's Albania). They later penetrated as far south as Turkey, where they were swallowed up into the larger mixed race mass occupying that country. The Slavs in eastern Europe not only bore the brunt of the Mongoloid Hunnish invasion of Europe, but also were occupied for nearly one thousand years by the Muslim Turks.

## *Celtic Innovations—Chain Mail and Soap*

The Roman conquest of southeastern Europe, France, and Britain effectively destroyed the Celtic cultural heritage. The Celts were not as literate as the Romans and thus had less of the organizational skills or abilities of their conquerors. However, the Celts were the inventors of chain link armor, iron horse shoes, and seamless iron tires for their chariots. Another important Celtic innovation was soap.

In their art forms, the intricacy of which has become legendary, the links the Celts had with other Indo-European tribes is revealed. The Celtic style is marked by a preference for stylized plant motifs, usually of Greek origin, and fantastic animals, derived from the Scythians and other Russian steppe Indo-Europeans.

Other favorite designs were elliptical curves and opposing curves, spirals, and chevrons, also derived from Russian steppe art. Almost all of the original Indo-Europeans worshipped the sun, and the sun wheel image, circle with a cross through it, dominated many designs. The modern Celtic cross, regarded today as a Christian symbol, was directly copied from this original Indo-European root and was originally a very pagan symbol. Today Celtic as a language has survived at only the extreme ends of the area occupied by the Celts: Wales, Scotland, and a few areas in Ireland.

### *The Original European Religion*

The influence of the Indo-European gods was such that their names and some of the customs associated with their worship live on to this day.

Many of the original Indo-European gods' names were either taken over by Christianity (Hel, the name of

**250 BC BRONZE OF ROSEMETRA SHOWS EARLY GERMANIC TYPE**

The racial makeup of early German tribes is illustrated by this bronze head of the Celtic goddess, Rosemetra, circa 250 BC.

the goddess of the underworld was, for example, plagiarized directly by Christianity) or were kept in various forms, so that five of the seven days of the modern week are named after them, as detailed below. That this is so should not be surprising: these gods were the main religion of the white people of Europe for at least six thousand years, compared to the less than one thousand years that Christianity has existed in northern Europe to date.

The chief characteristics of this original white religion and its array of gods were:

- The world itself was the product of the great world-tree, Yggdrasil, which reached through all time and space. Yggdrasil was, however, always under attack from an evil serpent, Nidhogg. The fountain of Mimir, source of hidden wisdom, lay under one of the roots of the tree.
- Worship of any of these gods was usually conducted in the open—often near holy trees or within arrangements of stones, with the Indo-Europeans using and building megalith sites in Europe for this purpose.
- Odin (also known as Odhinn—called Woden by the Anglo-Saxons, and Wodan or Woutan by the Germans) was the king of the gods. His two black ravens, Huginn ("Thought") and Muninn ("Memory"), flew all over the world to report on the doings of men and gods alike.
- Odin's court was in the great citadel of Valhalla, where all brave warriors went after dying in battle. When Odin took to travel he used his eight-footed steed, Sleipner. He armed himself with his spear, Gungnir, and his most precious jewel, the ring called Draupner.
- Odin was also the god of wisdom, poetry, and magic, and he sacrificed an eye for the privilege of drinking from Mimir, the fountain of wisdom. Odin had three wives.

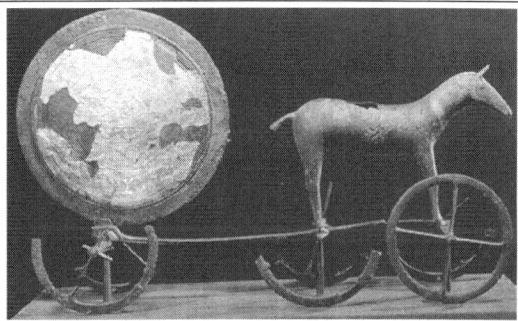

*Ancient German religious ceremonial chariot, with bronze and gold worked disc and horse, circa 1400 BC. The workmanship gives lie to the "barbarian" accusation so often heard from the Romans. Found in the Trundholm Bog on the Danish island of Seeland.*

- Thor was the eldest son of Odin and the strongest of the gods. He had a magic hammer, which he threw with the aid of iron gloves and which always returned to him.
- Odin's other son was Balder (or Baldur), the god of the sun and of light and joy, who was killed after the evil god Loki tricked his blind

twin brother, Hoder, the god of darkness, into killing him.

- Frei or Freyr was the son of the fertility god Njord. Freyr was the god of fruitfulness, prosperity, and peace, and also the bestower of sunlight and rain. He wakened the earth from the long sleep of winter, and prayers for a bountiful harvest were addressed to him.

Frey was the patron god of Sweden; his chief shrine was at Uppsala. His sister was Freya.

- Freya or Freyja was the goddess of love, fertility, and beauty, sometimes identified as the goddess

**THURSDAY—FROM THE GOD THOR**

*Thor, son of Odin, striking down enemies with his mighty hammer, Mjollnir. Thursday is named after him. Four other days of the week are also named after Nordic gods.*

of battle and death. Blonde, blue-eyed, and beautiful, Freya traveled on a golden-bristled boar or in a chariot drawn by cats. In Germany, Freya was sometimes identified with Frigg, the wife of Odin.

- Frigg or Frigga, was the goddess of the sky and wife of Odin, the chief of the gods. She was worshipped as the protector of married love and housewives. A bunch of keys was her symbol.

- Tiu was the god of war and battles. He was represented as having only one hand. Some versions say it was because he could only give victory to one side, and others that it was bitten off by the wolf Fenris.

- Hel was the goddess of the dead. She dwelt beneath one of the three roots of the sacred ash tree, Yggdrasil, and was the daughter of Loki. Odin condemned Hel into the underworld and placed her in charge there, never to emerge again.

- Loki was a giant who represented evil and was possessed of great knowledge and cunning. Loki and Hel would lead the forces of evil against the gods, in the final battle between good and evil, the "Ragnarok," or end of the days.

- Besides these major deities, there were a number of lesser gods: Hermod, Bragi, Forseti, Idun, Nanna, and Sif.

**FREJYA—GODDESS OF LOVE AND BEAUTY**

*Frejya, the Indo-European goddess of love and beauty, riding her chariot drawn by cats. A nineteenth century painting.*

- The Valkyries were a band of warrior-maidens who were sometimes portrayed as Odin's daughters. They included Brunhilde who was immortalized in a Richard Wagner opera. The Valkyries helped Odin choose which warriors deserved to go to Valhalla after dying in battle.

At Valhalla, the warriors would spend their time fighting or feasting until "Ragnarok."

### Five Days of the Week Named after the Northern Gods

Tuesday is named after Tiu, the god of war; this day is still called Tisdag in Sweden and Tirsdag in Denmark. Wednesday is named after Wodan, or Wotan/Odin (Wodansday). In Sweden and Denmark, the day is called Onsdag.

Thursday is named after Thor (Thorsday), while his mother, Frigg, is remembered in the day called Friday (Frigg's day). Baldur, god of the sun and light, is remembered on Sunday. While the name of the day Saturday is not derived from northern gods, it is drawn from the pagan Indo-European pre-Christian Roman celebration of Saturnalia. Monday, or day of the moon, is the only day not directly named after a pre-Christian god.

## *Indo-Europeans in the Middle East*

In their wanderings south and east, the Indo-European tribes took with them various species of north European grain together with ploughing instruments and cattle species—remains of which have been found all the way from northern Europe into modern day Turkey and further into the Middle East.

Indo-European tribes started arriving in the Middle East shortly after the first Old European society had been established in that region, in the fertile river valley between the Tigris and Euphrates Rivers in present day Iraq.

The great Indo-European invasions of the Middle East took place in fits and starts. Some of the more famous were: the Indo-Aryans to present day India, the Aryans to Afghanistan, the Hittites to the Middle East, the Sumerians and Gutians to Mesopotamia, and the Galatians to present day Turkey. Names of countries in this region—Iran, Iraq, and Afghanistan—are derived from the word "Aryan." Further migrations spread even further into China.

The great difference between the western and eastern migrations of the Indo-Europeans was that in the west they found genetically similar populations with whom they mixed, while in the east

**NORDIC INVADERS OF THE STEPPES**

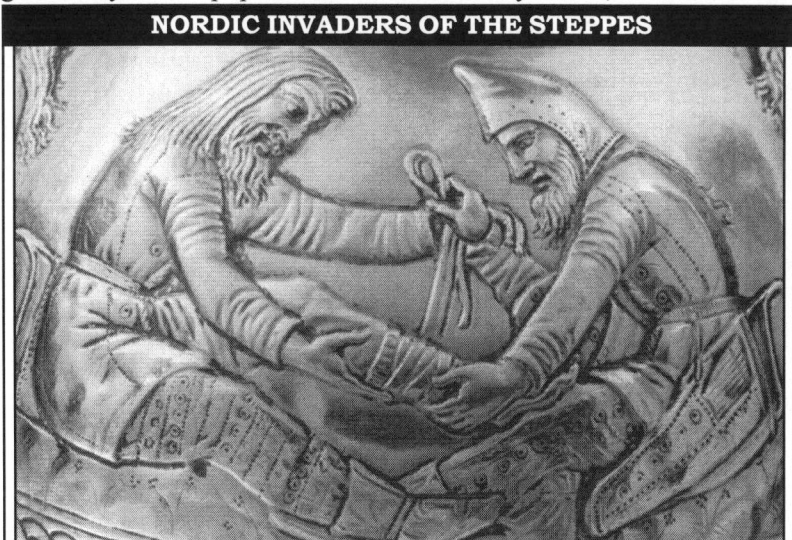

*Scythians, as depicted by themselves on a steel bowl found in a grave site near the Black Sea. At different stages the Scythian area of influence stretched from eastern Europe to the Middle East. Eventually they were overwhelmed by the nonwhite/ mixed race peoples, although it is still possible to see light hair and light eyes— flashbacks to the invaders of these lands many thousands of years ago.*

they mixed with, and were eventually submerged by, genetically dissimilar peoples.

Some of the more notable Indo-European tribes who invaded the Middle East:

- The Amorites were an Indo-European tribe who invaded Asia Minor (Turkey) from the Aegean Sea around 1500 BC, and were noted amongst the local people for worshipping a hammer wielding "Thunder God"— obviously related to the north European Thor. Egyptian paintings of the time depict the Amorites (the Egyptians called them the "Amurru") as fair, light eyed men with Nordic features who were still launching attacks on the Egyptian state as late as 1300 BC. A large number of Amorites settled in Palestine, becoming one of the first Indo-European tribes to mix with the Semitic speaking Jewish tribes in that region, hence they later became associated with Semitism.

- The Scythians overran what is today Palestine, Israel, and Lebanon in the seventh century BC, and some of their light eyed and light haired descendants can still be found amongst the Druse peoples of Lebanon. The Scythians moved through Asia as far as Afghanistan, with forward groups penetrating to the Indus River in India. Many early writers such as Polemon of Ilium, Clement of Alexandria and others, recorded that the Scythians were similar to the Celts in appearance, always being described as "fair or ruddy" in hue.

- The Philistines were an Indo-European tribe who also invaded the Middle East, coming from Crete and bearing many cultural similarities to the Mycenaean culture. The Philistines established an unpopular iron rule over the Jewish tribes they found in the region.

- The Cimmerians were a smaller Indo-European tribe who reached the Middle East around the eighth century BC, and established a short-lived kingdom in the region known today as northern Iran.

- The Indo-European Phyrgians reached modern day Armenia around the eighth century BC, and established another short-lived kingdom.

- Around 900 BC, yet another Indo-European tribe, known as the Persians, reached Azerbaijan, from where they entered modern day Iran, followed closely by the Indo-European Medes tribe.

The Persians, who were more numerous, overpowered the Medes and together these two tribes established what became known as the Persian Empire, ruling over a large number of Asiatic and Arabic racial types.

All of these tribes eventually disappeared through interbreeding with the non-Indo-European peoples in the regions they occupied. It is still possible to see genetic throwbacks amongst the peoples of the Middle East—with fair eyes and fair hair—in that region.

The Indo-European language survived the extinction of many of the tribes from that group, primarily because of the power and dominance of their reigns in the areas of their settlement. Common Indo-European root words are still easily found in a variety of languages spoken in those regions in which they left their mark. As a result, modern academics, cowed by the racial implications of the concept "Indo-European" generally only accept this word as having a linguistic meaning.

## *Aryana—The Aryan Origin of Afghanistan*

Around 2000 BC, a sun-worshipping Indo-European tribe calling themselves Aryans invaded central Asia and occupied territory as far as the north of India. These invaders, who used the Sanskrit written

### ANCIENT IMAGES OF INDO-EUROPEANS IN THE MIDDLE EAST

Right: *A Hittite spearman, in a plumed helmet and carrying a shield, is part of an impressive frieze in the palace at the Hittite city of Carchemish.*

Below right: *A Hittite chariot rides over a conquered Semite. In common with all Nordic Indo-Europeans, the Hittites brought the horse with them into the Middle East. The racial conflict which followed the Indo-European invasion of the region is accurately captured in this detail from the frieze at the great city of Carchemish.*

Below left: *An original statue of Idrimi, the first king of the Mitanni, an Indo-European kingdom in northwestern Mesopotamia, established 1475 BC. It lasted until about 1275 BC, being severely mauled at the hands of a rival Indo-European tribe, the Kassites.*

language, were what became known as the original Aryans. Far off distant racial cousins of the Aryans went west, penetrating as far as Ireland, giving the name "Eire" to that land—also a derivative of the word Aryan.

After 2000 BC, waves of Aryans flooded into modern day Afghanistan, setting up a nation which became known as Aryana, or "Land of the Aryans."

By the middle of the sixth century BC the Persian Empire had incorporated Aryana into its boundaries, and by 330 BC, Alexander the Great had occupied the region. By this time most of the original Aryans in Aryana had been absorbed into the local native population, although it is still possible to this day to see light eyed and light haired individuals amongst the modern Afghanistan population.

During the first century AD, the Kushans, an Asiatic race, occupied Aryana, destroying the last vestiges of the original Indo-Aryan culture and race. Thereafter Aryana fell under the rule of a large number of different nonwhite races, until the seventh century AD when Arab Muslim armies occupied the region.

In 1220 the region was once again overrun by Mongols under Genghis Khan, who devastated the land. By this time the people of Aryana had passed into history—and only that country's name is remembered today.

## The Aryans and India

Another branch of the Aryans penetrated as far east as India, where they also settled and built a civilization. Although the Aryans established a powerful white civilization in northern India, it would be incorrect to think that the native Indians had not created anything of their own. Mixed with original white Mediterraneans, the Indus civilization created by the Harappans was already in existence by the time the Aryans invaded.

*Aryan survivors in modern Iran: Left: Two children from a northwestern village of Iran, and right: A Qashqai girl from the Fars region in southern Iran near the Persepolis ruins.*

The invading Aryans were more advanced and referred to the conquered Indians as "Dasyu"—the "dark ones" or slaves. Indo-Aryan poetry (the *Rigveda*) is full of stories of war against the Dasyu, and reflects the stark racial divisions between the conquering Aryans and the conquered Indians.

## Racial Conflict in the Rigveda

**NORDIC REMNANTS IN AFGHANISTAN**

The *Rigveda*, the original holy book of the Aryan conquerors of India, contains a great many references to the race of the conquerors and the conquered. According to this book, the leader of the Aryan invasion was one Indra, and his role in "slaying the Dasyus" (the Negroids in India) is a prominent theme:

*Afghan children in a refugee center, in Toza-Lokai refugee camp, October 2001. Note the blond child, compared to the other children, some of whom show distinctly Asiatic racial traits.*

"*Thou, Indra, art the destroyer of all the cities, the slayer of the Dasyus, the prosperer of man, the lord of the sky*" (RgV. VIII 87.6). It goes on to use the word "black" in a number of instances to describe the Dasyu: "*Indra, the slayer of Vrittra, the destroyer of cities, has scattered the Dasyu (hosts) sprang from a black womb*" (RgV. II 20.6).

### The "Aryan Color" in the Rigveda

The *Rigveda* praises the god who "*destroyed the Dasyans and protected the Aryan color.*" (Rg.V. III 34.9) It then goes on to thank the god who "*bestowed on his white friends the fields, bestowed the sun, bestowed the waters*" (Rg.V. I 100.18).

Black skin is repeatedly referred to with abhorrence. Starting with a description of the "black skin" ('Krishnam Vacham') in RgV. IX 41.1, Sam. V I. 491 and II. 242, and in RgV. IX 73, it is said that "*stormy gods who rush on like furious bulls and scatter the black skin,*" and it claims that "*the black skin, the hated of Indra*" will be swept out of heaven (RgV. IX 73.5).

Rg.V. I 130.8 tells how the "black skin" was conquered: "*Indra protected in battle the Aryan worshipper, he subdued the lawless for Manu, he conquered the black skin.*" The *Rigveda* thanks God for "*scattering the slave bands of black descent,*" and for stamping out "*the vile Dasyan color*" (Rg.V. II.20.7, II 12.4). It also contains this choice remark which sums up the Aryan's opinion of their nonwhite subjects: "*Black skin is impious*" (Sans., Rg.V. II. 12.4).

Other extracts from the *Rigveda* further illustrate the sharp racial divisions in this time:

- Indra - 1.130.8 - *"Indra in battle helps his Aryan worshipper, he who hath hundred helps at hand in every fray, in frays that win the light of heaven. Plaguing the lawless he gave up to Manu's seed the dusky skin; Blazing, 'twere, he burns each covetous man away, he burns the tyrannous away."*

- Indra - 4.16.13 - *"Thou to the son of Vidathin, Rjisvan, gavest up mighty Mrgaya and Pipru. Thou smotest down the swarthy fifty thousand, and rentest forts as age consumes a garment."*

- Indra - 5.29.10 - *"One car-wheel of the Sun thou rolledst forward, and one thou settest free to move for Kutsa. Thou slewest noseless Dasyus with thy weapon, and in their home o'erthrewest hostile speakers"* ("Noseless Dasyus" would suggest a reference to flat nosed Negroid types).

- Soma Pavamana - 9.41.1 - *"Active and bright have they come forth, impetuous in speed like bulls, driving the black skin far away."*

- Soma Pavamana - 9.73.5 - *"O'er Sire and Mother they have roared in unison bright with the verse of praise, burning up riteless men, blowing away with super-natural might from earth and from the heavens the swarthy skin which Indra hates."*

## Rigveda *Describes Aryan Gods as Blonds*

- Indra - 10.23.4 - *"With him too is this rain of his that comes like herds: Indra throws drops of moisture on his yellow beard. When the sweet juice is shed he seeks the pleasant place, and stirs the worshipper as wind disturbs the wood."*

Indra - 10.96.8 - *"At the swift draught the Soma-drinker waxed in might, the Iron One with yellow beard and yellow hair. He, Lord of Tawny Coursers, Lord of fleet-foot Mares, will bear his Bay Steeds safely over all distress."*

- Indra - 1.9.3 - *"O Lord of all men, fair of cheek, rejoice thee in the gladdening lauds, present at these drink-offerings."*

### *Indra's Weapon: Thor's Lightning Bolt?*

In what could easily be another indicator of the common cultural origins between the *Rigveda* and the Indo-European gods, Indra's greatest weapon is said, in the Hindu holy book, to be a lightning bolt—

identical to the weapon of Thor, the northern European god:

- Indra - 1.100.18 - *"He, much invoked, hath slain Dasyus and Simyus, after his wont, and laid them low with arrows. The mighty Thunderer with his fair-complexioned friends won the land."*

- Indra - 1.101.1 - *"Sing, with oblation, praise to him who maketh glad, who with Rjisvan drove the dusky brood away. Fain for help, him the strong whose right hand wields the bolt, him girt by Maruts we invoke to be our Friend."*

- Indra - 1.103.3 and 4 - *"Armed with his bolt and trusting in his prowess he wandered shattering the forts of Dasas. Cast thy dart, knowing, Thunderer, at the Dasyu;*

**NEGROID DEMONS IN HINDUISM**

*From a Hindu temple in India: In Hindu mythology, the white goddess Durga slays the Negroid demon Mahishasura. In Hindu mythology most of the gods have white skins and European like features, while the demons are distinctly Negroid. The Hindu holy book, the* Rigveda, *is very graphic in its description of racial conflict.*

*increase the Arya's might and glory, Indra. For him who thus hath taught these human races, Maghavan, bearing a fame-worthy title, Thunderer, drawing nigh to slay the Dasyus, hath given himself the name of Son for glory."*

### Aryan Origin of Caste System

At the time of the writing of the *Rigveda*, a clear distinction was drawn between the two types of people in the Indus River Valley: the "fair" conquering immigrants and the "dark" native people.

Within three hundred years, however, physical mixing had proceeded to the point where these two racial classes had been subdivided further. Membership in each class was determined solely by the color of an individual's skin. This came to be known as the caste system. The word "caste" was the term given by Portuguese travelers many centuries later, from the Latin word castus, meaning pure. The original Sanskrit for the caste system was "varna," which means color.

## BOLLYWOOD—THE LAST OF THE ARYANS

*The last of India's Aryans can be found in that country's film industry, Bollywood.*
Left: *The Indian actress, Pooja Bhatt, shows European eye and skin color. Her*
*features contrast with those of a more typical Indian female, alongside.* Right: *The*
*male Indian actor Aamir Khanall, whose Aryan ancestry contrasts strongly with the*
*more typical Indian male, alongside.*

   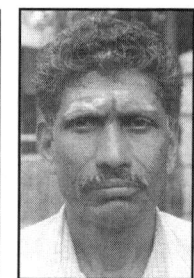

As assimilation and integration between the Aryans and the Dasyu increased, the caste system became more and more complex, till four major divisions were created, with membership in each group dependent upon the coloring of the individual. This four tier system still exists in India today, with the highest caste, the Brahmans (or "priests"), being the lightest in color, and the Sudas or "untouchables" being the darkest.

Within a few hundred years the original Aryans had become so assimilated that their contribution to Indian civilization can be considered to have ended. Their legacy lives on in the language, religion, and poetry of India—and the caste system. Blue or gray eyes can, however, still be found in the Indian upper classes, which tend to be concentrated in the northern parts of that country, where the original Aryan settlement took place.

Many of these lighter colored Indians become successful actors and actresses in India's film industry which is nicknamed "Bollywood." In accordance with the caste system, the more European looking the actors, the more successful they tend to be. Genetic studies conducted in India have confirmed not only the Indo-European invasion, but also the considerable genetic gap between the castes.

## THE HISTORY OF THE SWASTIKA

The swastika was a letter of the ancient Indo-European Sanskrit language, and originally was a symbol of the sun, meaning "well being." This emblem was carried by Celts, Germans, and Slavs throughout their wanderings, and became the Celtic cross. It was incorporated into the Indo-Aryan religion, and then transported to the Hindu religion. As an enduring symbol of the Indo-European peoples wherever they went, the swastika is found in all the lands where these people settled. Some examples:

**1. Left: The Swastika in India:**
*The swastika can be seen on a carving called an ayagaptha, in Mathura, India.*
*The emblem is one of the last remains of the tribe of Indo-Europeans—who called themselves Aryans—who invaded India. In that land, they were eventually absorbed into the overwhelming nonwhite mass, creating the caste system still present in that country to this day.*

**2. Right: The Swastika in Classical Greece:**
*An example of how the swastika was also used as a symbol in classical Greece. Here it can be seen as a decoration on the clothing of a picture of Athene, the goddess of wisdom, the arts, and war—and also patron of the city of Athens. This detail is from a Greek vase dating from approximately 500 BC.*

**3. Left: The Swastika in Classical Rome:**
*The Indo-European origins of the Romans—in particular the Latini tribe—are apparent through their liberal use of the swastika as an emblem. Here the swastika can be seen underneath the figures on the Ara Pacis Augustae: the altar built to commemorate the peace established by Augustus, consecrated 4 July 13 BC.*

**4. Right: The Swastika in the Viking era:**
*A swastika bearing detail from a bucket handle on the well preserved Viking ship, called the Osberg ship, circa 800 AD. The handle depicts a figure carrying a shield with four swastika sun emblems in its corners.*

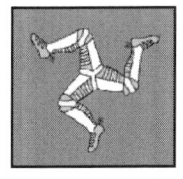

**5. Left: The Isle of Man Triskelion, circa tenth century AD:**
Top: *The flag of the Isle of Man, called a triskelion, a direct derivative of the swastika.*

*According to that island's history, this symbol was of Norsk [Norwegian] origin, and was displayed on the armorial bearings of the kings of Norway. The triskelion also appears on this sixth century BC Greek vase—evidence of cultural links through race and time.*

**6. Right: Christian Symbolism, circa twelfth century AD:**
*Although pagan in origin, the swastika was so set in Western culture that it was absorbed into Christian symbolism. Here it can be seen on a twelfth century Welsh church engraving, which depicts Christ carrying a swastika banner. The swastika was also developed into the "Celtic cross" which was often used as a Christian tombstone.*

**7. Left: The Swastika in Western Architecture:**
*The swastika was a popular motif in Western architecture, and was widely used in major public buildings in Europe and North America, from the Opera Building in Paris through to the front door of the Metropolitan Museum of Art in New York City. Alongside is the entrance to the "Met" in New York City, and below, a close-up view of the swastika motif, displayed over the heads of thousands of visitors.*

# CHAPTER SIX

## To the Ends of the Earth—Lost White Migrations

**In addition to the great Indo-European migrations, several other waves of white migration occurred, varying in number, influence and reach—the most spectacular being a white settlement in North America dating from approximately 7000 BC.**

Knowledge of these migrations had been lost for centuries. Due to relatively recent archaeological finds, many have now been rediscovered. In this way Nordic and white Mediterranean remains (sometimes preserved naturally, sometimes preserved through artificial means) have been discovered in China, the Canary Islands, and in North America. Some are thousands of years old.

The discovery of these mummies shows without question that early white migrations across seas and continents took place; it is just the exact number of individuals who undertook these migrations which is still a matter of debate.

### The Tocharians—Ancient Whites in China

The Tocharians comprised one of the most famous eastern migrations of Celtic peoples into the Far East, reaching the Takla Makan Desert (situated

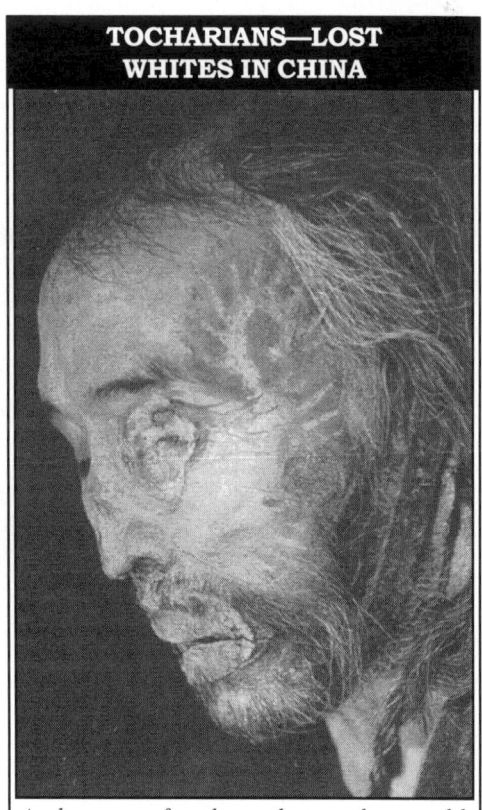

**TOCHARIANS—LOST WHITES IN CHINA**

*A close up of a three thousand-year-old, unmistakably white, Tocharian male, one of many unearthed from the graveyards in the Takla Makan Desert in western China. This mummy is on display at the Xinjiang museum, Uromqi, China.*

between Kazakhstan, Kyrgyzstan, and Tibet) in China around 1500 BC. Remarkably, this great migration was unknown until the 1977 AD discovery of 3,500-year-old graves of these people.

As a result of the natural dryness of the environment, many of the corpses are almost perfectly preserved, with their reddish-blond hair, long noses, round eyes, and finely woven tartan clothing (usually associated with the Celts in Scotland), showing undeniably white racial traits.

The Chinese civilization always contained stories of blue eyed and blond haired leaders who were the originators of Buddhism and the first leaders and organizers of Chinese society. These stories were always regarded as pure legend until the 1977 discovery of the graveyards of the Tocharians. The mummies are unequivocally Nordic racial types. The graveyards lie near the ruins of the great Tocharian cities, built along the famous Silk Route. It is beyond doubt that whites settled in China, and the Chinese legends of white influence on that civilization have a basis in fact.

These people have become known by the language which they spoke: Tocharian. The civilization which they built consisted of great cities, temples, and centers of learning and art. They were also the builders and maintainers of the original Silk Road—the path for trade between the West and China. It was originally thought that the Chinese built the great cities along the Silk Road, but the discovery of the remains of the original people of this region shows that the impressive ruins which still lie undisturbed along that road, are the remains of a great lost white civilization.

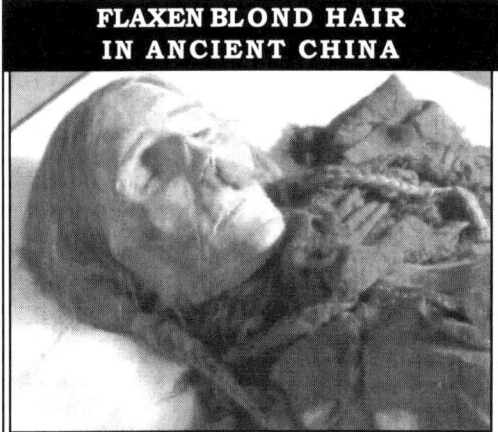

**FLAXEN BLOND HAIR IN ANCIENT CHINA**

*A Tocharian female mummy with long flaxen blonde hair perfectly preserved in ponytails. She has been dated from 1500 BC, and was discovered in the Zagunluq Cemetery, Takla Makan Desert. Items of woven material, identical to Celtic cloth, definitively proved the Indo-European origins of the Tocharians, who not only built the fantastic Silk Road cities which today lie deserted, but who are also credited with bringing Buddhism, horses, the saddle, and ironworking to China.*

The first white mummy in the region was discovered by accident in 1977 after shifting sands uncovered a female

## THE "BEAUTY OF LOULAN" RECONSTRUCTED

Left: *In 1980 a blonde haired mummy was found in Loulan, China. The mummy was radiocarbon dated as being from 1800 BC.* Right: *A reconstruction of the mummy, named the "Beauty of Loulan" as used on separatist literature in the region, which to this day, shows a large degree of non-Chinese ancestry amongst its population.*

corpse whose body had been mutilated, presumably in some act of war. Excavation around her corpse uncovered a further sixteen mummies, so perfectly preserved by the desert that traces of tears were found on the face of a mummified infant. Fully dressed bodies were found wearing finely woven woolen textiles with Celtic patterns, leather shoes, and jewelry. The desert conditions proved so exceptional that even pieces of bread used as offerings were preserved intact alongside what is the world's oldest saddle. In one grave, excavators discovered a saddle cover and a pair of trousers with drawings of humans on one leg—one face had blue eyes.

By the early 1990s, over a thousand Nordic corpses had been uncovered from the graveyards in the region (called Wapu), but by 1998, the Chinese government had halted further archaeological expeditions to the area, quite likely for fear of exposing yet more ancient European faces to the world. The current inhabitants of the surrounding lands, who are obviously not pure Chinese and who speak a form of Turkish rather than Chinese, have been agitating for independence for some time. The discovery of the white mummies has served to highlight their racial and ethnic differences from the Chinese and the issue has become a political hot potato for that country's government. However, some of the mummies which have already been uncovered are still on display in a local museum, while others lie in storerooms slowly deteriorating.

## Ancient Europeans in Eastern China

Ancient white influence was not limited to the western parts of China. A genetic study published in the journal *Molecular Biology and Evolution* (Vol. 17, pages 1396–1400, 2000) titled "Genetic Structure of a 2,500-Year-Old Human Population in China and Its Spatiotemporal Changes" came to a remarkable conclusion. The Chinese and Japanese scientists who authored that report found that the city of Linzi (located in the far eastern seaboard province of Shandong), had over the past 2,500 years undergone massive changes, and that even today, that *"population showed greater genetic similarity to present-day European populations than to present-day east Asian populations."* The report continued: *"The 2,000-year-old Linzi population had features that were intermediate between the present-day European/ 2,500-year-old Linzi populations and the present-day east Asian populations. These relationships suggest the occurrence of drastic spatiotemporal changes in the genetic structure of Chinese people during the past 2,500 years."*

This report proved conclusively that ancient Europeans had penetrated China right through to the Pacific Ocean. Some Chinese legends maintained that the first Chinese emperors, who brought unity and civilization to China, had fair hair or blue eyes.

## Chinese Leaders with Blue and Green Eyes

The new finds are forcing a reexamination of old Chinese books that describe historical or legendary figures of great height, with deep-set blue or green eyes, long noses, full beards, and red or blond hair. Scholars had once scoffed at these references, but it now transpires that they were correct.

One of these accounts can be found in the song to the great General Lü by the Chinese poet Li He (circa 790–816 AD) in his "Romance of the Three Kingdoms:"

> *General Lü, The valiant-hearted,*
> *Riding alone on Scarlet Hare,*
> *Out of the gates of Ch'in,*
> *To weep at Gold Grain Mound*
> *By funeral trees.*

*Inscrutable that vaulted azure,*
*Arching over earth,*
*This is the way the world wags*
*In our Nine Provinces.*
*Gleaming ore from Scarlet Hill!*
*Hero of our time!*
**Green-eyed general,** you well know
*The will of Heaven!*
(Emphasis added. Translation from
*Goddesses, Ghosts, and Demons—The*
*Collected Poems of Li He* (790–816),
Translated by J.D. Frodsham, North Point
Press, San Fransisco, 1983.)

*A swastika carved on the underside of a bowl, recovered from the Silk Road cities, is a clear cultural indication of the Indo-European origins of the Tocharians. Like all other Indo-Europeans, the Tocharians brought with them the Sanskrit language, and the sun wheel was their alphabetic symbol for "well being." From the Tocharian influence, the swastika has spread throughout China to this day.*

### The Disappearance of the Tocharians

Over time, these white people mixed with the neighboring Mongoloid tribes and slowly vanished from history as a distinct group. The physical features of the people currently living in western China clearly show part white and part Mongoloid traits, with blond hair not unknown. Thus it was that the white civilization of ancient China vanished through racial mixing, with only the crumbling ruins of their cities and their corpses remaining as silent witnesses.

### The Guanches of the Canary Islands

Off the coast of West Africa lie the Canary Islands, a region which became home to a mysterious group of Nordics in antiquity who were known as the Guanches. While it is unknown for sure how they arrived on the islands, what is certain is that they shared a number of cultural characteristics with the ancient Egyptians and that their building style appears to have been replicated in South and Central America. It is possible to see what the Guanches looked like due to the fortuitous existence of some of their mummies which are on display in the Canary Islands' national museum. The corpses on display are estimated to be between six hundred and one thousand years old.

An examination of one of the mummies' bodies showed incisions that virtually matched those found in Egyptian mummies, although the string used by the Guanche embalmers to close the wounds was much coarser than what the Egyptian experts used. The Guanches also

## GUANCHE AND MAYAN PYRAMIDS—SIMILARITIES

Left: *One of the pyramids of Guimar, Canary Islands.* Right: *A Mayan pyramid on the Atlantic coast of Mexico, at Chichen Itza. The resemblance is unmistakable. There is strong evidence to suggest that whites used the Canary Island current to cross the Atlantic Ocean and influence the Central and Southern American civilizations in pre-Columbian times.*

possessed the art of writing, although this has not yet been the subject of any major study.

### Guanche Pyramids on the Canary Islands

The most stunning link between the Guanches and the Egyptians comes in the form of pyramids. The Guanches built several small step pyramids on the islands, using exactly the same model as those found in ancient Egypt and Mesopotamia. The pyramids have an east-west alignment which indicates that they probably had a religious purpose, most likely associated with the rising and setting of the sun. Carefully built stairways on the west side of each pyramid lead up to the summit, which in each case has a flat platform covered with gravel, possibly used for religious or ceremonial purposes.

### Guanche Type Pyramids Found in Mexico

The famous explorer, Thor Heyerdahl, who "rediscovered" the pyramids on the Canary Islands and who set up an academic body to study the phenomena, argued that the pyramids may be remains from explorers who sailed the Atlantic in ancient times, and who may have possibly forged a link with the pre-Columbian civilizations of the Americas. As the original inhabitants of the Canary Islands were fair haired and bearded, it was possible, Heyerdahl suggested, that long before the fifteenth century, people of the same stock as those who settled the Canary Islands also sailed the same route along the Canary Current that took Christopher Columbus to the Americas.

This theory formed the basis of Heyerdahl's famous "RA" expeditions in which he showed that it was possible to cross the Atlantic

## RED-HAIRED GUANCHE MUMMIES ON DISPLAY IN CANARY ISLAND MUSEUM

*Two Guanche mummies, with red hair and other Nordic features—the original inhabitants of the Canary Islands. It is unknown at what date they settled the islands, but they show cultural similarities with the ancient Egyptians. It seems likely that they were original Cro-Magnon types.*

in an Egyptian reed boat. In fact, Columbus's starting point was the Canary Islands, where he obtained supplies and water on Gomera, the island next to Tenerife.

The Guanches on Tenerife in 1492 did not permit Columbus to land on their island. They were not impressed by the physical appearance of the bearded Europeans, who looked like the Guanches themselves.

When Columbus and the Europeans who followed in his wake landed in the Americas, they were welcomed and initially worshiped as gods, since the beardless Indians they encountered believed that the Spanish belonged to the same people as the legendary founders of their civilization, bearded men from across the Atlantic Ocean.

According to the Aztec and Olmec (Central American Amerind) legends, their god, Quetzalcoatl, had Nordic features (eyes and hair color) and a beard. This god came from over the sea and taught the Amerinds how to raise corn and build structures.

There is a marked similarity between the step pyramids on the Canary Islands and those in Central and South America, strongly suggesting yet another great lost white migration, this time to Central and South America, perhaps a thousand years or more before Columbus.

There is also clear evidence from the Mexican side of the Atlantic Ocean that whites—blond haired whites—reached that part of the world long before the Spanish explorations of the late 1490s.

On the walls of the Temple of the Warriors, Chichen Itza, located on the east coast of Mexico, is a series of paintings depicting white prisoners captured by dark skinned natives, and then a white man with long blond hair being sacrificed by the nonwhites. These paintings date from before Christopher Columbus sailed the Atlantic in 1492.

## DID THE GUANCHES CROSS THE ATLANTIC?

*The best evidence for early Guanche crossings of the Atlantic comes from Mexico itself. The Amerind "Temple of Warriors" located on the east coast of Mexico, dates from pre-Columbian times, yet its murals contain a series of images which clearly show white prisoners being sacrificed.* Top right: *White prisoners, captured and stripped naked by dark skinned natives.* Center right: *A white prisoner, with long blond hair, being sacrificed by Chichen Itza warriors.* Below right: *The same mural, reconstructed in life size, with models, on display at the Parque Etnografico Museum on the Canary Islands by Thor Heyerdahl.*

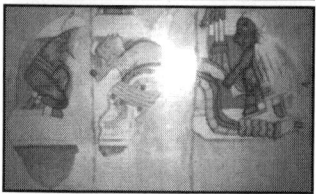

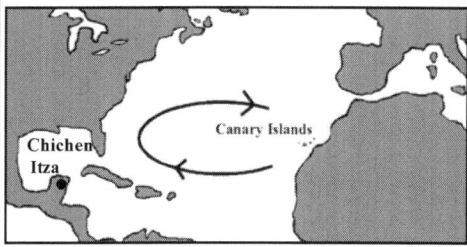

*The position of the Canary Islands and the route of the Canary Current to and from the Americas. The existence of the red haired Guanches on the Canary Islands, combined with the red haired pre-Columbus mummies found in South America and the marked similarity in pyramid building styles, indicate that whites probably used the Canary Current to cross the Atlantic, most likely between 2000 and 500 BC. Note the position of the pre-Columbian centre of Chicen Itza, where the murals alongside originate.*

## The Disappearance of the Guanches

Guanche artifacts, such as cave murals, tombs, stone and mortar walls, broken pottery, and other everyday items are abundant on the island. Similar artifacts have been found on the African continent—notably in Morocco, indicating that at some stage the Guanches crossed the sea to Africa. There they started mixing with Arabic and other nonwhite racial types. This is likely the cause of some flashes of blond hair and light colored eyes found amongst the Berber population of northwest Africa to this day.

The pyramids and other structures on the islands seem to have been constructed by an advanced people. By the time of the Spanish invasion, the Guanches had lost much of their civilized apparel, and Spanish accounts have it that they were attacked by naked tribesmen, who sometimes inflicted serious military defeats upon the invading

Spaniards. It was only in 1496 that the Spaniards finally defeated the last of the Guanches. The arrival of the white Spanish in the mid-fourteenth century saw the remaining Nordic Guanches absorbed into the new settler population. The blond, blue-eyed, tall stock has been preserved in part, and can still be seen today in many individuals on the island. Culturally speaking, the Guanche civilization was completely absorbed by the imported continental European culture, so that the Canary Islands remain Spanish territory to this day.

### White Types in North America 7000 BC?

One of the most enigmatic of the lost great white migrations is the existence of skeletal remains in North America. These date from as early as 7000 BC, appear to be white in nature, and most certainly are not "Native American" or Amerind (whose racial traits are Mongoloid or Asiatic—the original homeland of the Amerind peoples).

It is beyond dispute that white tribes reached China. Compared to the distances those whites traveled, it would have been a relatively

**THE FIRST WHITES IN NORTH AMERICA CIRCA 7000 BC?**

**The Nine Thousand-Year-Old Spirit Cave Mummy, Nevada, USA**

*A reconstruction of the face of the Spirit Cave Mummy, based on a cast of the skull, showing the various stages used in the reconstruction process (as published in* Newsweek, *US edition, April 26, 1999). The Spirit Cave Mummy was the first—but not the last—ancient remain found in America that were clearly not Amerind and which forced a rethink on exactly who are "Native Americans." Discovered in 1940, but only analyzed racially in 1994, this nine thousand-year-old mummy was discovered in a cave in Nevada, USA. The clearly Caucasian facial structure indicates that whites were on that continent, either prior to, or simultaneous with, the originally Mongoloid Amerind population.*

short hop across the rest of Asia to the Bering Straits (which divides Asia and North America) and then into the North American continent. This was exactly how the Amerinds got to North America; there is no reason why advanced groups of whites could not have traveled this route even before the Amerinds.

It is equally possible that early whites could have sailed from western Europe, hugging the last ice pack along its coastline past present day Greenland. Other evidence (reviewed below) supports this possibility.

### Spirit Cave Mummy—Used Diamond Plaited Textile Matting

In 1940 a mummified and well preserved body was unearthed in the Spirit Cave complex, located in the American state of Nevada. The mummy's scalp was complete and skin remained on the back and shoulders.

On the head there was a small tuft of straight dark hair, which changed to reddish-brown when exposed to light. Artifacts discovered in the Spirit Cave totaled some sixty-seven items, including knives, baskets, and animal bones.

The mummy was lying on a fur blanket dressed in a twisted skin robe with leather shoes on its feet and a twined mat sewn around its head and shoulders. A similar mat was wrapped around the lower portion of the body. Two bags contained cremation ashes and bone fragments.

The style of weaving used in the textiles is known as diamond-plaited matting. This is a complex system requiring a high degree of sophistication in material manufacture technology that would have rivaled any on the planet at the time.

The mummy became known as the Spirit Cave Mummy, and was placed in the Nevada State Museum's storage facility for decades. Only in 1994 was the mummy "rediscovered" and the startling truth revealed. Tests showed that the corpse was 9,400 years old—a forty-five- to fifty-five-year old male—and, most importantly, not an ancestor of any modern Indian tribe.

The age was determined by performing seven separate radiocarbon-dating tests on samples of bone, hair, and the two reed mats in which he was buried.

The Spirit Cave Mummy's white racial traits are undeniable. It has a long, small face and a large cranium, in sharp contrast to the Mongoloid features of American Indians. The Spirit Cave Mummy represents some form of non-Amerind, and most likely white, settlement or incursion into North America around the year 7000 BC. the Nevada State Museum went public with its findings on the mummy in 1996. It immediately sparked a furor, with the American Indians demanding that the corpse be reburied in accordance with tribal custom—falsely claiming the Spirit Cave Mummy as one of their own.

The Amerind tribe involved, the Paiutes, laid claim to the

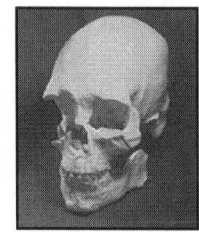
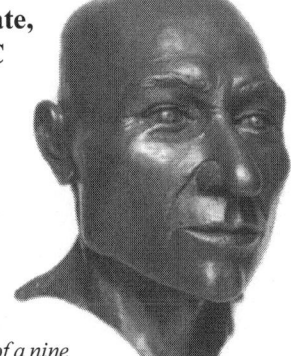

**Kennewick Man— Washington State, USA, 7000 BC**

Above left: *The skull of a nine thousand-year-old white racial type discovered in North America: Kennewick Man, found in the Kennewick River in Washington State, USA. Artifacts found in the surrounding area suggest he was part of a larger community.*

Above right: *A reconstruction of the face of Kennewick Man, based on the skull. The features are clearly indicative of white racial characteristics.*

corpse under an American law, the Native American Graves Protection and Repatriation Act of 1990, which allows for the return and reburial of bodies of "Native Americans." An extended legal dispute arose over the issue of ownership. As part of the legal wrangling, the Paiute have consistently refused to allow DNA testing of the corpse.

This is not the only case where American Indians have blocked the study of obviously non-Amerind remains. Another case, that of Kennewick Man was similarly held up by Indian objections, and in 1993 another skeleton was found near Buhl in the state of Idaho. The latter remains were some 10,600 years old, making them the oldest ever found in North America. The skeleton was turned over to local Indians, the Shoshone-Bannock tribe, and reburied before any comprehensive testing could be undertaken.

In this way several unique anthropological specimens have already been given to, and buried by, Indian tribes. In Montana, naturally shed human hair discovered by one archaeologist elicited an Amerind claim. Although the hair had not been buried in any kind of ritual, the US federal government has prevented testing of the hair to commence.

The reason for the American Indian sensitivity over the issue is obvious. Proof that whites, even if only in small numbers, walked the continent of North America before the Amerinds themselves would undermine the latter's claim to be the original "Native Americans." For the sake of political correctness, much valuable scientific data is being suppressed.

### Kennewick Man 7200 BC

On July 28, 1996, another dramatic find was made in the state of Washington in the northwestern United States: on that day a well-preserved skeleton was found in the Columbia River in Kennewick. This skeleton has become known as Kennewick Man.

The nearly intact skeletal remains, found with a stone arrowhead lodged in the pelvic bone, are so clearly non-Amerind and so close to white, that forensic anthropologists and local police first thought them to be those of a nineteenth century white male, about forty-five years old, who was killed by an arrow.

Radiocarbon dating of a finger bone, however, showed it to have great age—at least nine thousand years old—putting the individual on the North American continent around the year 7200 BC.

Like the Spirit Cave Mummy, Kennewick Man's white racial traits are the cause of much controversy. Local American Indian tribes filed claims for possession of Kennewick Man. After a protracted legal dispute, scientists won the right to forensically examine the remains.

Initial examination of Kennewick Man's skull indicated a likely white, even Nordic, cranial structure, differing greatly from the Mongoloid skull shape of American Indians.

The man was a little over five and a half feet tall and of slender build. The skull is dolichocranial (cranial index 73.8) rather than brachycranic, the face narrow rather than broad and flat. (The average cranial index for Nordic racial types is 74.)

Other features are a long, broad nose that projects markedly from the face and high, round orbits. The mandible is v-shaped, with a pronounced, deep chin. Many of these characteristics are definitive of modern day white peoples.

Other nearby finds of bone needles close to the Kennewick Man's remains assume that he may possibly have worn tailored clothing. These astonishing finds reveal that Kennewick Man was not alone, but that he lived in a community of some sort. In October 1999, the US Government issued a report on Kennewick Man, claiming that the skeletal remains possibly resembled the Ainu racial type (found in Japan). The Ainu also have strong Caucasian features, suggesting some type of ancient white ancestry, although this has to date not been borne out by genetic research.

## Fork Rock Cave—Nine Thousand-Year-Old Sandals

In Oregon there is a cave known as the Fork Rock Cave which has been the center of a number of significant non-biological finds. In 1938, seventy pairs of sandals made of sagebrush were discovered, and radiocarbon dating technology dated them at 9,000 years old. Charcoal was also found with a radiocarbon date indicating it was 13,200 years old.

The sagebrush sandals were intricately woven, and the other items found in the cave included projectile points, scrapers, drills, a wooden trigger for a trap, small pieces of basketry, and awls to make leather (or tailored clothing for the Kennewick Man and his peers), all of which indicated highly skilled workers. These differ vastly from Indian artifacts both in ancient North America and in modern Indian findings.

**LOVELOCK CAVE SKULLS**

*Skulls recovered from the Lovelock Cave, where, according to Amerind tradition, the last of a red haired tribe, the Si-Te-Cah, were exterminated. The "long," or doliocranic, nature of the Lovelock Cave skulls also indicate their white ancestry.*

### The Si-Te-Cah—The Amerinds' White Enemies

In fact, red haired enemies feature in local Indian legends—or what were thought legends until the discovery of what became known as the Lovelock mummies. The Paiute Indians—the same ones who object to the scientific investigation of the Spirit Cave Mummy—had a number of legends dealing with red haired enemies whom they called the "Si-Te-Cah."

Significantly, the name Si-Te-Cah means "tule eaters"—tule being the fibrous reed which is the base material of the mats in which the Spirit Cave Mummy was buried. Tule is no longer found in the region and was likely imported along with the people who used it.

According to the Paiute legends, the red haired peoples were warlike, and a number of the Indian tribes joined together in a long war against them. Eventually, the last of the Si-Te-Cah were trapped in what is now called Lovelock Cave. When they refused to come out, the

Indians piled brush before the cave mouth and set it aflame. The Si-Te-Cah were incinerated.

Sarah Winnemucca Hopkins, daughter of Paiute Chief Winnemucca, related many stories about the Si-Te-Cah in her book *Life among the Paiutes.* On page seventy-five, she wrote: *"My people say that the tribe we exterminated had reddish hair. I have some of their hair, which has been handed down from father to son. I have a dress which has been in our family a great many years, trimmed with the reddish hair. I am going to wear it some time when I lecture. It is called a mourning dress, and no one has such a dress but my family."*

In 1931, further skeletons were discovered in the Humboldt Lake bed. Eight years later, a mystery skeleton was unearthed on a ranch in the region. In each case, the skeletons were exceptionally tall—much taller than the surrounding Amerinds. There is a small display on the Si-Te-Cah in the Lovelock museum today, but it ignores the evidence which indicates that the Si-Te-Cah were not Amerinds. The Nevada State Historical Society also displays some artifacts from the cave.

### Wizards Beach Man—Pyramid Lake, Nevada

Yet another non-Amerind skeleton has been found at a place called Pyramid Lake, Nevada. The remains are known as Wizards Beach Man. This skeleton has been dated at 9,225 years old. Once again the skull shape is distinctly "long" (that is, European) and very different to the Mongoloid shape of original Amerind racial types.

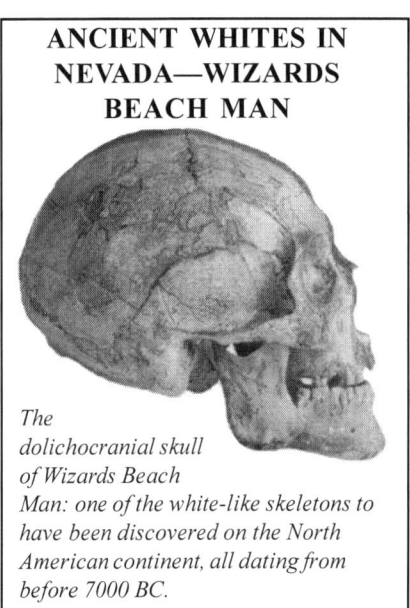

**ANCIENT WHITES IN NEVADA—WIZARDS BEACH MAN**

*The dolichocranial skull of Wizards Beach Man: one of the white-like skeletons to have been discovered on the North American continent, all dating from before 7000 BC.*

### Peñon Woman—Thirteen Thousand-Year-Old Skull

In December 2002, it was announced that a skeleton, which had been in Mexico City's National Museum of Anthropology since 1959, had been identified as being more than thirteen thousand years old, the oldest skeleton yet found in the Americas. Dubbed "Peñon Woman III," the skeleton's skull—doliocraniac or "long-faced"—was what attracted the attention of scientists, as the Amerind population has broad Mongoloid

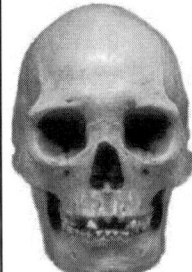

**THIRTEEN THOUSAND-YEAR-OLD DOLIOCRANIAC SKULL—MEXICO**

Left: *The skull of Peñon Woman III, the oldest skeleton yet discovered in the Americas, shows evidence of Caucasian white origins, as evidence from the doliocraniac, or '"long" form of the skull, which contrasts strongly with the broad, flat skull shape of Amerinds whose originating population was Asiatic. The skull has been dated at more than thirteen thousand years old.*

shaped skulls. Scientists speculated that the skull was possibly of Ainu extraction, just like the Kennewick Man.

### *Lineage X—The White Link Shown by Genetic Tracking*

Those who argue for an ancient white settlement of North America based on the large number of non-Amerind, white-looking, skeletal remains found on that continent, were boosted by a 1998 announcement on the existence of a genetic link between Amerinds and Old European white populations.

The genetic findings were announced in 1998 by Theodore Schurr, a molecular anthropologist from Emory University in Atlanta, at a meeting of the American Association of Physical Anthropologists in Salt Lake City (*Science,* Vol. 280, April 24, 1998).

The data, from a genetic marker named Lineage X, suggests definite links between ancient whites and Native Americans. It implies that ancient European peoples who reached North America after first presumably migrating through Asia, still retained a distinct genetic makeup which then passed into New World populations through later physical mingling.

According to these Lineage X findings, white populations from Europe were most likely amongst the North American continent's earliest settlers. The Lineage X markers and possible source populations have been studied by Emory researchers Michael Brown and Douglas Wallace, Antonio Torroni of the University of Rome, and Hans-Jurgen Bandelt of the University of Hamburg. Lineage X, a site of genetic variation, is found in mitochondrial DNA (mtDNA) and thus is passed only through the maternal line. It is one of five markers or haplogroups in mtDNA now identified in Native Americans, of which the other four (A–D) are shared by Asians and Amerinds, in accordance with widely accepted theories of their ancient links.

The fifth genetic marker, Lineage X, occurs at low frequencies in both modern and ancient remains of Native Americans and in some European and Middle Eastern groups including Italians, Spaniards, Finns, Turks, and Bulgarians. Crucially, Lineage X does not occur in any Asian population, including those of Tibet, Mongolia, Southeast Asia, or Northeast Asia. Brown and his coworkers had expected to find it in Asia, like the other four Native American markers, and are now pressed to account for the gap in their data. This and other evidence persuasively indicates that groups of whites migrated from Europe to North America over nine thousand years ago, and at a later stage mixed with Amerind stock to cause this fifth genetic marker to appear in North America.

## Megaliths in North America

If the general theory of a white presence in ancient North America is accurate, then it would be logical that such a population would have left some type of buildings or settlements. In this regard, the existence of megalithic structures and even small square-building cities on that continent needs to be reevaluated in light of the new discoveries as outlined above.

### MEGALITH SITES IN NORTH AMERICA

*Megaliths are concentrated on the eastern seaboard of the USA. Here are a few Megaliths found in the state of Massachusetts. All illustrate the unquestioned existence of stone megaliths—structures foreign to the American Amerinds.*

*The remains of a stone circle, Burnt Hill.*

*"The Shrine," Shutesbury.*

*Harvard Chamber, Harvard.*

*The Shutesbury Chamber.*　*Palmer Chamber, Palmer.*　*A lime kiln, Bolton.*

The most dramatic of the early structures on the North American continent is to be found at a site called "Mystery Hill," located near the town of Salem, in the American state of New Hampshire. There, a thirty acre megalith site—in many respects identical to those found in western Europe, and equally as old—has been open to the public since 1958.

While diggings at the "America's Stonehenge" site has produced artifacts from most time periods, the most significant find has been an etching which experts have identified as "Celtic" in nature, raising that tantalizing possibility that it was the subject of an early settlement from the European mainland.

In addition to these buildings, a number of ironworking sites have been discovered in North America. Ironworking was foreign to the Amerinds. The presence of nine thousand-year-old seemingly white skeletal remains and these ancient structures serves as powerful evidence of Pre-Amerind whites in North America. All indications are that most of these whites were exterminated in conflict with the

**MYSTERY HILL—MEGALITHS IN AMERICA CIRCA 7000 BC**

*"America's Stonehenge," located at Mystery Hill, New Hampshire, USA. Although the site has been open to the public for decades, it is still one of America's most "unknown" structures—because of the racial implications it contains. The building technique and style is identical to the megalith structures found in western Europe and is completely foreign to the American Indians ("Amerinds"). The fact that the "America's Stonehenge" site is still unknown to the wider public is an example of the malicious suppression of an important archaeological site for the political implications which it carries. Compare these pictures to the megalith pictures in Chapter 3 of this book. The complex consists of a number of large shaped standing stones, covering some thirty acres. Like Stonehenge in England, the structures can be used to determine the occurrence of specific solar and lunar events of the year. A number of stones found in the area show manmade markings, with some of them showing links to early European scripts. In addition to these buildings, a number of ironworking sites have been discovered. Ironworking was foreign to the Amerinds and was a trademark of the Indo-European peoples. The presence of nine thousand-year-old white-like skeletal remains and these ancient structures serve as powerful evidence of pre-Amerind whites in North America. All indications are that these whites were lost in conflict and miscegenated with the Amerinds.*

Amerinds—with survivors being physically absorbed into the Amerind population.

## Ironworking Sites in North America

Archaeologists and historians are of the unanimous opinion that the Amerinds did not have smelting or iron casting technology or ability, yet in a number of areas in North America remains of iron smelting furnaces have been found. They all follow designs which had previously only been found in Europe. The ability to work iron was one of the single biggest advances which originated with the Indo-Europeans.

The most famous of these iron furnaces is to be found on Spruce Hill, a flat top mountain in the Scioto Valley in south central Ohio. The collapsed walls of a surrounding fort and other buildings—some 200,000 tons of cut rock—are still to be seen on the site, which was first fully explored by Arlington Mallery in 1948, and detailed in his book *The Rediscovery of Lost America* (E.P. Dutton, New York, 1979).

Mallery went on to discover fourteen other ironworking sites, which clearly were foreign to the Amerinds, in the Deer Creek Valley, about ten miles from Spruce Hill.

What makes the iron smelting sites so significant is the fact that they are identical to sites found in Europe. At some stage of prehistory, it seems likely that Europeans managed to sail the divide between Europe and North America. Most likely the route taken would have followed the far north, from Scandinavia to Greenland, and then possibly along the ice pack coast down into the northeastern seaboard of the North American continent.

## The Mystery of the Anasazi: Were They White?

The mysterious ruins of the cliff dwellings in Nevada and else-where in the western United States have baffled archaeologists and historians. Square stone structures were foreign to the Amerinds, and local Indian legends claimed that the buildings were first created by a mysterious people called the Anasazi, who inhabited the area before the Amerinds.

Given the Lineage X and other skeletal evidence proving the existence of whites in America, either prior to or at the very least simultaneous with, the Amerinds, a strong circumstantial case could be made for white origins of the very European looking buildings which are currently shown off to tourists as Amerind-created structures. Only

**PRE-INDIAN NEVADA CLIFF DWELLINGS**

*The famous cliff dwellings of Nevada, USA. These very un-American Indian stone structures were, according to the Amerinds, built by the Anasazi people, who predated them. American Indians are not known for square stone buildings anywhere else.*

a racial examination of surrounding gravesites will provide the final answer to the issue.

There are hundreds of similar structures to be found all over the Southwest. While all are attributed to Amerinds, the question can be rightly asked: if Amerinds did indeed build these structures, why were they living in buffalo skin tents when Europeans colonized that country after the 1500s?

### The First Whites in America Disappear

The evidence indicates that the first whites in America were killed in open warfare with Amerinds (who may have arrived simultaneously or afterwards), and that the survivors were absorbed into what became the numerically dominant Amerind groups.

The existence of the Lineage X gene string adds credence to this. As mtDNA is transmitted only through the female line, it is obvious that the white males were killed by the nonwhites, and the white females were taken alive by the Amerinds for sexual purposes. This can be the only reason why mtDNA gene strings have been found amongst the Amerinds. The first whites in America disappeared, along with their culture, through a process of racial integration, leaving behind only skeletons and other artifacts as evidence of their existence.

### The Great White Secret of Easter Island

For centuries, the stone statues on Easter Island in the Pacific Ocean have baffled historians, but the great Scandinavian explorer and authority, Thor Heyerdahl, in his book *Aku-Aku: The Secret of Easter Island* (George Allen & Unwin, London 1988), uncovered astonishing facts about the island and the ancestors of the people on the island.

Sadly, Heyerdahl's discoveries have been largely ignored by historians, primarily because of the racial implications they carry.

Heyerdahl discovered, as is detailed in the book mentioned above, that the leading family on Easter Island to this day has a familial propensity for red hair, fair skin, and thin noses. This is in stark contrast to the rest of the island's population, who are for the greatest part dark, flat nosed, and black haired.

The red haired people on Easter Island today claim descent from a white people known as the "long ears," so called because they wore large earrings which elongated their earlobes, and who arrived on the island by boat at some stage in history, the exact date of which is unknown.

According to the oral tradition of the red haired descendants on Easter Island—who are now of mixed descent—these first red haired white people on the island set up a kingdom under one Hotu Matua.

These white settlers then set up buildings and as part of their construction work carved and set up the famous stone statues, which all have long ears and long noses—again in vivid contrast to the flat nosed natives. The stone statues have been dated at approximately 1,600 years old, meaning that the settlement of the island by these mysterious red haired whites must have occurred around the year 500 AD.

All the while, the tradition goes, the red haired long ears used the dark skinned native inhabitants of the island, whom they called "short ears," as labor. According to the legend, the white long eared people were: *"[A]n energetic people who always wanted to work, and the short ears had to moil and toil and help them make the walls and statues, which led to jealousy and dissatisfaction"* (Heyerdahl, ibid., page 122).

*"The long ears' last idea was to rid the whole of Easter Island of superfluous stone, so that all the earth could be cultivated. This work was begun on the Poike plateau, the easternmost part of the island, and the short ears had to carry every single loose stone to the edge of the cliff and fling it into the sea.*

*"This is why there is not a single loose stone on the grassy peninsula of Poike today, while the rest of the island is thickly covered with black and red scree and lava blocks."*

Heyerdahl continues the narrative of the oral tradition on Easter Island (ibid., page 123): *"Now things were going too far for the short ears. They were tired of carrying stones for the long ears. They decided on war. The long ears fled from every other part of the*

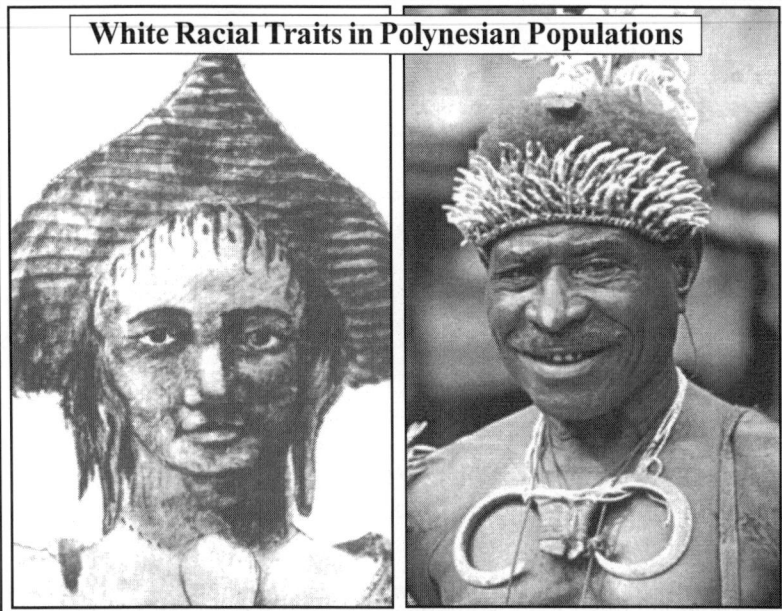

## White Racial Traits in Polynesian Populations

*Racial types in the Pacific: Left, an inhabitant of Easter Island, as drawn by Europeans visiting the island for the first time in the 1700s. Right: A contemporary Polynesian chieftain. The mixed white/Polynesian racial ancestry of the Easter Islander is apparent in eye, nose, and mouth shape.*

island and established themselves at the easternmost end, on the cleared Poike peninsula. Under the command of their chief Iko, they dug a trench nearly two miles long which separated the Poike plateau from the rest of the island.

"This trench they filled with a great quantity of branches and tree-trunks till it was like a gigantic far flung pyre, ready to be set on fire if the short ears on the plain below tried to storm the slope leading to the plateau. But one of the long ears had a short ear wife—her name was Moko Pingei and she was living up on Poike with her husband. She was a traitor and had arranged a signal with the short ears down on the plain. When they saw her sitting, plaiting a large basket, the short ears were to steal in a long line past the place where she sat.

"One night the short ears' spies saw Moko Pingei sitting and plaiting a basket right at one end of Iko's ditch, and the short ears stole one by one past the place where she sat, at the very edge of the cliff. They sneaked on along the outer edge of the plateau until they at last had completely surrounded Poike.

"Another army of short ears down on the plain marched openly up towards the ditch: the unsuspecting long ears lined up

91

*to face them and set fire to the whole pyre. Then the other short ears rushed forward from their ambush, and in the bloody fight which followed, all the long ears were burned in their own ditch.*

*"Only three of the long ears succeeded in leaping through the fire and escaping . . . One of them is called Ororoina and another Vai, but the name of the third is forgotten. They hid in a cave which the inhabitants can point out to this day.*

*"There they were found, and two of them were stabbed to death with sharp stakes, while the third and last, Ororoina, was allowed to remain alive as the only surviving long ear. Ororoina was taken to the house of one of the short ears who was named Pipi Horeko. There he married a short ear of the Haoa family and had many descendants . . . the last of which are still living on the island now"* (Heyerdahl, ibid., pages 123–24).

This is the oral tradition, as recounted in Heyerdahl's book. Most certainly it in some way represents at least a partially accurate

**RED HAIRED GIANTS OF THE PACIFIC**

*Many of the statues on Easter Island have separate hair pieces cut out of red rock from a different part of the island. This supports the island's inhabitant tradition that red haired people erected the statues. The leading family on the island to this day have a propensity for red hair—evidence of an early white migration to the region—a claim which they make in their oral history as well. The explorer Thor Heyrdahl documented all this and more in his book* Aku-Aku, The Secret of Easter Island.

version of events as the easternmost part of Easter Island, Poike, is indeed the only place on the island which is strangely clear of stones. It is also cut off from the rest of the island by a ditch, in which evidence of a great fire has been found.

**EASTER ISLAND—WHITES' LAST STAND**

*Easter Island—with the Poike Peninsula and the long ear ditch marked. The Poike Peninsula was where the red haired whites allegedly made their last stand around the year 400 AD.*

The fact that the leading family on the island to this day shows red hair and some European features, even if they have been mixed to a certain degree with the nonwhite natives, is the clearest sign that the "long ears" were indeed white people.

It was after this great race war on Easter Island that many of the long ears' statues and buildings were pulled down by the nonwhite natives. Some were simply too big to pull down, and it is those which remain standing today.

### "Red Haired" Statues—Colored Stone

Originally, many of the famous statues had separate sculptured hair pieces as well. Sadly, many have been knocked off over the course of time, but some remain or have been restored by modern archaeologists. The reason why the hair pieces were carved of separate pieces of rock lies in their color.

These hair pieces were cut of red colored stone which was hewn from a part of the island quite separate from the place where the main statues themselves were cut. The long ears even cut the statues in their own image, with red hair (Heyerdahl, ibid., pages 88–91).

### South American Red Haired Incas

The red haired whites of Easter Island must have come from somewhere. Heyerdahl turned to study surrounding regions and he found evidence of mixed race peoples, some with red hair, on the Marquesas Islands, near Easter Island. However, Heyerdahl also found, by researching original Spanish accounts of the conquest of South America, that red haired Incas were also present in South America as late as the 1500s. The conquistador, Pedro Pizarro, reported in his account of the great Spanish invasion of South America in the 1500s, that while the masses of Andes Indians were small and dark, the members of the ruling Inca family were tall and had whiter skins than the Spaniards. He mentioned in particular certain individuals in present day Peru who were white and had red hair (Heyerdahl, ibid., page 351).

Heyerdahl reported that this is reflected in the mummies found in South America. On the Pacific coast, in the desert sand of Paracas, there are large burial caves in which numerous mummies have been perfectly preserved. Some of the mummies were found to have the stiff black hair of the Indians. Others, which have been kept in the same conditions, have red, often chestnut-colored hair, *"silky and wavy,*

## THE NAZCAS—THE WHITE MUMMIES OF PERU—500 BC

*The long suppressed white origins of much of what has been regarded as "Native American Indian" culture is apparent from the finds in the Paracas burial ground in Peru. One of the most famous ancient wonders of the South American continent are the huge emblems on the Nazca plains in that country* (bottom right) *which have been dated at approximately 500 BC.*

*The emblems, many only properly visible from the air, are one of the wonders of that continent. They are usually attributed to the "Nazca Indians" but the well preserved bodies of the Nazca upper classes and priests have been uncovered in the neighboring Paracas region. Of the approximately four hundred mummies uncovered so far, almost all of them are clearly white in racial origin, with red hair being prominent.*

Right: *One of the Nazca Paracas mummies, disinterred from its sand tomb after two thousand years. The feathered hat and fine cotton cloak embroidered in multicolored wools have been very well preserved by the natural dryness of the sand grave—as has the long straight red hair, a trait only found in the Nordic subbranch of the white race. The pattern on the clothing is of particular interest—as it is most often used in modern times to depict "native South American culture"—when it originated with the whites of ancient South America. It is possible that these peoples were the origin of the Aztec and Inca legends of white skinned gods who allegedly came from across the ocean and taught the Amerinds to raise buildings and crops.*

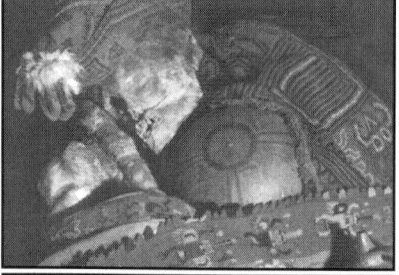
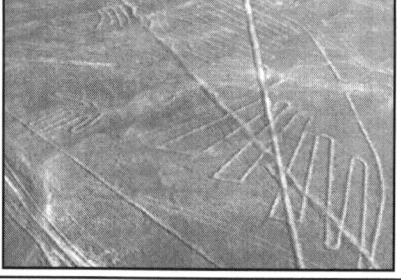

## SPANIARDS DISCOVER MIXED RACIAL TYPES IN CENTRAL AND SOUTH AMERICA

*Evidence of white/Amerind mixed racial types as recorded by the Spanish at the time of their conquest of Central and South America. Left: A drawing, made by the conquistador Felipe Guaman Poma de Ayala, of a Quipu keeper, an important member of the administrative hierarchy of the Incas. Ayala depicted the Inca nobleman with long light colored hair and light skin. This compares dramatically with the Spanish illustration of dark haired and dark skinned Incas, right, made by Don Antoniao Mendoza in 1540 AD for the king of Spain, to illustrate life and customs in Mexico at the time.*

*as found amongst Europeans; they have long skulls and remarkably tall bodies. Hair experts have shown by microscopic analysis, that the red hair has all the characteristics that ordinarily distinguish a Nordic hair type from that of Mongols or American Indians"* (Heyerdahl, ibid., pages 351–52).

Pizarro asked who the white skinned redheads were. The Inca Indians replied that they were the last descendants of the Viracochas, who were a divine race of white men with beards. They were so like the Spanish that the Incas thought the Europeans were the Viracochas who had come sailing back across the Pacific (Heyerdahl, ibid., page 253). According to the principal Inca legend, the sun god Con-Ticci Viracocha had taken leave of his kingdom in present day Peru and sailed off into the Pacific with all his subjects.

When the Spaniards came to Lake Titicaca, up in the Andes, they found the mightiest ruins in all South America—Tiahuanaco. They saw a hill reshaped by man into a stepped pyramid, classical masonry of enormous blocks—beautifully dressed and fitted together, and numerous large statues in human form. They asked the Indians to tell them who had left these enormous ruins.

The well known chronicler, Cieza de Leon, was told in reply that these things had been made long before the Incas came to power. They were made by white and bearded men like the Spaniards (Heyerdahl, ibid., page 253). The white men had finally abandoned their statues and gone with the leader, Con-Ticci Viracocha, first up to Cuzco, and then down to the Pacific. They were given the Inca name of Viracocha, or "sea foam," because they were white skinned and vanished like foam over the sea. The Spaniards recorded that the ruling Inca families called themselves Orejones, or long ears, in contrast to their subjects. Pizarro pointed out that it was especially the long ears who were white skinned (Heyerdahl, ibid., page 253).

On Easter Island, tradition has it that the long ears came from over the sea. Their first king had long ears when he reached the island in a seagoing vessel. This ties in well with the completely separate Inca legend which says that Con-Ticci Viracocha had long ears when he sailed off westwards across the sea.

## White Origins Suppressed

Heyerdahl's pioneering work shows that, drawing upon a number of different evidential strands (red haired South American mummies, red haired people on Easter Island, and Inca legends), it is highly likely that a group of white racial types were present in the area in pre-Columbian times.

These early whites, possibly linked to Canary Island Guanches, swept across the Atlantic Ocean, settled and built cities and civilizations in South America, and then spread out into the Pacific Islands, or so the evidence argues.

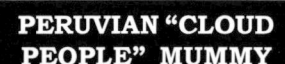

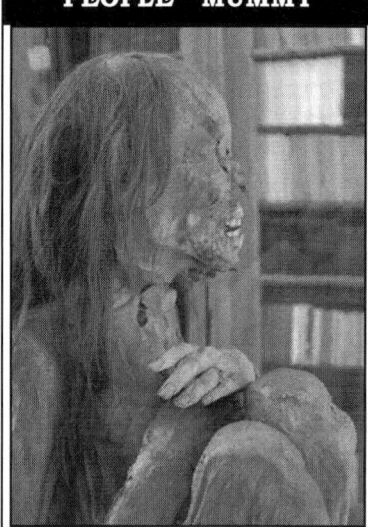

*A long red haired mummy from Peru, part of the mysterious light skinned "Cloud People" who predated the Indians of South America.*

There, they were apparently either killed off by the nonwhite natives or were absorbed into the native population, leaving behind only flashes of their coloring amongst the inhabitants of the region.

The mysterious long eared and red haired statues of Easter Island and some of the great ruined cities found in South America appear then, to be the legacy of lost white migrations.

It is from these ancient people that the legends of white and bearded gods, which pervade Inca and Aztec mythology, appear to originate.

**Right:** *Statues and carvings found at the ruins of Monte Alban, Mexico, a major pre-Aztec center, have clear white racial features, including this one of a bearded man. Facial hair is a distinctly non-Amerind (Mongoloid) racial trait. This figure —and many others like it—contrast strongly with the almost Negroid characteristics of later Olmec statues from the region. Monte Alban is near the city of Oaxaca de Ju Rez and flourished from about 500 BC to 750 AD. Monte Alban had long since been deserted at the time of Spanish conquest of the region in the 1500s.*

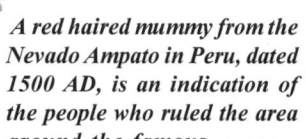

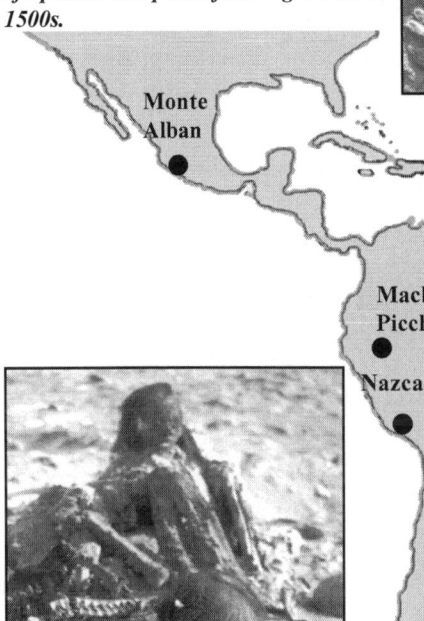

*A red haired mummy from the Nevado Ampato in Peru, dated 1500 AD, is an indication of the people who ruled the area around the famous Machu Picchu site.*

*The builders of the Nazca Plains signs in Peru were red haired racial types, as evidenced by the numerous mummies and bodies which have been found there.*

**Right:** *the sadly desecrated cemetery of Chaucilla, near Nazca, has dozens of ancient red haired corpses jutting out of their open graves, mute testimony to Peru's ancient white past.*

97

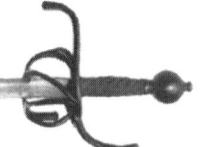

# CHAPTER SEVEN

# Inexorably Overwhelmed—Whites in the Middle East

**The racial makeup of the original inhabitants of the Middle East—from Turkey to modern day Iran, including the areas known today as Iraq, Syria, Lebanon, Palestine, and Egypt, was by the year 4000 BC, predominantly original white Mediterranean, with Alpine and Proto-Nordic subgroups scattered amongst them.**

These original white inhabitants were strengthened by the arrival of large numbers of Indo-Europeans who started spreading south from their ancestral homeland in southern Russia from around 3000 BC onward. In addition to these white peoples, another group was to play a significant role in the history of the Middle East—the Semitic speaking peoples (this encompasses a wide range of peoples, including groups known to history as the ancient Jews and Arabic peoples).

They eventually came to predominate the entire area, entering the original white territories as laborers, traders, immigrants, and military conquerors.

From a racial point of view it is worth noting that neither the original Old European Mediterranean white peoples nor the original Semitic peoples exist in their original form anymore.

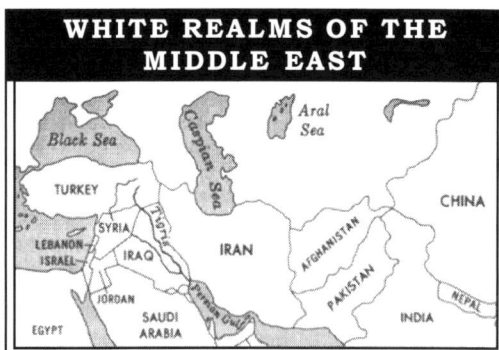

*A map of the region under discussion in this chapter. Almost every country shown here was subjected to invasions by Indo-Europeans, who then set up white civilizations—only to be later submerged into a mass of Semitic, Mongoloid, and Hamitic (mixed) peoples who came to work in the nations as slaves or laborers.*

While retaining certain physical characteristics, both of these groups have mixed substantially with each other and additional racial groups as a result of the ebb and flow of historical events in the region.

It is also untrue to consider modern Jews as purely "Semitic." The Jews of ancient times were most certainly as pure a Semitic people as could be found, but in modern times they are a mix of a great many races, from black right through to all of the white subraces. Semitic peoples also encompassed a large number of other tribes in the Middle East—as is still the case today.

Nonetheless, the history of the ancient Middle East is dominated by centuries of physical struggle between successive waves of white and Semitic peoples. Each group established civilizations which in turn were overrun by their rivals, or, just as often, by a racially similar tribe.

Control of the Mesopotamian River Valley swung between these groups for thousands of years, with each successive invasion bringing with it an impetus of new blood and culture.

For a long period the white tribes were able to hang on to the higher lands to the northeast of the Tigris/Euphrates River basin, while various Semitic tribes

**EARLIEST DECIPHERABLE DOCUMENT**

*A Sumerian clay tablet, from about 2800 BC. It is one of the earliest decipherable documents in the world. Writing was done on clay tablets with the impressions being made by wooden wedged instruments. The tablet would then be baked to harden it—a process which preserved it for nearly five thousand years.*

occupied parts of previously Indo-European held territory within the Middle East. As a result of this continual crossover of civilizations and shared geographical area, the racial distinctions of the peoples became blurred. Toward the close of this epoch it becomes more difficult to identify clear racial groups as opposed to named cultures.

Ultimately, the disappearance of the distinct racial groups in the region led to the torch of civilization being passed to what were then more homogeneous societies—first in Egypt, and then to the classical Greek and Roman civilizations.

### Sumeria: First White Settlement

The region between the Tigris and Euphrates Rivers is commonly called the Fertile Crescent because of the closeness of fresh water supplies. However, the term is a misnomer. Rainfall in the region has always been sparse, and large parts of this region are arid desert. The region was, contrary to popular myth, never ideal farming territory, and the dryness was only alleviated in part due to the proximity of the river water. In spite of this, by the year 5000 BC, original Mediterranean whites and some early Nordic tribes (together known as Ubaidians) established settlements in the Tigris and Euphrates River basin. These settlements gradually developed into the chief cities of the region, and today this territory lies in the country of Iraq.

### Second White Invasion 3250 BC—Origins of Sumer

These original whites were conquered by a new white tribe, the Sumerians, in 3250 BC. These people gave their name to the region: Sumer. In the centuries that followed their immigration, the country grew rich and powerful. Art and architecture, crafts, and religious and ethical thought flourished.

The Sumerian language became the prevailing speech of the land and their system of writing, the Sumerian script, where pictures were used to represent objects, set the standard for all written languages of the time. Although initially very basic—a stick drawing of a fish would represent a fish and so on—this written language laid the basis for all pictographic languages, including the later Egyptian and Sanskrit forms. Writing was done on clay tablets with impressions being made by wedge shaped instruments.

This pictographic writing eventually developed symbols for abstract concepts such as love, hate, go, and so on. The Sumerian script dominated all writing forms for at least four thousand years until the Greek script became preeminent.

From the very beginning, the settlement of the Sumer delta possessed metal working facilities (they were particularly good at copper working) and wheeled vehicles, a significant breakthrough at the time. It is presumed that the wheel originally developed from the potter's wheel, which the Sumerians also possessed and apparently innovated.

To the southeast of Sumer lay the Saudi Arabian peninsula—the original heartland of the Semitic speaking peoples. The original whites were soon surrounded by Semitic tribes, and within a few hundred years Semitic immigrants began to take up residence in the region, both as peaceful immigrants and as raiders.

### The First Semitic Invasion: The Akkads

The first large scale Semitic invasion took place in 2335 BC, when the white Sumerians were overrun by the Akkadian people. The Semitic Akkad occupation of Sumer led to the establishment of a new

**MAGNIFICENT MONUMENTS—BUILT
ONLY OF CLAY BRICKS**

*Despite not having natural stone resources, the Sumerians created huge monuments of clay brick which still stand. This is the main step ziggurat at Ur, built circa 2100 BC, shortly after the first major Indo-European invasion. The temple building was created in the shape of a step pyramid.*

kingdom, known as "The Kingdom of Sumer and Akkad." It was shortly after the Akkadian invasion that the first Jews were recorded as entering Sumeria in large numbers.

After a few generations the Semitic tribes started intermarrying with the original white tribes, and although this process was not absolute, the distinctions between the two groups became blurred. This mixing of the races in the region led to an increasingly hybrid population—a trend which continues to this day. Art forms left by the early Babylonians revealed their racial makeup as primarily a Mediterranean people. With the passage of time a distinct Semitic influence became apparent.

The Mediterranean origin of these early people has been confirmed by the British anthropologists Dudley Buxton and Talbot Rice, who examined skulls excavated at the Sumerian palace at Kish in Mesopotamia. Similar skulls were found by the French anthropologist H.V. Vallois at Sialk, halfway between Teheran and Isfahan, northeast of Kish, and in the Indus River Valley by R.B.S. Sewell and B.S. Guha of the Zoological Survey of India. All the remains were positively identified as belonging to the (now nearly extinct) Mediterranean white subrace (*Race,* John R Baker, Oxford University Press, 1974, page 511).

### *Civilization of Sumer Peaks—After the First Indo-European Gutian Invasion*

The kingdom of Sumer and Akkad then fell before the first, and by all accounts ferocious, Indo-European invasion—that of the Celts. Known as Gutians in the Middle East, they fell upon the kingdom of

Sumer and Akkad less than one hundred years after it was established, around the year 2200 BC.

The Gutians sacked and destroyed the mixed Semitic/ Mediterranean Sumer and Akkadian civilization and established their own rule and civilization in the region. Soon they had provinces extending to the Mediterranean Sea.

It was after the Gutian invasion that Sumerian civilization was to reach some of its greatest heights. These included:

• The very first written law code in the world, which is still existent and dates from 2095 BC;

• The construction of the great Sumerian pyramids, called ziggurats (the most famous of which is the ziggurat at the Sumerian city of Ur, built in 2100 BC) which served as temples and community centers, many of which are still standing today; and

• A complex system of canals, weirs, and water routes by which the agricultural settlements alongside the rivers were kept irrigated.

After a few generations the Gutians themselves became submerged into the wider population of Sumer, whose great cities and wealth had acted as a magnet for all the surrounding Semitic tribes. Increasing numbers of Semite traders, labourers, and slaves were drawn to Sumer, creating over time a mixture of Old European, Semitic, and Indo-European peoples. This is reflected in their art forms and in the wide range of racial features on display in that region to this day.

### *The Second Indo-European Invasion: The Amorites*

The region was invaded once again by another Indo-European group, the Amorites, around the year 2000 BC. The Amorites had originally entered the Middle East from the Balkans and had occupied Palestine, mixing with a certain number of the Jewish tribes they subjugated there. It is a matter of conjecture as to exactly how much Semitic (therefore darker) physical characteristics they had by the year 2000 BC. Very likely it was not much, as the Egyptians still described them as fair haired and blue eyed some seven hundred years after they had invaded Sumeria.

### *Advanced Sumerian Culture*

Sumerian religion had four creating deities: An, god of heaven; Ki, goddess of earth; Enlil, god of air; and Enki, god of water. There were three sky deities: Nanna, god of the moon; Utu, god of the sun;

**BLUE EYED RACIAL TYPES IN ANCIENT SUMERIA**

Left: *A religious ceremonial figure of a Sumerian deity from circa 3000 BC, at Tell Asmos, a provincial Sumerian town. The figure is remarkable for it has blue eyes—set with the stone lapis lazuli. This blue stone was greatly prized by the Sumerians, who imported it from its only source, 3,200 kilometers away in north Afghanistan. Blue eyes are an exclusively white racial trait. Center: This female head, also from Tell Asmos, has equally blue eyes. Right: Gudea, the governor of the province of Lagash, circa 2150–2050 BC. Several statues of Gudea have been recovered from Lagash, which is now known as Telloh.*

and Inanna, the queen of heaven. Inanna was also the goddess of love, procreation, and war.

The Sumerians had a reasonably advanced mathematical system with tables for multiplication, division, and even square and cube roots. They also possessed knowledge of geometry.

The most famous surviving piece of literature from this period is the *Epic of Gilgamesh,* a fictional story of an old king of the city state of Erech who sets off in search of immortality. It also includes a chapter dealing with a flood of the earth, and is clearly the origin of the Christian and Jewish Old Testament story of Noah and the flood.

### Babylon and Hammurabi

The chaos caused by the Amorite invasion lasted until 1763 BC, when a strong and capable king arose and united the inhabitants once again. At this time the city of Babylon was built, and the region became known as Babylonia.

Hammurabi was the first famous king of Babylon who managed to end the chaos and unite all the tribes into a nation. He is probably most remembered for his Code of Laws, dating from 1750 BC, which is widely, but incorrectly, held to be the first written legal code in the world

## ROYAL TOMB AT UR 2500 BC

Below right: *The ornate headdress and jewelry of the Sumerian queen Shub-ab, about 2,500 years ago. Discovered along with several skeletons in a tomb complex* (left) *in the ancient city of Ur, the beautifully preserved jewelry was remounted on an actual female skull discovered in the same complex, whose features were rebuilt according to the skull shape.*

Below centre: *A sculpture of a white female head from Uruk, Sumeria, circa 3500 BC. Iraq Museum, Baghdad.*

(it was the second, the first being the code drawn up by the earlier white Sumerians).

Hammurabi's Code of Law was engraved in stone and set up in the great cities of the region, and to this day the code is regarded as the father of all legal codes of the world. An original copy of one of his codes is on display in the Louvre Museum in Paris, France.

While some of the laws seem harsh to the modern mind (death for being unable to repay debt, for example), the wording of the prologue to the Code of Law provides a fascinating glimpse into the conflict between the Semitic and Indo-European populations in the region.

In the prologue, Hammurabi announces that he has come to *"rule the black-haired people."* He is also referred to as "the white king" and the *"White Potent,"* apparently in reference to his coloring.

The original introduction to the Hammurabi Code states the following:

*"Hammurabi, the exalted prince, who feared God, to bring about the rule of righteousness in the land, to destroy the wicked and the evil-doers; so that the strong should not harm the weak; so that I should rule over the black-headed people like Shamash, and enlighten the land, to further the well-being of mankind . . . Hammurabi, the prince, called of Bel am I, making riches and increase . . . who enriched Ur . . . the white king . . . the mighty, who again laid the foundations of Sippara . . . the lord who granted*

## HAMMURABI'S CODE OF LAW 1750 BC

Right: *The Stela of Hammurabi's Code of Law, 1750 BC. The code has been preserved intact on this stela, now in the Louvre Museum in Paris. At the top of the stela is a picture of King Hammurabi before Shamash, the Indo-European sun god, who was also the god of justice. The introduction to the code is directly below the pictures, in which Hammurabi asserts that he has come to rule over the "dark-haired people."*

*The 282 laws cover offenses against other people and property; disputes concerning land, trade, fees, professional services, and family. Some of the punishments would be considered harsh by*

*modern standards, but on the whole the laws present a picture of a well ordered society which lived by recognized standards and offered protection to all its citizens.*

Left: *A detail from the stela showing the great white King Hammurabi in profile. His racial features are clear in this contemporary depiction.*

*new life to Uruk, who brought plenteous water to its inhabitants . . . the White, Potent, who penetrated the secret cave of the bandits"* (Translated by L. W. King, The Eleventh Edition of the *Encyclopedia Britannica*, 1910).

Although the Code of Law drew a distinct line between Hammurabi himself and the "black haired" peoples, it also showed that by this time large numbers of the population had become distinctly Semitic. Nonetheless, building upon the technological and cultural precedents set by the Sumerians, the Babylonians maintained the complex systems of canals, dikes, weirs, and reservoirs constructed by the original white inhabitants. As an indicator of the symbolism Babylon has come to acquire, to this day the black Rastafarian movement talks about all white civilizations as being "Babylon."

### The Third Indo-European Invasion: The Kassites and the Hittites

Babylon was then invaded by a new wave of Indo-Europeans. Called the Kassites and Hittites, the newcomers had conquered most of the region by 1595 BC. Under Kassite rule, which lasted another 450 years, Babylonia once again became a power of considerable importance. The Kassites were the first people to use the chariot as a weapon of war, a skill later taken on by nearly every other nation in the Middle East and Europe.

## Semitic Population Increases—Jews into Captivity

By this time the number of Arabic Semites in the region was reaching overwhelming proportions. This balance was tipped even further by a renewed Semitic invasion which started in the ninth century when the Chaldeans managed to occupy the region. Although Semitic himself, the Chaldean king, Nebuchadnezzar (who became king in 604 BC), achieved fame for carrying off several thousand Jews into captivity in Babylon. The Chaldeans in turn were attacked by the originally Indo-European Assyrians in the north, and the city of Babylon was eventually sacked by the Assyrians around the year 700 BC.

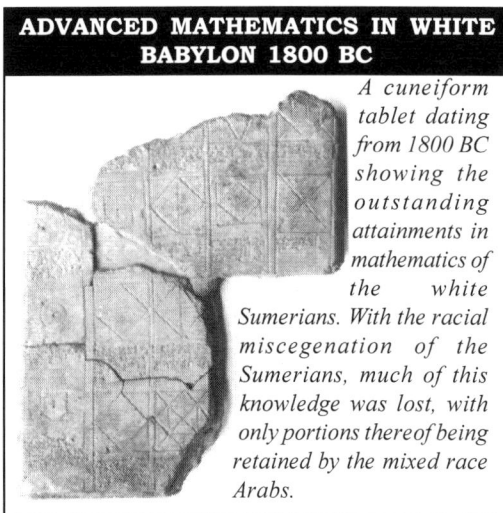

**ADVANCED MATHEMATICS IN WHITE BABYLON 1800 BC**

*A cuneiform tablet dating from 1800 BC showing the outstanding attainments in mathematics of the white Sumerians. With the racial miscegenation of the Sumerians, much of this knowledge was lost, with only portions thereof being retained by the mixed race Arabs.*

## Syria and the Hittites

An Indo-Aryan tribe called the Hittites established an empire in present day Turkey around the year 2000 BC, after sweeping south and west from their original homeland in Southern Russia. In 1700 BC, Hittite armies began pushing south, conquering Syria and the Tigris and Euphrates River Valley, which led to the destruction of the Babylonian empire by 1600 BC. At its height, the Hittite Empire covered an area stretching from the Black Sea to Syria.

By conquering Syria, the Hittites had taken away an Egyptian colony, and the Egyptian pharaoh, Ramses II, attacked the Hittites from bases in Palestine in 1269 BC. The Hittites defeated Ramses, and a peace treaty followed, in terms of which the Hittites kept possession of Syria.

The Hittites are credited with being the first people to work iron in the region, and are famous for borrowing much of their legal system from the law codes they found when they conquered the

Babylonians. They also were responsible for the spread of Mesopotamian culture around Asia Minor (Turkey) and even to the early Greeks.

By 1500 BC, the Hittites had, like many of the Indo-European tribes (and also the Semites), started to mingle with the other peoples in the region, eventually producing the population of today in the Middle East, an indefinable mix of white, Semite, black and even Mongoloid strains.

**JEWS PAY HOMAGE TO ANCIENT ARYAN ASSYRIANS**

*An engraving from the palace at Ashurbanipul at Nineveh, Assyria, at the height of the Assyrian Empire. The Jewish king, Jehu (kneeling), pays homage to the Assyrian ruler, Shalmaneser III, in 841 BC.*

So weakened, the Hittite empire came to an end, being overrun by new waves of Indo-Aryan invaders, the Assyrians, from the north. With the collapse of the Hittite Empire in 1200 BC, no one power was strong enough to dominate the Middle East, and a number of independent states flourished for about five hundred years.

One of the Indo-Aryan invasions which contributed to the fall of the Hittites was led by a tribe known as the Philistines. This tribe conquered large parts of the Middle East, including today's Palestine (from where the name of that country originates) and eventually Babylon as well. The Philistines established what was by all accounts a harsh rule over the Semites, which led to the subjugated Jewish tribes developing a fanatical hatred for them.

This dislike of Philistines was repeated in the Bible, which in turn was absorbed into European culture. In this way, the insult of calling someone a "Philistine" became part of everyday English language.

### *Phoenicians—Foremost Traders of Their Time*

A number of other smaller white cultures sprang up in this region, each of them contributing in their own way to the advancement of civilization. Amongst them were the Phoenicians, who through trade established themselves as a powerful nation in the Mediterranean. Their home base was in present day Lebanon, an area which they had occupied

## PERSIANS SHOWN AS NORDIC TYPES 310 BC

Above: *The famous Alexander Sarcophagus (also known as the "Sarcophagus of Sidon"), circa 310 BC, is of value because it shows details of Persian soldiers dating from the time of Alexander the Great. They are in color—many Persian warriors are depicted as having light eyes and hair with fair or red mustaches. The sarcophagus reputedly belonged to Alexander the Great himself, Archaeological Museum, Istanbul.* Right top: *A detail from the Alexander Sarcophagus: A Persian soldier, the original painted with fair hair and blue eyes.* Right: *The white racial features are clear in this "Head of a Dead Persian," Roman copy of a figure from a victory monument of Attalos I at Pergamon, c. 230–220 BC, Terme Museum, Rome.*

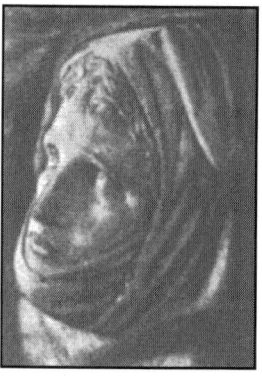

by the year 2700 BC. Although originally a Mediterranean people, there is evidence to suggest that during their long stay in Lebanon and Palestine, the Phoenicians absorbed a fair amount of Semitic blood, being ruled by the Hebrews for a significant period of time. However, the Phoenicians were also ruled by the Egyptians and Hittites in turn, and by this time had started to exhibit the physical characteristics associated with Nordic, Mediterranean, and Semitic peoples.

The Phoenicians are credited with the creation of the modern alphabet, although this is a slight exaggeration. The Phoenicians took the semi-alphabet script developed by the Egyptians, adopted it, and used it as a means for their trade.

This basic alphabet was picked up by later Greeks and developed into Greek script. From this Greek script the modern alphabet was developed over a much longer period of time. At best then, the Phoenicians can claim to having been one link in the process of the development of the modern alphabet.

The Phoenicians became famous as traders, establishing settlements all over the Mediterranean basin, including the Italian peninsula and Spain. In 800 BC, the Phoenicians founded the city of

Carthage in present day Tunis, just opposite the bottom of the Italian peninsula. Carthage came to be populated by a large number of different peoples, but retained its essentially Mediterranean/Nordic mix right until the time of its wars with Rome.

The most famous Carthaginian military leader, Hannibal, who was the scourge of Rome for many years, was a very clear Nordic subracial type, who came from a noble family in Carthage. Although Carthage was eventually destroyed by the Romans, it lasted longer than the Phoenician cities in Lebanon which were razed in 750 BC by new Indo-European led invaders, the Assyrians.

### *Persia—Original Indo-European Civilization*

The leaders of Persia called themselves Aryans. Darius the Great, King of Persia (521–486 BC), in an inscription in Naqsh-e-Rostam (near present day Shiraz, Iran) proclaims: "I am Darius, the Great King . . . A Persian, son of a Persian, an Aryan, having Aryan lineage . . ."

The Iranian plateau was settled about 1500 BC by Indo-European tribes, the most important of which were the Medes, who occupied the northwestern portion, and the Persians. The Persians were dominated by the Medes until the accession to the throne by the Persian Cyrus the Great in 550 BC. He overthrew the Medean rulers, conquered two neighboring kingdoms (including Babylonia in 539 BC), and established the Persian Empire as the preeminent power of the Middle East.

Cyrus tried to be a benevolent ruler. In Sumeria he allowed the dominant religion of the time to approve his assumption of the Babylonian kingship, while in Jerusalem he launched the rebuilding of the Jewish temple. The result of his endeavors was an empire of diverse peoples which ultimately led to Persia's undoing.

Cyrus's son, Cambyses II, extended the Persian realm even further by conquering the (by then thoroughly mixed race) Egyptians in 525 BC. Darius I, who ascended the throne in 521 BC, pushed the Persian borders as far eastward as the Indus River, had a canal constructed from the Nile to the Red Sea, and reorganized the entire empire, earning the title Darius the Great.

From 499 to 493 BC Darius the Great engaged in crushing a revolt of the Ionian Greeks living under Persian rule in Asia, and then launched a punitive campaign against the Greeks for supporting the rebels. His forces were disastrously defeated by the Greeks at the historic Battle of Marathon in 490 BC.

His successor, Xerxes I, also tried to defeat the Greeks, but was in turn defeated in the great sea engagement, the Battle of Salami, in 480 BC, and in two successive land battles the following year. The forays of the Persian king Xerxes I were the last notable attempt at expansion of the Persian Empire. By this stage the Aryan tribes had absorbed the Semitic and Asiatic immigrants into the region, and had started to unravel as a homogeneous nation.

**NUBIAN SLAVE ATTACKED BY LION**

*A panel recovered from the Assyrian capital city of Nimrud, dating from the reign of King Ashurnasirpal II (883–859 BC). The carving shows an African being attacked by a lioness. The design appears to be Phoenician, even though it was found in the Assyrian city.*

## Indian Depictions of Persians as Nordics and Mixed Racial Types

At the time when the Greek writer Xenophon praised what he called "tall beautiful Persian women" (during the sixth century BC), the Persian envoys to India were depicted in still existent paintings in the Ajanta caves outside Bombay as light skinned, blue eyed and blond, or dark skinned, and blue eyed with fair beards (Ujflvy, *L'Anthropologie,* vol. ii., 1900). This was the first tangible sign that the Indo-European Persians had started mixing with the darker natives of their land.

By the fourth century, this process had spread so dramatically that only a very few of the ruling class could still claim pure Indo-European ancestry. Finally, the already largely mixed race Persians were overrun by the new white force in the region: the Indo-European Macedonians under Alexander the Great in a series of battles between 334 and 331 BC.

The Persians became known for the efficient administration of their huge empire, but are probably best remembered for their religion called Zoroastrianism. Founded by the prophet Zarathustra, the basic concept of a battle between good and evil supernatural powers was later plagiarized by the early Christians and worked into the biblical New Testament (the concepts of heaven and hell are not mentioned at all in the Christian Old Testament).

## *Assyrian Empire—World's First Postal System*

The next large empire in the Middle East was established by the originally Indo-Aryan Assyrians (the word Assyrian is a corruption of the word Aryan) who, from their base in modern day Syria, captured Babylon in 910 BC. In 722 BC, the Assyrians captured Palestine and by 671 BC their empire extended as far as the Nile Delta.

The Assyrians, like the Hittites, had mastered the art of ironworking and iron weapons (a skill which had come down from the Indo-Aryan north and had spread with the Indo-Aryan invasions). As such they had a massive advantage over their opponents.

The Assyrian king of this time, Ashurbanipul, was a cultured man and reputedly had a library—probably mostly looted from the Sumerians and Babylonians—of some 22,000 clay tablets at the capital city of Khorsabad. The Assyrian empire was the first to build a network of national roads and a postal service. They also had the first coherent administrative system which served as a role model for many later civilizations.

By the middle of the seventh century BC, the Assyrian empire was on the decline, weakened by a steady dissolution of their original racial homogeneity through increasing mixing with the ever growing number of Semites in the region. Eventually a combination of neighboring Indo-European tribes (Persians, Medeans, and Scythians) overthrew the Assyrians, and in 612 BC the capital, Nineveh, was destroyed.

The downfall of the Assyrians left four small powers in the Middle East. These were the Medeans, the Persians, the Lydians, and the Chaldeans. All but the last of these were still majority white in racial makeup, although large—and soon to be overwhelming—numbers of Semites, Arabics, and even Mongoloids had been integrated into their societies.

### *The Medeans and Scythians*

The people known as the Medes had already established an informal empire just to the east of the Assyrians, south of the Caspian Sea, in modern day Iran. The Medeans were also noteworthy for their help in the destruction of the Assyrian Empire and were in turn overrun by their former colony, Persia, in 550 BC.

Like so many Indo-European cultures of the region at that time, they not only had to contend with the local white/Semitic mixed population, who continually agitated against them, but also with other Indo-European invaders who continually penetrated the region from the north. The most noted of these new invaders were the Nordic Scythians, who were the first to use mounted cavalry in battle.

The Scythians overran what is today Palestine in the seventh century BC, and some of their fair haired and light eyed descendants can still be seen amongst the Druses of Lebanon.

To add to all this confusion, beginning about 1400 BC, a new wave of migrations changed the face of practically all of western Asia. From the Balkan Peninsula came a wave of different Indo-European tribes, who became known as the Sea Peoples. They overran the Hittite Empire in Turkey and launched attacks on Syria, Palestine, and Egypt.

Yet another Indo-European people called Mushki, who settled in eastern Anatolia, became a constant threat to Assyria in the northwest.

## Whites Submerged Circa 250 BC

The fall of the Persian Empire marked the end of the great majority white civilizations in the Middle East. By this time, all of the settlements had lost whatever racial homogeneity they once had, and were to larger or smaller degrees societies comprised of a plethora of mixed races. They produced the wide and varied physiognomy visible to this day in the region—a mix of Semitic and original white stock.

From the time of the fall of the Persian Empire, the Middle East ceased to be an area which was majority occupied by peoples who could claim to be white in the original racial sense of

**ASSYRIAN KING ASHURNASIRPAL II (883–859 BC)**

*A statue of the Assyrian king, Ashurnasirpal II, from Nimrud in present day northern Iraq. The king's hair and beard are shown worn long in the fashion of the Assyrian court at this time. His features are quite clear in this large statue. Ashurnasirpal holds a sickle in his right hand, of a kind which gods are sometimes depicted using to fight monsters. The cuneiform inscription across his chest proclaims the king's titles and genealogy, and mentions his expedition westward to the Mediterranean Sea.*

## THE GREAT PALACE AT PERSEPOLIS, PERSIA CIRCA 500 BC

*The great ceremonial city of Persepolis, founded by Darius I (522–486 BC), was a magnificent center which served as capital of the great Persian Empire until it was overrun by the numerically superior mixed races of the Middle East. Today only the ruins of this once great city stand witness*

*to the passing of yet another white tribe.* Above: *A reconstruction of what the great*

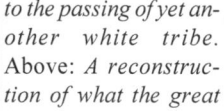

*hall looked like in its glory. A double staircase, decorated with reliefs, led to the magnificent audience hall where the Persian emperors received foreign envoys and visiting dignitaries. Today it is a ruin, the original Persians gone.* Alongside right: *The ruins of the city as they can be seen today.* Alongside left: *An archer of the Persian army of Darius is portrayed on enameled tiles found in the remains of the great city of Susa. The soldier is depicted with blue eyes. Currently on display at the Louvre Museum, Paris. Originally composed of Old European types mixed with Nordic Indo-European invaders, the Persians were slowly absorbed into the increasing mass of mixed race inhabitants of the Middle East until only a few original white racial types remained in the region. This is evident in the physiognomy of the present day population of that country. The very name Iran (Persia's new name) was derived from the word Aryan.*

the word. Nonetheless, to this day there remain significant Indo-European "genetic throwbacks" amongst the Persians, today called the Iranians. These can also be found amongst modern-day Indians, Afghanis, Iraqis, Syrians, Lebanese, and Palestinians.

Persia was overrun by the Arabic Muslims in 651 AD, and through the integration which followed, the last major traces of the pure Indo-European peoples in the Middle East were diluted.

Indeed, much of what later became known as Muslim culture, architecture, writing, and other skills, was taken from the Persians into the Semitic speaking world.

# CHAPTER EIGHT

## *Nordic Desert Empire—Ancient Egypt*

**Although situated in North Africa, Egypt had been settled by three white groups prior to 3500 BC, namely Old European Mediterranean types, Proto-Nordics, and Nordic Indo-Europeans, with the latter group penetrating the territory as part of the great wave of Indo-European invasions which took place from 5600 BC onward.**

Living in typical Neolithic settlements, this period of history is called the pre-dynastic period and is formally considered to have come to an end in 3100 BC.

### *"Ginger" and Other Inhabitants of Early Egypt*

Racially speaking, the inhabitants of Egypt at this period in time were divided into three groups. Skeletal evidence from grave sites show that the original white Mediterraneans and Proto-Nordics were a majority in the area.

A well preserved body found in a sand grave in Egypt dating from approximately 3300 BC, on display in the British Museum in London, was nicknamed "Ginger" because of his red hair—a racial trait only found in persons of Nordic ancestry.

However, diggings also reveal a significant minority of Semitic (Arabic) peoples were living in the Nile Delta valley alongside the whites, and in the very far south (in what later became southern Egypt and the Sudan) lived

**NORDIC EGYPTIAN CIRCA 3300 BC**

Below: *A well preserved body from the pre-dynastic period in Egypt, circa 3300 BC. Buried in a sand grave, the natural dryness of the surroundings kept the body preserved. His red hair (and thus Nordic features) have been so well preserved that he has been given the nickname "Ginger" at the British Museum where he is kept on public display.* Right: *"Ginger's" head, showing the red hair.*

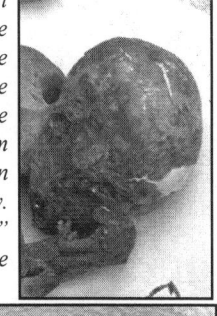

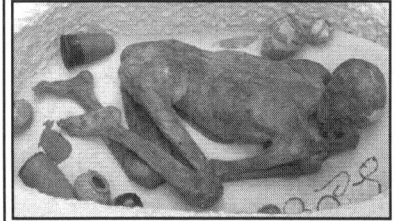

115

a large number of blacks, known as Nubians. The existence of these two nonwhite groups within Egypt was later to have a major impact on the history of that civilization, and also do much to destroy the "environmental" theory of the origin of civilizations, as all three groups shared the same environment, yet produced very different levels of achievement.

### ORIGIN OF PRE-DYNASTIC EGYPTIANS CIRCA 5600 BC

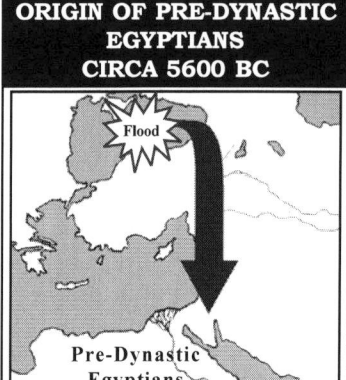

Above: *Entering Egypt at the time of the great Indo-European migrations from the Black Sea basin circa 5600 BC, Nordic peoples such as "Ginger" (see page 115) settled the Nile River Valley and laid the basis for what was, by 3000 BC, to become the first Egyptian Dynasty.*

Right: *The earliest representation of First Dynasty life is to be found on the "Palette of Narmer" which dates from around 3000 BC.*

*The image on the palette is thought to be that of Menes, the first great white king of Egypt, who united Lower and Upper Egypt.*

*Menes, also known as Narmer, is shown striking the head of an enemy who has clear Semitic features.*

## The Old Kingdom 3100–2270 BC

In terms of contemporary time frames, the Egyptian state first formally emerged shortly after the establishment of the civilization between the Tigris and Euphrates River Valley. By the year 3100 BC, a measure of unity had started to take hold in Egypt, coalescing into northern and southern kingdoms. Around that year, a dynamic leader named Menes united these northern and southern kingdoms and established a capital city at Memphis on the Nile River. The year 3100 BC therefore marks the start of the Dynastic Period, called the Old Kingdom by historians.

Menes developed the idea of using channels to divert the waters of the Nile to irrigate land—and this irrigation system exists along the Nile River to this day. Menes was such a gifted and charismatic leader that he was deified by later Egyptians, and a cult developed which pictured him as a direct descendant of the gods, a tradition which then spread to other pharaohs. It is very likely that the word "man" originated with Menes.

During his reign construction was started on the greatest city of ancient Egypt, Memphis, which became the capital of this first kingdom. Also about this time, Egyptian pictograph writing appeared, probably inspired by the Sumerian script. The Old Kingdom traded

**IMHOTEP'S FIRST GREAT PYRAMID AND NECROPOLIS—SAQARA 2600 BC**

Above: *The first great pyramid of Egypt: the step pyramid of Saqara, circa 2600 BC, with its equally impressive mortuary center in the foreground. The architect, Imhotep, was later made into a deity out of respect for this technological achievement.*

extensively with surrounding lands, obtaining wood from Lebanon and copper from mines in the Sinai Peninsula.

It was also during this Old Kingdom period that the great pyramids and Sphinx at Giza were built, starting around the year 2500 BC. The project was launched by Pharaoh Cheops (also known as Khufu), who, because of the pyramids, remains one of the most famous pharaohs of this First Kingdom. His daughter, Queen Hetop-Heres II, of the Fourth Dynasty, is shown in a colored bas relief in a tomb to have been a distinct blonde. Her hair is painted a bright yellow stippled with little red horizontal lines, and her skin is white (*The Races of Europe,* Carleton Stevens Coon, New York City, Macmillan. 1939, p.98).

The Cheops pyramids are not the oldest Egyptian pyramids. The step pyramid at Memphis predates them by at least a century, and was designed by a court architect, Imhotep. This great structure, nearly 216 feet (66 meters) high, must have seemed overwhelming to ordinary Egyptians at the time, who at best lived in two story mud brick houses, and it is no surprise that the architect was eventually deified.

### The Giza Sphinx and Pyramids 2500 BC

The Cheops pyramids are impressive today and by the standards of the time they must have appeared to be a superhuman achievement. Twenty years in the building, these pyramids used between five and six million tons of stone, some blocks being moved over five hundred miles, with almost perfect masonry work on site so that the alignment variance of the stones even today is less than one percent. The greatest pyramid reaches 479 feet (146 meters)—higher than St. Peter's Cathedral in Rome (which remains the biggest Christian cathedral in the world).

### Egyptian Religion Provides Insight into Race

Charms and magical prayers were collected into a book known as *The Egyptian Book of the Dead.* Many Egyptians ensured that these books were put into their tombs to assist in a successful resurrection. The focus of Egyptian religion was primarily concerned with the achievement of life after death. The practice of mummification was started on the basis of a myth that the god of the Nile River, Osiris, had been murdered by his evil brother, Seth.

According to the myth, Seth cut Osiris's body into pieces. These pieces were gathered together by Osiris's grieving widow Isis, and reassembled, thus resurrecting him. The Nile god then became the first mummy, and every mummified Egyptian became a second Osiris. This resurrection theme was to become dominant in other religions, and adopted by Christianity. Thus the tradition of mummification started: a jump start to everlasting life in the hereafter. The process of mummification has also provided modern day historians with a spectacular and unique chance to see the physical characteristics of Egyptians exactly as they were.

The evidence is overwhelming that these first Egyptian societies were white—a Proto-Nordic/Alpine/Mediterranean mixture. The leadership elite, in particular the pharaohs themselves, were mostly Nordic. The mummified remains of numerous pharaohs and common folk from this first great Egyptian civilization have unmistakable white features.

For example, the well preserved body of Pharaoh Ramses II has red hair, and there are large numbers of mummies whose blond hair has been extraordinarily well preserved through the centuries.

This tradition of Nordic pharaohs was to last almost till the second part of the Third Kingdom, circa 1050 BC, by which time racial demographic shifts had taken place in Egyptian society in favor of nonwhite groups.

All this is not to say that no other races lived in the area. There were a significant number of Semitic Arabic racial types, who had settled there from their homeland in the Arabian Peninsula. These nonwhite peoples were, however, for many years—centuries even—excluded from mainstream Egyptian society because of their race. They were

## THE MYTH OF THE "BLACK SPHINX"

*The Great Sphinx at Giza, outside Cairo, circa 2500 BC. Due to the fact that the Sphinx's nose is missing, the myth of the "Black" Sphinx has arisen. An increasing number of black supremacists have claimed that the Sphinx had Negroid racial features, and that whites (usually blamed on Napoleon Bonaparte's troops) used the Sphinx as cannon target practice to shoot off its flat nose so as to hide the fact that it was Negroid.*

*In reality, the Sphinx was erected by the white Pharaoh Khafre, whose face was used as the model for the sculpture. A contemporary sculpture of Khafre—most likely the exact one from which the Sphinx was modeled—is illustrated alongside. When Napoleon invaded Egypt at the end of the nineteenth century, he commissioned French artists to make an inventory of the Egyptian relics he found there, and their pictures show the Sphinx damaged even then—proof that the French never used the Sphinx as target practice.*

*The Sphinx was used as target practice by nonwhite Muslim invaders, several centuries before Napoleon. This damage, combined with centuries of natural sand abrasion, was the real cause of the weathered face of this great monument from white Egypt.*

most often used as laborers, along with blacks captured by the Egyptians in warring expeditions even further south into modern day Sudan. Their numbers steadily increased during their stay in Egypt, and they became a significant demographic element in that land.

### Egyptian Achievements—Created 365 Day Calendar

Aside from the stupendous achievement of building the pyramids, the white civilization of Egypt is credited with many achievements, some of which benefit to this day. The Egyptians were the first to divide the solar year into 365 and one quarter days based on a twelve month cycle. The Egyptians also became famous for their medical skills, although the difference between magic and science does not appear to have been fully made. Evidence exists of advanced surgery having been carried out as far back as the First Kingdom, and many techniques and herbal remedies were taken over by the classical Greeks and survived right into medieval European times.

In contrast to Mesopotamian writing, Egyptian writing (hieroglyphics, meaning "sacred signs") remained pictorial in content throughout the span of this civilization. Egyptian writing was only deciphered in 1822 after the discovery of the Rosetta Stone.

### The Middle or Second Kingdom 2060–1785 BC

The period 2270–2060 BC was marked by great instability in Egypt, where the unity of the country fell to pieces. Only in the year 2060 BC was Egypt again politically united. It managed to attain a part of its Old Kingdom splendor, although it never built anything the size of the Great Pyramids of Giza again.

This period of political unity did not last longer than seventy years, and around the year 1785 BC, a divided Egypt was conquered by a Semitic tribe known as the Hyksos. They had little trouble subjecting the Egyptians, aided through the use of iron weapons and the horse and chariot, neither of which the Egyptians had seen before. The Hyksos had been attacked with this weapon by the Indo-European tribes who had developed the chariot on their route south from their respective homelands in the north.

It took some two hundred years for the Egyptians to rebuild their strength and the Hyksos were finally expelled in 1580 BC—after the Egyptians had mastered the new weapon of horse and chariot and turned it against them. The Egyptian records show that the Minoans from Crete had helped fight the Semitic Hyksos invaders—further evidence of the close links between the Egyptians and the Old European

**ENDURING MONUMENTS TO EGYPT'S GREATNESS**

*Unequaled for sheer scale and magnificence, the Great Pyramids of Giza stand as towering monuments to the architects and engineers who oversaw their creation. Using over six million individual blocks in the greatest pyramid, that of Cheops, the masons used a limestone casing which slotted together with perfect symmetry and precision, as illustrated in the picture above right.*

# TUTANKHAMUN'S WHITE FAMILY ALBUM

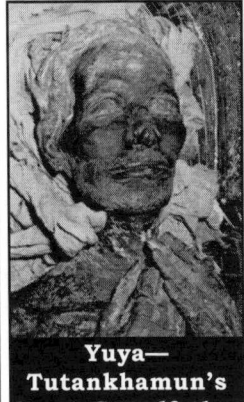

| Yuya—<br>Tutankhamun's<br>Great Grandfather | Thuya—<br>Tutankhamun's<br>Great Grandmother | Tiye—<br>Tutankhamun's<br>Grandmother |
|---|---|---|

*Possibly the best known Egyptian King is Tutankhamun, who reigned around the year 1350 BC. It is Tutankhamun's gold mask (below left) which has come to symbolize Egypt in many peoples' minds. His tomb was found almost intact in 1924.*

*Tutankhamun was descended from a long line of Nordic ancestors, as illustrated here in this family album of mummies. Above left: Yuya, Tutankhamun's great*

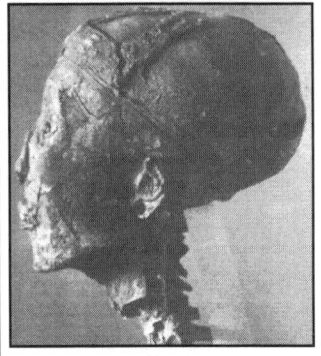

*grandfather, dating from approximately 1400 BC. Yuya's blond hair and Nordic facial structure have been well preserved by the embalming process. Above center: Thuya, Tutankhamun's great grandmother, wife of Yuya and mother of Tiye. Above right: Yuya's daughter, Queen Tiye. She was the wife of Pharaoh Amenhotep III, and grandmother of Tutankhamun. (Confusion existed over the identity of Tiye's mummy until scientific analysis of a lock of her well preserved hair was found in her grandson's tomb.)*

*Bottom left: The skull of the poorly preserved mummy of Tutankhamun himself. Note his distinctly "long" head, which contrasts strongly with the famous gold mask that does not bear any resemblance to the boy king.*

*In fact, there are three different Tutankhamun masks, each with different physical characteristics. Tutankhamun's mummy was encased in a number of coffins, with each sarcophagus bearing a different mask. The most likely reason for the different looking masks is that the king died so unexpectedly that his funeral apparel had not yet been made, and other Egyptians donated their funeral masks for use in the king's burial.*

## WHITE ROYALTY AS RACIAL IMAGES IN EGYPTIAN ART

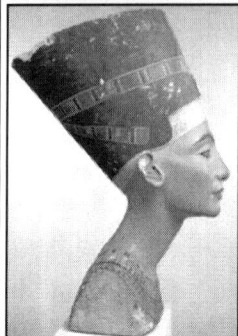  

Left: *The famous bust of the beautiful white queen Nefertiti, Eighteenth Dynasty, circa 1350 BC. This bust was discovered in 1912 during excavation work at Tel el Amarna. It now resides in the Egyptian Museum in Berlin. Nefertiti was married to the father of Tutankhamun, although she might not have been Tutankhamun's biological mother.* Center: *The unmistakably white visage of Pharaoh Amenemhet III, of the Twelfth Dynasty (circa 1991–1786 BC). Amenemhet reclaimed swampland and was one of the last of the great pyramid builders of Egypt.* Right: *An original wooden statue of the Egyptian King Hor (circa 1783–1633 BC), on display at the Cairo Museum, Egypt, is inlaid with lapus lazuli eyes.*

civilization. The result of two hundred years of Hyksos rule had left its mark upon the Egyptian population. As reflected in its art, the white population after this time began to show increasing signs of nonwhite admixture. This white/Semitic mix came to characterize virtually the entire Middle East.

However, an important element of the Egyptian population was by this stage showing clear nonwhite ancestry. It was with the Third Kingdom and its expansion into areas heavily populated by Nubians (blacks from Sudan) and Ethiopia (occupied by masses of Arab/Semitic peoples) that large numbers of these nonwhites came to be prominent in Egyptian society, either as slaves or freemen.

### *Last Surge of Power—The New Kingdom (The Third Kingdom) 1580–1085 BC*

The third (and last) great surge in Egyptian power came with the expulsions of the Semitic Hyksos. Adopting the horse and chariot, energetic and expansionist pharaohs set about consolidating Egypt and establishing an empire. Syria, Phoenicia, Palestine, Nubia, and northern Sudan (the latter with large black populations) were all conquered and incorporated into the Egyptian Empire. The greatest expansionist king was Thutmose III (circa 1501–1447 BC). A series of tall pointed stone columns (called obelisks) were built to commemorate his various campaigns. Only four of the obelisks survived the strife of Egypt's history, and today they stand in Istanbul, Rome, London, and New York, silent reminders of the greatness of a bygone age.

The greatest pharaoh of this time was Amenhotep III (1411–1375 BC) who built Thebes up into the most magnificent city of the age. Amenhotep built many other huge structures, including the temple of Luxor at the city of Thebes.

**BLUE EYED EGYPTIAN 2800 BC**

*A blue eyed statue from the earliest Egyptian dynasties: An Egyptian noble lady from the Fourth Dynasty—around 2800 BC. Inlaid with lapus lazuli blue eyes, it was placed inside the lady's tomb.*

### *Tutankhamun—Stood on His Black and Semitic Enemies 1350 BC*

Tutankhamun, the boy king (who died when he was eighteen) reigned around 1350 BC. Although he died too young to become a pharaoh of any great significance in his own time, he gained fame when his tomb was discovered intact in 1924 (one of the few tombs to be found in such a good state—most had been the subject of grave robbers centuries before). It is the gold burial mask of Tutankhamun, which has come to symbolize ancient Egypt.

However, the real significance of the artifacts in the tomb has been largely ignored: amongst Tutankhamun's possessions were some of the most graphic racial images in Egyptology.

One of Tutankhamun's thrones, the ecclesiastical chair, has on its footrest the "Nine Bows"—the Egyptian name for the traditional enemies of Egypt. The finely crafted figures on the footrest are of nine blacks and Semites tied together in chains. They were positioned on the footrest so that when the pharaoh sat on his throne, his enemies would be under his feet.

Another graphically racial image found in Tutankhamun's tomb is found on one of his walking sticks. The handle is made up of a bound

Semite and a bound black—when the Egyptian king went for a walk with his royal walking stick, he held the enemies of Egypt in his hand.

### The King Walks on Egypt's Racial Enemies

Yet another candid racial image from Tutankhamun's tomb is found in a pair of his sandals. Inlaid with a picture of a Semite and a black, the pharaoh would trample his enemies underfoot when he walked.

Tutankhamun's famous wooden chest, which was found in the antechamber of his tomb, contains yet another striking scene. On its sides, it shows the Egyptian king riding a chariot and trampling the enemies of Egypt: blacks and Semites.

By Tutankhamun's time then, the Egyptians were clearly aware of the growing numbers of their racial enemies creeping up on them. These graphic references to Egypt's racial enemies are ominous when it is considered that by the time of Tutankhamun, nonwhite slaves had already become commonplace.

In addition to this, a significant number of Egyptians were now of mixed race, the Hyksos occupation having left behind a number of Egyptian/Semitic types. Significantly, Tutankhamun's widow attempted to strike an alliance with the Indo-European Hittites who had in the interim became the leading power in the Middle East, by arranging her

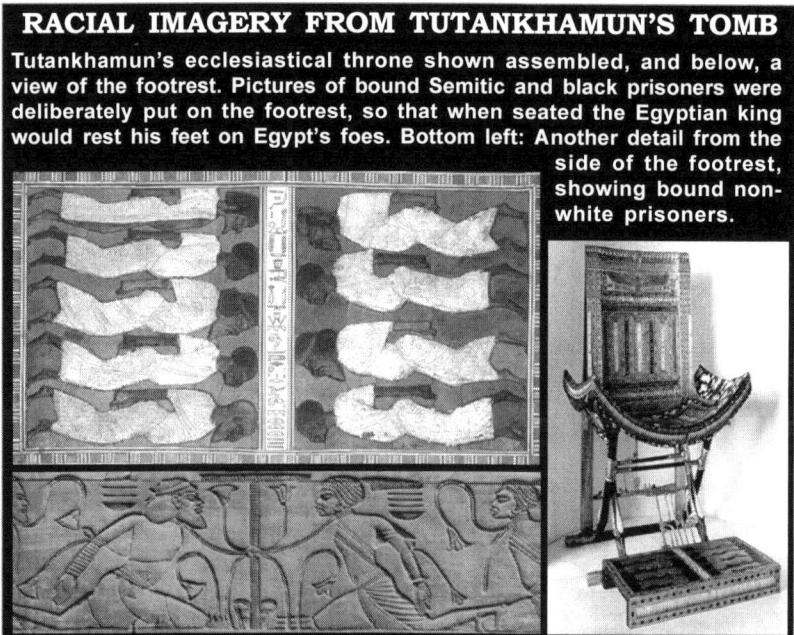

**RACIAL IMAGERY FROM TUTANKHAMUN'S TOMB**
Tutankhamun's ecclesiastical throne shown assembled, and below, a view of the footrest. Pictures of bound Semitic and black prisoners were deliberately put on the footrest, so that when seated the Egyptian king would rest his feet on Egypt's foes. Bottom left: Another detail from the side of the footrest, showing bound non-white prisoners.

# THE PHARAOH WALKS ON THE ENEMIES OF EGYPT

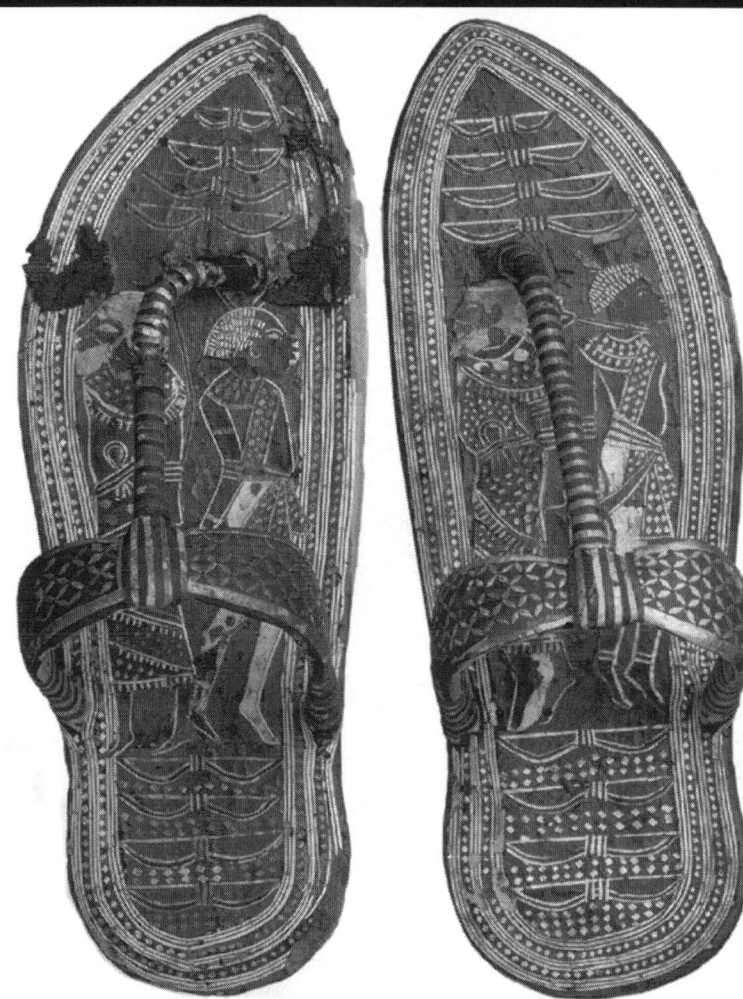

*The boy king Tutankhamun, who died when he was eighteen years old (circa 1325 BC), has become one of the most famous Egyptian kings, not because of his deeds, but because his tomb was discovered virtually intact in 1924. The great significance of his tomb lies in the fact that we are accorded a unique opportunity to see perfectly preserved everyday items from the king's personal belongings—including,* above, *a pair of sandals. The Egyptian king's sandals have bound black and Semitic prisoners inlaid into the soles. The meaning is clear—when the pharaoh walked in these shoes, he would trample the racial enemies of Egypt underfoot. This powerful symbolism was commonly used in other artifacts, such as walking sticks and even game sticks. The last white Egyptians finally vanished some four hundred years after Tutankhamun, around the year 800 BC, racially absorbed into the nonwhite masses.*

own marriage to a Hittite prince. (The marriage never took place, as the husband to be was killed just prior to the ceremony.)

### The Fall of White Egypt

From the time of Tutankhamun onwards, the final decline of Egypt was irreversible. Later kings tried to reverse the trend and they sometimes succeeded, temporarily, in rolling back the waves of conquest and counter conquest in Palestine and Syria. One pharaoh even managed to take a Hittite princess as a bride.

But there were fresh enemies: Egypt was now attacked by new Indo-European invaders emerging from the Aegean, the so-called Sea People. As their name implied, they arrived by boat and raided Egyptian settlements, leaving again by the means that they arrived. These Sea Peoples were mainly comprised of Philistines from Asia Minor and Achaeans from mainland Greece. Egyptian illustrations of the time show prisoners being taken with light hair and light eyes—Sea People raiders unfortunate enough to fall into captivity in Egypt, where they could expect no mercy.

### White Egyptians Disappear 800 BC

Ever since the time of the Hyksos invasion and the fall of the Second Kingdom, the demographic shift amongst the Egyptian population had been against the original whites. Slowly at first, but then speeding up, nonwhites or mixed racial types began to make up more and more of that country's population—drawn in as slaves, laborers, immigrants, or invaders.

These other racial types were of two sorts: Semites (whom the Egyptians called "Sand Dwellers") and blacks, from the region of Nubia in the far south (present day Sudan). A review of Egypt's relations with Nubia is therefore crucial to understanding what happened to the white Egyptians, and why they vanished.

### Race War with Nubia

Clashes between the Egyptians and the black Nubians had long been a feature of Egyptian history, with the first campaigns against the Nubians launched by Old Kingdom pharaohs around 2900 BC. In 2570 BC, Pharaoh Sneferu launched a concerted attack upon Nubia. Egyptian records show that seventy thousand prisoners were taken.

# TUTANKHAMUN VANQUISHES EGYPT'S NON-WHITE ENEMIES

Right: *A general view of Tutankhamun's wooden kist.* Above and Below: *Two close-ups of the detail on the front and rear of the chest, showing the king trampling blacks and Semites under his chariot.*

*Note also the black slaves fanning Tutankhamun at the rear of his chariot—the use of nonwhite labor being the primary reason why that civilization was eventually overrun by those very nonwhites.*

*These scenes are very famous, and are commonly used as an illustration of ancient Egypt. Very often the blatant racial imagery is deliberately obscured or even retouched—with the blacks and Semites removed from the picture so as to hide the message which the Egyptian king wished to convey—that he was a conqueror of the black Nubians and the Semites.*

*Many items found in Tutankhamun's tomb—even decorations on the king's golden chariot—showed blacks and Semites being subjugated by the victorious white Egyptians.*

*These artifacts serve to illustrate what the Egyptians thought of their black neighbors, but it did not stop them from using the blacks as slaves or mercenaries. This practice of using nonwhite slaves eventually led to the fall of Egypt, after those people gradually came to form the majority of the population of that land.*

In 1296 BC Egypt conquered Nubia and built a series of massive forts to protect its southern borders against the Nubians, with the most famous of these being the fort at Buhen, which had walls which were over 364 feet (110 meters) high and almost 15 feet (4.5 meters) thick.

Along the banks of the southern Nile huge stones were erected upon which, in hieroglyphics still visible today, the passage of blacks past those points was forbidden—the first public "Whites Only" signs in history.

At the time of the Hyksos invasion of Egypt, many local Nubian kings allied themselves with the Hyksos and inflicted defeats upon the weakened Egyptians, including the destruction of the southern forts.

When the Hyksos were finally driven out, the white Egyptians exacted a terrible revenge upon the blacks, launching many campaigns of conquest and suppression against them, all the while bringing back thousands into Egypt as slaves—a racial time bomb which was to eventually destroy Egyptian civilization.

## Egyptian Writings about Blacks

The white Egyptians left many written references to the black population in Nubia and in their own country. In fact, at one point, their writings record a law that forbade blacks from entering their country at all. An overview of these written inscriptions is highly worthwhile and devastates claims by pro-black historians, who, in an attempt to distort the historical record, claim that the ancient Egyptian civilization was black in racial origin. The most complete record and translation of these scripts was undertaken by Professor James Henry Breasted, Professor of Egyptology and Oriental History in the University of Chicago in his work *History of Egypt, from the Earliest Times to the Persian Conquest,* Second Edition, 1909. For anyone interested in a detailed overview, based on original Egyptian sources, this book is well worth reading. All the writings quoted below have been extracted from Breasted's work and are based on original Egyptian records.

## Egyptian Racial Writings: The Sixth Dynasty

An inscription that was written by Count Uni, governor of the South, and an official of the Old Kingdom, reads as follows:

*"His majesty made war on the Asiatic Sand-Dwellers and his majesty made an army of many ten thousands: in the entire South . . . among the Irthet blacks, the Mazoi blacks, the Yam blacks,*

## EGYPT'S ENEMIES IN ANCIENT EGYPTIAN ART

Above: *Tile inlays from the mortuary temple of Ramses III, western Thebes, Medinet Habu, circa 1170 BC. The palace entrances were decorated at the bottom on both sides with representations of Egypt's enemies.* From Left to Right, *a Libyan, a Nubian, and a Syrian. The first and third are Semites, the center figure a black from the far south. As the racial demographics swung increasingly against the original white Egyptians, so more and more of these nonwhite types came to dominate Egyptian society—to the point where Egypt was finally submerged by them.*

Top Right and Center: *Details from a walking stick recovered from the tomb of the boy king, Tutankhamun (circa 1350 BC). Bound Semitic and black prisoners decorate the curved handle end of the stick, symbolizing the fact that when the Egyptian king went for a walk, he would hold the enemies of Egypt in the palm of his hand.*

Above: *Semites, clearly identified as racially foreign with distinctive physical characteristics, present tributes to the Egyptian pharaoh, a painted scene from the tomb of Sobekhotep at Thebes.*

Above: *Blacks, from Nubia, presenting gold tribute to the white Egyptians, dating from the Third Kingdom's occupation of Nubia as a permanent colony, circa 1840 BC. Nubia was an important source of gold, wild animals, and slaves for the Egyptians—and the eventual cause of the latter's downfall, after they came to dominate the population makeup of that land.*

Above: *An original Egyptian model of blacks used as mercenaries by the ancient Egyptians.*
*Along with slavery, this was the main channel through which Africans entered white Egyptian society.*

*among the Wawat blacks, among the Kau blacks, and in the land of Temeh."*

This is an example of an Old Kingdom (2980–2475 BC) pharaoh using thousands of blacks as mercenaries. The army was sent into southern Palestine and *"returned in safety after it had hacked up the land of the Sand-Dwellers. His majesty sent me to dig five canals in the South, and to make three cargo-boats and four row boats of Acacia wood of Wawat.*

*Then the black chiefs of Irthet, Waway, Yam, and Mazoi drew timber therefore, and I did the whole in only one year. The pharaoh came to inspect this work and at the coming of the king himself, standing behind the hill country, while the chiefs of Mazoi, Irthet, and Wawat did obeisance and gave great praise."*

This writing shows very clearly the use of blacks as labor, and illustrates how they were slowly but surely drawn into Egyptian society.

### Egyptian Writings: The Twelfth Dynasty

A sandstone stela found in the sanctuary of Wadi Halfa contains an account of the Nubian expedition of Pharaoh Sesostris I, which carried this king's wars to their southernmost limits. At the top of this stela there is a relief showing Sesostris I standing facing the Lord of Thebes, who says: *"I have brought for thee all countries which are in Nubia, beneath thy feet."*

The inscription of Prince Amenim, which is carved into the stone in the doorway of his cliff-tomb in Benihasin, describes the black lands as "vile." It reads as follows ("Kush" was one of the black lands): *"I passed Kush sailing southward . . . then his majesty returned in safety having overthrown his enemies in Kush the vile."*

The inscription on the stela of Sihathor, an "Assistant Treasurer," is now in the British Museum, and reads as follows: *"I reached Nubia of the blacks . . . I forced the Nubian chiefs to wash gold."*

### "To Prevent That any Black Should Cross. . ."

The final conquest of Nubia was attained by Sesostris III in 1840 BC. This king conducted four campaigns against the blacks and erected several forts at strategic points, making Nubia a permanent colony of Egypt.

The first Semneh stela inscription recounting the subjugation of Nubia by Sesostris III reads as follows:

# NORDIC NOBILITY IN ANCIENT EGYPT

## Father and Son: Two Great Pharaohs of Ancient Egypt

*Left: The well preserved mummy of the great Ramses II (1292–1225 BC), is on public display at the Egyptian Museum, Cairo. This picture shows well his red hair. Although touched up by the embalmers with henna, (as he was eighty years old when he died, and his hair would have been white by then), traces of the original red hair color were found when examined microscopically. People with red hair in ancient Egypt were associated with the god Set, and Ramses' father was Seti I (below), whose name means "followers of Set." It is likely that Ramses came from a family of redheads.*

**RAMSES II**

Below left: *Although the mummy of Ramses II is well preserved, the most lifelike of all the surviving Egyptian mummies is that of his father, the Nordic Pharaoh Seti I, whose features remain crystal clear to this day.*

Below right*: Seti's mummy can easily be compared with a relief of his face, made in his lifetime at the temple at Abydos. Seti was the son of the great Ramses I, and became pharaoh in approximately 1320 BC. His mummy was so well preserved because it was covered from head to foot in a black resin, which effectively halted the decomposition process.*

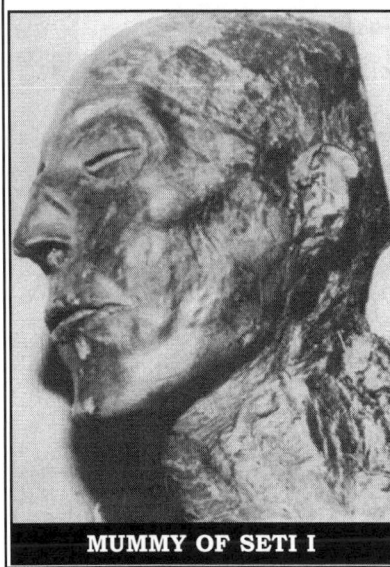

**MUMMY OF SETI I**

**BAS-RELIEF OF SETI I**

131

*"Southern boundary, made in the year 8, under the majesty of the king of Upper and Lower Egypt, Sesostris III . . . in order to prevent that any black should cross it, by water or by land, with a ship, or any herds of the blacks; except a black who shall come to do trading in Iken, or with a commission. Every good thing shall be done with them but without allowing a ship of the blacks to pass by Heh, going downstream, forever."*

### Egyptian Racial Writings: The Eighteenth Dynasty 1580–1350 BC

The inscription of Ahmose reads: *"Now after his majesty had slain the Asiatics, he ascended the river . . . to destroy the Nubian Troglodytes; his majesty made a great slaughter among them."*

The Tombos Stela of Thutmose I reads: *"He hath overthrown the chief of the Nubians; the black is helpless, defenseless, in his grasp. He hath united the boundaries of his two sides, there is not a remnant among the curly-haired, who came to attack; there is not a single survivor among them . . . They fall by the sword . . . the fragments cut from them are too much for the birds."*

In the annals of the great warrior king, Thutmose III, at the sixth Karnak pylon, there is a list that contains no less than 115 of the names of the towns and districts of the conquered Nubian regions.

Another pylon at Karnak contains references to about four hundred towns, districts, and countries conquered in Nubia. Inscribed on one of the tablets is the famous "Hymn of Victory" which reads as follows: *I have bound together the Nubian Troglodytes by the tens of thousands. The northerners by hundreds of thousands as prisoners."*

Another remarkable inscription is to be found on the Semneh stela of Amenhotep III, which is also in the British Museum in London. It reads as follows: *"List of the captivity which his majesty took in the land of Ibbet the wretched.*
*List of Prisoners and Killed*
*Living blacks 150 heads*
*Archers 110 heads*
*Female blacks 250 heads*
*Servants of the blacks 55 heads*
*Their children 175 heads*
*Total 740 heads*
*Hands thereof 312*
*United with the living heads 1,052."*

### *The Red Haired Ramses II—Last Significant White Pharaoh*

Egypt's last display of national vigor came with the red haired Pharaoh Ramses II (1292–1225 BC). Ramses II managed to reestablish the already decaying Egyptian Empire by recapturing much land in Nubia. He also fought a series of battles against invading Indo-Europeans, the Hittites.

This culminated with the Battle of Kadesh in northern Syria. Ramses signed a treaty with the Hittites in 1258 BC, which ended the war. In terms of the treaty, Ramses took as his wife an Indo-European Hittite princess.

## THE END OF ANCIENT EGYPT— OVERRUN BY THE BLACK NUBIANS

White Egyptian Pharaoh
Tuthmosis III, 1450 BC

Black Nubian Pharaoh
Shabako, 710 BC

Above left: *A statue of the white Pharaoh Thutmose III (1490–1436 BC) clearly shows his racial features, which contrast strongly with a statue of the black Nubian King Shabako, above right, late Twenty-fifth Dynasty, circa 710 BC. The last white Egyptians had vanished prior to 800 BC, physically integrated into the mass of Nubian and Semitic peoples who had come to dominate that land. The resultant mixed race population was unable to withstand new invaders, some Semitic and some black. The most prominent of the black Nubian invaders then set themselves up as new Egyptian kings, later called the Twenty-fifth Dynasty, dating from 746–655 BC. Unable to maintain the originally white civilization they had inherited, the Twenty-fifth Dynasty sputtered out of its own accord and was finally destroyed by an Assyrian invasion. The fall of Egypt is officially dated as from the end of the Twenty-fifth Dynasty—but the true Egyptians had long since vanished.*

His other achievements included the building of the rock-hewn temple of Abu Simbel, the great hall in the Temple of Amon at Karnak, and the mortuary temple at Thebes.

After this king, Egypt entered into a steady period of decay, caused directly by the elimination of the original Egyptians, and their replacement with a mixed population made up of black, Semitic, and the remnant white population. This racially divergent nation was never again to reach the heights achieved by the First, Second, or the first part of the Third Kingdoms. In these later years there were competing claimants to the pharaoh's throne, many of whom, racially speaking, bore no resemblance to the original pharaohs at all.

## Mixed Race Pharaoh Is the Last Pharaoh

The true Egyptians had all vanished at the very latest by 800 BC, and the divided and weakened Egypt was easy prey to numerous invaders, some Semitic, some Nubian, and some Indo-European, none of whom established any sort of permanent rule.

The Nubian invaders set up a new kingdom known as the Twenty-fifth Dynasty (746–655) and claimed to be the inheritors of the previous kingdoms. This one hundred year dynasty saw a number of Nubian and mixed race rulers, all claiming to be pharaohs and attempting to revive some of the older practices, such as mummification.

## Ancient Egypt's End: Overrun by Nonwhites

These nonwhite "Egyptians" were an illusion—the true white Egyptians had vanished, along with their society, and the Nubian dynasty sputtered out of its own accord.

The last pharaoh of this Nubian dynasty, Taharka, whose mixed race ancestry is clear from sculptures, was driven from his throne by invading Assyrians, and it is from this fall of Taharka that historians formally date the fall of Egypt, although in reality the last true Egyptian had disappeared nearly two hundred years previously.

The course of racial developments in Egyptian history has been backed up by anthropological research. The British anthropologist G.M. Morant produced a comprehensive study of Egyptian skulls from commoner and royal graves from all parts of the Egyptian lands and times.

His conclusions were that the majority of the population of Lower Egypt—that is in the northern part of the country—were members of the Mediterranean white subrace. In the south (or Upper Egypt) this population pattern was repeated but this time showed a certain percentage of black admixture (reflecting the proximity of the Nubian settlement).

Significantly, Morant found that with the passage of time, the differentiation in skull types between Upper and Lower Egypt became less and less distinct, until ultimately they became indistinguishable— the surest sign of the absorption of the white subrace into the growing nonwhite mass (*Race,* John R. Baker, Oxford University Press, 1974, page 519).

## White Greek Occupation 325 BC

After passing under Ethiopian, Assyrian, and Persian rule, Egypt was finally occupied in 325 BC by the Greek Macedonian Alexander the Great (whose tribe was one of the original Indo-European invaders of the Greek peninsula). The famous Queen Cleopatra, often associated with ancient Egypt, was one of these ruling Macedonians, and not an Egyptian.

Under Cleopatra's rule, Egypt became a Roman outpost. Although the Macedonians adopted certain cultural characteristics of ancient Egypt, the true Egyptians had long since passed from the world stage, absorbed into the mixed race mass of the Middle East.

# CHAPTER NINE

# Genesis of Western Thought—Classical Greece

**The Greek peninsula, and its northern borders, the Balkans, had previously been settled by the original European peoples during the Neolithic Age. These peoples had created the Old European civilizations, which were some of the most advanced in Europe at the time.**

From approximately 5000 BC onward, the Indo-Europeans had started flooding westward, at first conquering but then integrating with these original inhabitants. This massive influx brought about the fall of these Old European civilizations—and in their place rose the two great civilizations which have come to epitomize the classical world: Greece and Rome.

MYCENAE—FIRST GREAT GREEK CITY STATE 1900 BC

*The citadel of Mycenae, situated on the southernmost part of the Greek peninsula, reconstructed to what it looked like at its zenith. The genesis of classical Greek culture was born and nurtured here, one of the earliest Indo-European invasions of the Grecian lands.*

## Mycenaeans and Dorians—Founders of Athens and Sparta

The first of these new great civilizations was the Mycenaeans. Around 1900 BC they settled in large numbers on islands off the present day Turkish coast, establishing what became known as Ionia and the Ionian civilization.

The Mycenaeans were dispersed by another Indo-European invasion, that of the Dorians.

They established their capital at Sparta, a city which, along with Athens, was to become synonymous with the history of classical Greece.

## THE DROMOS—WHERE SPARTA'S MILITARY MIGHT WAS CREATED

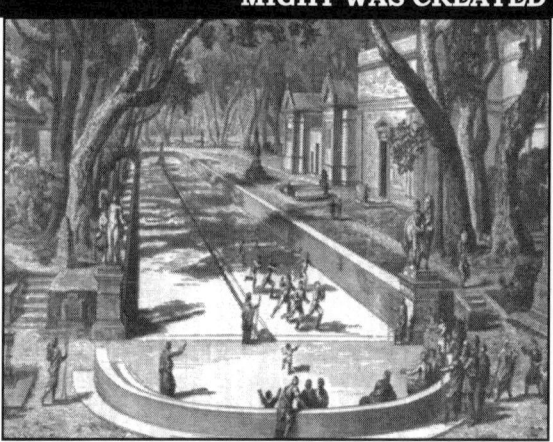

The source of Sparta's military power: The Dromos, or racecourse and gymnasium. The great expansion of Spartan power was largely attained by the disciplinary education of the Spartan youth, which, though it destroyed the possibility of family life, produced the harsh and inflexible character of the splendidly trained warrior to whom the military supremacy of Sparta was due. Spartan men were all full-time professional soldiers, sometimes to the exclusion of family life.

This obsession with military preparedness made them an exceptional fighting force, but ultimately led to their downfall. The manual labor in Spartan society was done by an ever increasing number of mixed race slaves imported for the purpose. This, combined with the high death rate amongst Spartan men, soon led to that nation's extinction.

By approximately 1000 BC, the waves of invading Indo-Europeans had come to an end, and a semblance of stability returned to central and western Europe.

Together with the original Europeans, the new Nordic settlers built upon the Old European civilizations, with the first great "city states" being built on the Greek peninsula.

### Hellenic Age—Height of Greek Civilization 800–400 BC

The four hundred years stretching from 800–400 BC are known as the Hellenic Age, and mark the height of classical Greek civilization. Around this time the Greeks also founded the city of Byzantium, later to become famous as Constantinople, today called Istanbul. It was only the later Romans who called the inhabitants of this region Greeks— they referred to themselves as Hellenes, hence the Hellenic Age.

In 776 BC, the first Olympic games were held at Olympia. Thereafter they took place every four years in honor of the god Zeus, and lasted in that form until 394 AD. During these celebrations, all the Grecian city states sent athletes to Olympia, wars were suspended, and legal disputes and the use of the death penalty were forbidden.

### Greek States—Oligarchy versus Democracy

Knowledge of the nature of the city state is crucial to an understanding of the history of classical Greece. Far from being a united people, the Greeks established themselves in walled, fortified, and quite often self sustaining cities, each fiercely independent and warring with each other at the proverbial drop of a hat. By 750 BC, two distinct ideologies had formed amongst the Greek city states. The first was an oligarchy—ruled by an educated elite. The second was a limited form of democracy—rule by the citizens. The city of Sparta was the leading exponent of the oligarchic system, while the city of Athens was the leading exponent of the democratic system. Four city states in particular achieved prominence: Sparta, Corinth, Athens, and Thebes.

The latter three cities were plagued by political uncertainty for long periods, with government forms alternating between democracies, monarchies, and oligarchies. Sparta was the only exception to this variance in political form: it remained steadfastly oligarchic and actively despised the democracies.

### Sparta and Race—World's First Eugenics

The Spartans strictly divided their society into three classes which were based solely on race. At the top were the Spartans, who were nearly all Nordic. The middle class was mainly comprised of the original Greeks and some later descendants of other Indo-European invaders (such as the Dorians). This middle class tended to be less Nordic in appearance than the Spartans. The lowest class of Spartan society was the darkest in the society, called helots, who were mainly Old Mediterranean racial types who had mixed with North African (Arabic, Nubian, and Semitic) slaves imported into the region at an earlier date.

The Spartans devoted themselves full time to military and physical training. Every Spartan man was a lifelong soldier, never taking part in any other function of society. The middle classes undertook all the commercial activity in Spartan society, while the lowest classes did the manual labor. The existence of this full-time and fully trained professional army class

*Master craftsmanship: A 2,500-year-old Mycenaean gold inlaid dagger.*

## OLYMPIA—ORIGIN OF OLYMPIC GAMES 440 BC

*The origin of the Olympic games: Olympia, the great religious and athletic center of Greece, as it looked circa 440 BC. So important were the games as homage to the gods, that wars between the Greek cities were temporarily halted in their honor.*

was unique in history, and the city of Sparta was the only Grecian city which did not have city walls—so feared were the Spartan soldiers, that none deemed it wise to attack.

The Spartans also practiced a crude form of racial eugenics (improvement of the racial line)—allowing only the best specimens amongst them to survive to adulthood. All new babies were examined by a council of elders and any mentally retarded or severely deformed children were deliberately left to die. The Spartans also regularly engaged in what was known as the Crypteia—the wholesale slaughter of hundreds of helots at a time, officially recorded as a necessary measure to preserve their society. In addition, Spartan laws dictated heavy penalties for celibacy and late marriage, and exempted from taxes those who had more than four children. The end effect of all these measures was a gradual Nordicization of Spartan society.

This process was eventually reversed as the warlike nature of the Spartans finally whittled away their warrior class. Many were killed in battle before having time to procreate in sufficient number to keep up a steady population growth. So weakened, the Spartans were finally overrun by an Indo-European people from north Greece, the Macedonians. The Spartans are almost unique in that they did not disappear through racial integration, but rather through self extermination in endless wars.

Although not as formally defined, this same racial class mix prevailed in almost all of the southern Greek city states. The lowest

NORDIC RACIAL TYPES AS LEADERS IN CLASSICAL GREECE

*Left to right: Zeno of Cyprus, founder of Stoic philosophy; Pericles, the most famous Athenian leader of all time; Demosthenes of Athens, the finest orator of his day; and Sophocles of Athens, one of the most famous playwrights of ancient Greece.*

(and darkest) classes were always the numerically superior group, continually being supplemented by the importation of slaves and laborers from other territories.

## Athens—Evolution of Government

The city of Athens passed first through a period of oligarchy, then into autocracy, and finally into a limited democracy. There was no standing army although the Athenians could, once mobilized, put a very powerful military force into the field.

The two ideological systems which prevailed in the different city states—oligarchy and democracy—came into direct conflict with one another. This clash played a major role in destroying the power of classical Greece, although the real death knell for that civilization was the infusion of foreign blood. This influx of nonwhite foreigners into classical Greece came about through the large scale colonization of neighboring territories.

Although some territories upon which Greek colonies were established had racially compatible natives (southern Italy, the Mediterranean coast of France, and eastern Spain), many were not compatible at all. The importation of slaves into mainland Greece from areas such as Asia Minor, North Africa, and other parts of the Middle East continued unabated between the years 700–500 BC—which ultimately left its mark upon a significant section of the Greek population.

Originally the classical Greeks prided themselves upon possessing the "fairest . . . of all the nations" or so wrote the Jewish physician and sophist Adamantius during the fourth century AD (*Physiognomica*, iii. 32). As the darker elements in Grecian society grew in number, so did the desire to mimic the original Nordic blond haired type. The Greek writer Euripides, for example, wrote a tract on how Greeks dyed their hair blond, and many other Greek writers left tracts describing how hair could be dyed blond with natural chemicals.

The classical Greeks did, however, damage their own population growth by constant infighting and wars with outsiders. The greatest of these outside conflicts was with the Persians—a decade long war, which contained some of the most famous battles ever.

### *The Athenian Wars with Persia 490–480 BC*

The originally Indo-European Persians had started expanding their empire around 550 BC, and this expansion westward included occupying the Ionian city states, which had been founded by the remnants of the Mycenaean peoples.

After the Persian King Darius I ascended to the throne, the Ionians rebelled and reestablished their independence. For five years, from 499–494 BC, the Ionians held out against the Persians. The Persians then reconquered Ionia and as punishment destroyed the largest city in that region, Miletus.

During the Ionian rebellion the city state of Athens had sent material aid to Ionia, and this act led to the Persians deciding to punish the Athenians. There followed two Persian invasions of the Greek mainland.

The first occurred in 490 BC and ended with the defeat of the invading forces at the Battle of Marathon. The invaders were forced to retreat and wait another ten years before relaunching their forces.

### *Thermopylae—Spartans' Heroic Stand 480 BC*

The second invasion began when the Persian king, Xerxes I, brought together one of the largest armies in ancient history, crossing the Bosporus Strait on a bridge made of boats. The Greeks met the Persian army in 480

*An accurate representation of a Spartan soldier in full battle dress. The closed rank battle tactic introduced by the Spartans laid the foundation for the superiority of almost all European armies for the next two thousand years.*

BC at Thermopylae, where the Spartan leader Leonidas I and several thousand soldiers heroically defended a narrow pass.

A treacherous Greek showed the Persians another path that enabled the invaders to enter the pass from the rear. Leonidas permitted most of his men to withdraw, but he and a force of 1,400 Greeks fought until they were all killed by the overwhelmingly numerically superior Persian force. The Persians then proceeded to Athens, capturing and burning the abandoned city.

The Persian fleet then set sail after the Greek fleet, meeting them in battle off the island of Salamis near Athens. This battle, which saw over seven hundred ships from both sides engage one another for an entire day, ended in defeat for the Persians. The Persian king, who had watched the battle from a golden throne on a hill overlooking the scene, fled back to Persia. In the following year, 479 BC, the remainder of the Persian ground forces in Greece were beaten at the battle of Plataea.

In 478 BC a large number of Greek states formed a voluntary alliance, the Delian League, to drive the Persians from the Greek cities and coastal islands of Ionia. Athens, its status amongst the Greek city states enhanced by the victory at Salamis and Plataea, led the alliance. The victories of the league resulted in the liberation of the Ionian Islands from Persian rule by the year 466 BC.

### *Periclean Golden Age—Vote Based on Blood*

From the years 460–429 BC, Athens and many Grecian cities went through what is now known as its Golden Age. Athens was under the leadership of an immensely popular leader named Pericles, who, although a democrat (in the limited Athenian sense of the word—only adult males of a certain class were allowed to vote), was most certainly under no illusion of the potential threat to his society posed by the influx of nonwhite peoples.

In 451 BC, Pericles enacted a law limiting Athenian citizenship by biological descent—only those born of an Athenian mother and an Athenian father could be citizens. In other words, voting rights were granted on the basis of blood alone. During the time of Pericles, classical Greece reached the heights for which it is remembered today. Amongst his more famous achievements was the construction of the Parthenon on the acropolis in Athens, built from 447–432 BC and dedicated to that city's patron goddess, Athena Parthenos. This monument still stands today as a world famous beacon of classical Greece.

## THE PARTHENON ON THE ACROPOLIS IN ATHENS 438 BC

*The Parthenon on the Acropolis in Athens was built from 447–438 BC to commemorate the Greek victory over the Persian king Xerxes I.*

*At this time, Athens was at its zenith as a largely Nordic population, but it also included a large number of nonwhite slaves. Because of this, a law was passed in 451 BC which limited citizenship biologically—to those of Athenian descent only.*

*In this way the Athenians attempted to prevent non-Greeks from taking over their city. In this they failed, because they still used large numbers of nonwhites as slaves and for labor.*

Right: *The statue of Athena, the goddess of war, and the interior of the Parthenon, as it originally appeared. The interior was gilded and contained a massive statue—one of the wonders of Periclean Greece. The reconstruction is based on contemporary accounts.*

Below: *The Acropolis as it appeared during the city's golden age. Pericles, Athens' greatest ruler, and Phidias, her greatest architect, raised the city to such heights that her sheer aesthetic beauty has been unsurpassed to this very day. When the Romans occupied Greece—long after the latter's collapse—they were in awe of the sheer splendor of Athens, and took much of their architecture and artistic style directly from classical Greece. Inset: The Acropolis as it is today.*

## *The Inter-Greek Wars 431–404 BC*

The wars between the Greek city states, known as the Peloponnesian Wars (named after the peninsula), were the immediate cause of the collapse of the military might of classical Greece.

After the end of the Persian Wars, Greece had divided into two alliances: the Spartan League (mostly monarchies or oligarchies led by the city of Sparta) and the Athenian Empire (mostly democracies led by the city of Athens). Internal politicking, jealousy, general mistrust, and the conflict between democracy and oligarchy led to the outbreak of war between the two alliances.

The first phase of the war was inconclusive; whereas the Spartans had a strong land force, the Athenians were more powerful at sea. The city state of Athens was furthermore protected by massive and well built fortifications, which included the "Long Walls." These were an incredible set of approximately seven mile long walls lining a single road linking Athens with its major port, Piraeus, through which the Athenian navy could keep the city supplied in times of siege.

In 430 BC, a plague broke out in Athens and a quarter of the population, including Pericles, died. The Spartan League also suffered as the plague spread, and by 421 BC both sides were exhausted. A peace treaty was signed, but the peace was short-lived and a renewed conflict broke out in 415 BC, when the Athenians attempted an invasion of Sicily, where Spartan-aligned colonies had been established.

The Persians, still smarting from their defeat at the hands of the Athenians in 480 BC, then intervened, offering the Spartans money and skills to build a fleet to match that of the Athenians, on condition that the Spartan League guaranteed the Persians a free hand in Ionia.

The Spartan League accepted, and in 405 BC the new Spartan fleet scored a decisive naval victory at a harbor called Aegospotamoi in Thrace. The Spartans captured 170 Athenian ships and took about four thousand prisoners—a blow from which Athens could not recover. The Spartans then renewed their siege of Athens.

**BEAUTIFUL ORNAMENTAL GREEK VASES 300 BC**

*Magnificent examples of Greek craftsmanship: three vases—all over 2,300 years old—exhibiting artistry and skill which would be hard to match by modern standards.*

This time the Athenians were forced to surrender, an event which took place in 404 BC. They had no fleet to supply, and the resultant famine caused a collapse in the will to resist.

The Peloponnesian Wars were at an end, but they had exacted such a toll from all the Greek city states that the number of whites had been significantly reduced. This, combined with physical integration with the imported mixed race slaves from the Middle East and Africa, was the primary cause of the collapse of classical Greece.

By 400 BC, none of the formerly great city states could withstand the new power in the north, that of Macedonia. From this land, whose Nordic population had been almost unscathed by the wars, was to emerge the famous Alexander the Great, who conquered all the warring Grecian city states in 338 BC. The epic of Alexander and his empire is detailed in the following chapter.

## *Greek Academia—Origin of Western Thought*

Magnificent architecture is not the only legacy of classical Greece. Between the years 700–400 BC, there were great philosophical, cultural, and scientific achievements. Any review of classical Greece is incomplete without an overview of these great works.

- Greek philosophy is still held in high esteem. The father of philosophy was one Thales (636–546 BC) who lived in the Ionian city of Miletus. Thales was the first philosopher to offer an explanation of life in terms of natural causes, and not in terms of the whims of gods.

Left: *Euripides, Athenian playwright. Many of his plays—and those of his fellow Greek playwrights—are still performed today, so timeless and perfect were their construction.* Center: *Socrates, a philosopher of Alpine racial type. He was forced to commit suicide after enraging his fellow citizens.* Right: *The unmistakably Indo-European face of Homer, one of the greatest Greek poets and storytellers, most famous for his epic poem,* The Iliad. *All from the original Greek sculptures.*

- The geometrician Pythagoras (582–500 BC) came from Samos in Ionia, and is most famous for his geometric theory regarding right angled triangles.
- Another group of philosophers came to be known as Sophists, teachers of debate known as rhetoric. The Sophists insisted that truth in itself was a relative concept and denied the existence of any universal standards. The most famous Sophist was Protarus (490–421 BC) from whose name the word "protagonist" originates.
- In the fourth century a philosopher named Diogenes founded a school of philosophers known as the Cynics. They had no respect for rules and regulations of society and lived very simply. Diogenes lived this philosophy as well, using a storage jar as his home.
- The Stoic philosophers were named after the stoa (porch) where their founder, Zeno, taught. They believed that if people acted naturally they would behave well, because their nature was controlled by the gods.
- The most outstanding opponent of the Sophists was the Athenian born Socrates (470–399 BC) who believed in and quested after an eternal truth. Unfortunately for him his quest eventually led to his enforced suicide after his fellow Athenians accused him of disobeying religious laws and of corrupting the youth.
- The greatest of Socrates' disciples was Plato (427–347 BC) who achieved immortality by writing the first systematic treatise in political science, *The Republic*. Plato saw society as being divided into three classes: bronze (the workers), silver (the middle class), and gold (the ruling class). Significantly, Plato was the first renowned philosopher to recognize race as a factor in the rise and fall of civilizations. In *The Republic* he stated that the first requirement of continued statehood was the necessity of retaining racial homogeneity.
- Plato's greatest pupil was in turn Aristotle (384–322 BC) who wrote well on a large number of topics including art, biology, mathematics, politics, logic, and rhetoric. Aristotle also was the tutor of Alexander of Macedonia, who during his short life became ruler of most of the known world.
- Hippocrates (circa 420 BC) was a brilliant physician who revised much of what was known about medicine. His Hippocratic Oath is still used by doctors today as a code of professional ethics.
- Great Greek playwrights include Aeschylus (525–456 BC); Sophocles (496–406 BC), who was best known for his play *Oedipus Rex* (properly known as *Oedipus Tyrranus*), about a man who mistakenly marries his mother; Euripides (480–406 BC); and the comedian Aristophanes (445–385 BC).

**ORIGIN OF WESTERN DRAMA—THEATER OF DIONYSUS 440 BC**

*The center of Greek drama: The theater of Dionysus at Athens where the Great Tragedies were first performed over two thousand years ago (circa 440 BC).*

*The Greek theater at Epidaurus, circa 350 BC. Many of the amphitheaters can still be used for performances, so perfect are the acoustics and design of the construction.*

- One freed slave became famous as a story teller: Aesop (properly named *Aesopus*), who lived in the fourth century BC. He is best remembered for his collection of short stories, each with its own moral lesson.

### *The Greek Gods—Human-Like with Foibles*

Greek beliefs had several characteristics in common with many other Indo-European pre-Christian religions. The Greeks believed in gods who most often resembled humans in form and who also displayed human emotions. They had no holy book or specific directives, so interpretation and practice differed widely.

Their gods lived on a holy mountain, Mount Olympus, in a fairly ordinary society with a strict hierarchical structure. The main gods and their respective areas of responsibility reflect the very earthly nature of the religion as a whole:

• Zeus was the head of the gods, and the spiritual father of all the other gods and people. He was also very commonly known as Dias.

• Hera was Zeus's wife, and also the queen of heaven and the guardian of marriage.

• Hephaestus was the god of fire and metalworkers.

• Athena was the goddess of wisdom and war and official patron of the city named after her.

• Apollo was the god of light, poetry, and music.

• Artemis was the goddess of wildlife and the moon.

• Ares was the god of war.

• Aphrodite was the goddess of love.

• Hestia was the goddess of the hearth.

• Gaea was the goddess of the earth.

• Hermes was the messenger of the gods and ruler of science and invention.

• Poseidon was the ruler of the sea who, with his wife Amphitrite, led a group of less important sea gods, such as the Nereids and Tritons.

• Demeter, the goddess of agriculture, was associated with the earth.

• Hades, an important god but not generally considered an Olympian, ruled the underworld where he lived with his wife, Persephone. The underworld was a dark and mournful place located at the center of the earth, populated by the souls of the dead.

• Dionysus was the god of wine and pleasure, and as a result was one of the most popular gods.

• There were also creatures such as fauns (creatures with the legs of a goat and the upper body of a human), centaurs (the head and torso of a man and the body of a horse), and nymphs (beautiful, young, fairylike women).

The very name Europe is derived from that of the Greek goddess Europa, the daughter of the Phoenix, which was able to resurrect itself from ashes after being killed in fire.

The Greeks believed that the gods controlled all aspects of their lives, and that they were totally dependent upon the goodwill of the gods. Each city devoted itself to a particular god or group of gods, for whom temples were built. In this way Athena was protector of the city of Athens, and a gold statue of her was placed inside the Parthenon. Delphi was a holy site dedicated to Apollo. A temple built at Delphi contained an oracle, or prophet, who claimed to be able to see into the future; a similar temple was built at Didyma in modern day Turkey.

The most intriguing part of the Greek pantheon was that the gods, despite their superhuman powers, showed human foibles and errors of judgment—a strange mix of the supernatural and the very physical, showing clear similarities to the gods of the Indo-European religions.

### Greece Darkened—Citizenship to Foreigners and the "Colorate Gentes"

In 411 BC, forty years after Pericles had enacted his law limiting citizenship to those of biological Athenian descent only, the law was turned on its head. Citizenship of Athens was given to tens of thousands of foreigners who had entered the city, most of whom were from the Middle East. The argument used was that the city state had to make up the huge population losses suffered as a result of the Persian and inter-Grecian wars.

By this stage the racial mix of Athens and many other Grecian city states was beginning to show the effects of the importation of peoples from elsewhere in the Middle East, and significant sections of the population had become darker than even during Pericles' time.

**IN BLACK AND WHITE—THE DOWNFALL OF CLASSICAL GREECE**

Left: *The downfall of classical Greece—the importation of nonwhite slaves. In this 300 BC Grecian statue, a black African slave is shown polishing a boot. It was the importation of large numbers of racially foreign slaves which was to lead to the dissolution of the classical Grecian civilization. Contrast the slave with,* center, *a statue of a white Grecian male dating from classical times. Most modern white Greeks have very little or no original classical Grecian blood in their veins, and are descendants of later settlers, Crusaders and other invaders. (The fig leaf, so often seen in such statues, is a Victorian addition.)* Right: *A Greek statue of a Negro musician dating from between the fourth and third centuries BC, Bibliotheque Nationale, Paris.*

## THE AWE OF THE ANCIENT WORLD—DELPHI

Above: *The greatest religious center of the ancient world was Delphi in central Greece. Here the god Apollo himself dispensed advice to all those who sought it, through dedicated prophets and priests. Set halfway up the mountain Parnassus between majestic cliffs, the complex was the wonder of its age. In the center is the great Hall of Apollo. The surrounding buildings and works of art were given as tribute by kings and commoners alike in thanks for advice received or in hope of favors to come from the gods.* Below: *The ruins of Delphi today—testimony to how the people who built this magnificent edifice have passed from history.*

This darkening of the population (caused partly by the Nordic and original European elements of Grecian society warring themselves to death—and partly by the importation of masses of already mixed Middle Eastern peoples) runs directly in tandem with the decline and fall of classical Greece.

The gradual darkening of the Grecian peoples was noted by many famous Greek writers of the time. Hippocrates makes reference in his works to the "long heads" (that is, Nordic skulls) of the Macedonians, while Aristotle made copious references to the fairness of the Scythians and the Macedonians. The Greek soldier and historian Xenophon (430–354 BC) also made a point of referring to the blond haired and fair eyed Macedonians and Scythians in his book *Anabasis,* which described a Greek expedition against the Persians.

By the time of the Roman emperor, Octavian Augustus (who reigned directly after Julius Caesar), the Roman historian Manilius counted the Greeks as amongst the dark nations of the world, referring to them as part of the "colorate gentes" (*Astronomica,* iv, 719).

It is likely that Manilius was referring to the Hellenistic world in general, rather than the inhabitants of the Greek peninsula alone, as many people from the surrounding areas had by that stage adopted much of Greek culture, and were linguistically and culturally relatively indistinguishable from the Hellenes. There were, of course, still whites in Greece, both then and now.

### Later Byzantium Empire Drew Middle Easterners

Another factor which influenced the racial makeup of Greece was the later existence of the Byzantium Empire (Eastern Roman Empire), which drew all manner of Middle Eastern mixed types to the region. This process, which happened over a period of centuries, was to be aggravated by the Turkish invasion of Greece and the Balkans.

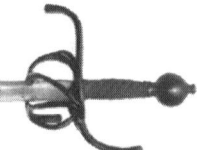

# CHAPTER TEN

## Conqueror and Creator—Alexander the Great

**The appearance of Alexander the Great on the stage of history is a remarkable example of how one person's strength of will in a leadership position can change the course of world events. From out of nowhere Alexander burst upon the ancient world and turned it on its head, and then, just as quickly, he vanished.**

To the north of Greece lay the territory of Macedonia, a nation whose origins lay in an invasion of the area by an Indo-European tribe during the great migrations which occurred from around 5000 BC onward. Archaeological investigations have revealed how Nordic the Macedonians were—particularly in contrast to the peoples who, by the time of the first Macedonian expeditions, made up the majority of the inhabitants of southern Greece.

**ALEXANDER THE GREAT: MILITARY TITAN WHO SPREAD CIVILIZATION**

*Alexander the Great, whose legacy is still felt to this day in the twenty-five cities which he founded. His incredible leadership skills enabled him to motivate his army to march to the ends of the earth—almost 20,000 miles (32,000 km) in eleven years.*

### Alexander Sarcophagus Depicts Racial Types

The famous Alexander Sarcophagus (also known as the Sarcophagus of Sidon, dating from 310 BC and presently in the Archaeological Museum in Istanbul) depicts Macedonians, including Alexander, as stereotypical Nordics with white skin, fair hair, and blue eyes.

### Philip II—Alexander's Father, Defeats Athens

The Macedonians were a relatively quiet people until their potential was unleashed by an energetic king, Philip II, in 359 BC. After firmly establishing Macedonian unity, Philip set about invading the Greek peninsula, occupying Athens in 338 BC. He then turned his attention to the Persian Empire to the est.

Before he could actually invade Persia, Philip was assassinated in 336 BC, soon after he discarded his queen, Olympias (who was Alexander's mother), and had taken a new wife, Cleopatra (not the one famed as an Egyptian queen).

It is cause for speculation that this domestic upheaval led to Philip's assassination, possibly arranged by his son, Alexander. Whatever the case, Philip was given a royal burial, and his tomb was discovered intact and in pristine condition in 1977 AD.

Philip's crown passed to his twenty-year-old son, Alexander, who in the year 334 BC set out to crush the Persians once and for all. In doing this he managed to unite most of the Greeks and became the undisputed master of the Greek peninsula.

### *Alexander Begins His Wars Against Persia 334 BC*

Alexander began his war against Persia in the spring of 334 BC by crossing the Dardanelles with an army of 35,000 Macedonian and Greek troops. His chief officers, all Macedonians, were Antigonus, Ptolemy, and Seleucus, who all played significant roles in history. At the river Granicus, near the ancient city of Troy, Alexander launched a surprise attack on a 40,000 strong Persian force.

The Macedonians defeated the Persians, losing, according to Alexandrian exaggeration, only 110 men. Whatever the truth, the victory was overwhelming, and as news of the decisive victory spread throughout Turkey, the entire subcontinent submitted to Alexander without putting up a fight.

Alexander then took on the main Persian army, commanded personally by King Darius III, at Issus, in modern northeastern Syria. Still only having around 35,000 soldiers, Alexander attacked the Persian army estimated by Macedonian records to be 500,000 strong—probably another exaggeration—but nonetheless indicative of the odds that Alexander faced. Incredibly enough, and probably due to his genius as a military leader, Alexander won the day at the Battle of Issus, in 333 BC, which saw the utter rout of the Persian forces.

### *Lebanon and Egypt—Alexandria Founded*

Pushing southwards, Alexander then stormed the fortified city port of Tyre in modern Lebanon, seizing the city after a siege of seven months. He then captured Gaza and in quick succession occupied Egypt, the disorganized and enfeebled nonwhite chieftains there offering little real resistance.

In 332 BC Alexander founded a new city in Egypt—which he modestly called Alexandria. This city would later become the literary, scientific, and commercial center of the Greek world. Cyrene, the capital of the ancient North African kingdom of Cyrenaica, submitted to Alexander soon afterward, extending his dominion to the city of Carthage (modern day Tunisia). There his troops set up a ruling aristocracy from whom the great general, Hannibal, would emerge to test the Roman Empire some two hundred years later.

### *Darius Killed—The Fall of Babylon 331 BC*

Turning northward again, Alexander drew up reinforcements and with an army of forty thousand infantrymen and seven thousand cavalry, marched on Babylon. Crossing the Euphrates and the Tigris Rivers, he met the Persian king, Darius, once again, who, according to Macedonian records, had drawn up a new army one million strong—certainly once again an exaggeration, but still without any doubt badly outnumbering Alexander's forces.

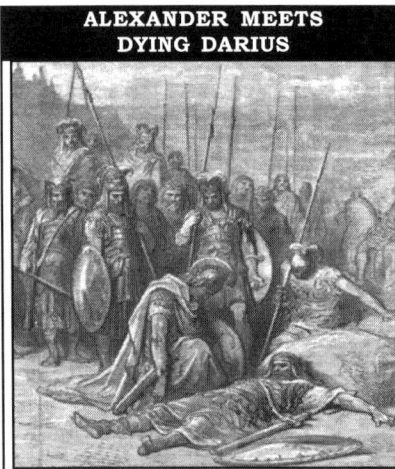

**ALEXANDER MEETS DYING DARIUS**

*Alexander and his great foe, Darius III of Persia, met at last. After his defeat, Darius fled to Medea, in 331 BC where he was murdered just before Alexander caught up with him. Here the final meeting is reconstructed according to original accounts—Alexander still paid respect to his dead foe who had long been the scourge of Greece and Macedonia.*

At the Battle of Gaugamela, on October 1, 331 BC, Alexander once again beat Darius, who fled and was killed by two of his own generals. The city of Babylon then surrendered and Alexander occupied the Persian capital city of Persepolis.

Within three years, Alexander had occupied a huge stretch of land, and all resistance crumbled before his ruthless army. His empire extended along and beyond the southern shores of the Caspian Sea, including modern Afghanistan and northward into central Asia.

## A SECRET OF ALEXANDER'S SUCCESS— THE SPEIRA UNIT OF 256 MEN

*The basic unit, or speira, in Alexander's army. The 256 men were ranked in close order, sixteen deep. In a charge, the spears of the first five ranks projected forward to break the enemy ranks—the rest of the men held their spears skyward to deflect arrows or other projectiles. Tactics such as these helped Alexander's army overcome overwhelming odds time and time again during their breathtaking march from Greece right through the Middle East, north into Asia, and then to India.*

### *In the Footsteps of the Aryans—Alexander Re-invades India 1,200 Years Later*

In order to complete his conquest of the remnants of the Persian Empire, which had once included part of western India, Alexander crossed the Indus River in 326 BC, and invaded the Punjab region, following the footsteps of the Indo-Aryans of some 1,200 years previously.

At this point Alexander's army rebelled and refused to go any further, seeing no point in marching endlessly on, getting further and further away from their homes without any respite in sight. Sensing that he had to get his men home quickly, Alexander then pulled off another incredible feat. He constructed a fleet of ships then and there and sailed down the Indus River, reaching its mouth in September 325 BC. He then sailed with his army to the Persian Gulf and returned overland across the desert, arriving in Babylon in 323 BC. It was while on this return journey that Alexander contracted fever and died in Babylon.

### *Alexander's Amazing and Enduring Legacy*

Alexander founded twenty-five cities—an amazing achievement all by itself. Many of them bore his name or local translations of his name, but one became most famous of all: Alexandria in Egypt,

## BATTLE OF GAUGAMELA—DARIUS'S FINAL DEFEAT BY ALEXANDER 331 BC

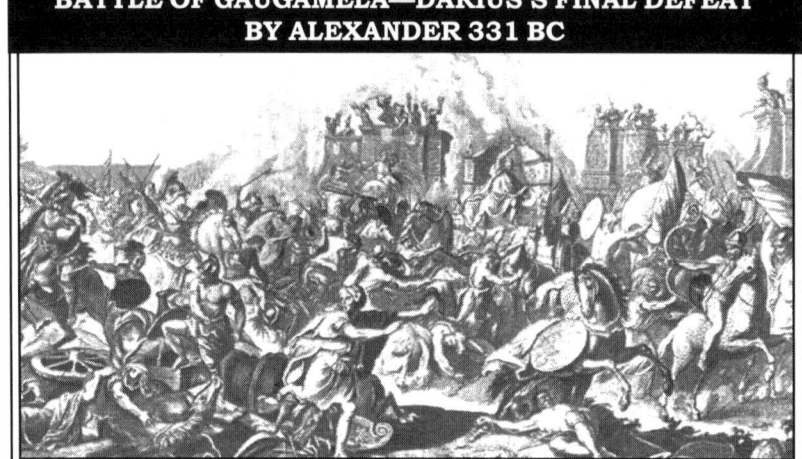

*Alexander's final defeat of Darius, the Persian emperor, at Gaugamela. In the two years following his first defeat at the Battle of Issus, the Persian emperor gathered together a new army, usually said to be one million strong—but when he confronted Alexander's superb army at Gaugamela on the Tigris River in 331 BC, his forces were once again annihilated.*

which is where he was buried. Founded in 332 BC, this city became the new capital of Egypt and in 300 BC a library and a place of learning was started, later to become world famous as the Library of Alexandria.

The library was said to have contained the greatest single concentration of contemporary knowledge in the world at that time.

Alexandria also became noted for its famous lighthouse. It stood at least 377 feet (115 meters) tall and had a fire and reflective mirrors at the top. Because it was one of the tallest manmade structures for many centuries, it was identified as one of the Seven Wonders of the Ancient World.

Although he only ruled for a short period of thirteen years (336–323 BC), dying at the age of thirty-three, Alexander etched his name into history by singlehandedly creating the greatest land empire the world had ever seen.

### *Alexander's Racial Unity Fails*

Despite having easily overcome the entire mixed race populations of the Middle East, Alexander publicly declared himself to be in favor of racial integration.

To this end he was an ardent exponent of ensuring the compliance of invaded nations by issuing orders that his Macedonian occupiers be integrated with the subject peoples. He ordered that all his generals should take wives from the conquered peoples, most of whom were racial mixtures of Semites, Arabs, Negroids, and original whites.

Alexander himself took a nonwhite wife, a Persian princess who was of mixed race. He also started dressing like the peoples he had conquered, and in 324 BC at a city called Susa he personally officiated at an arranged mass wedding of nine thousand of his senior army officers to Middle Eastern wives—the famous "marriage of East and West" meant to symbolize the new racial unity he was hoping to create.

Upon Alexander's early death, almost all of his senior officers who had been forced into these multiracial marriages renounced their imposed wives and set up pure white Macedonian ruling classes in the areas which had been placed under their control.

### Alexander's Empire Divided after His Death

At the time of his death there was no obvious successor to Alexander (as his one son was very young and the other was retarded— both were murdered in 305 BC and that ended the debate on succession), and within two decades his empire split into four units, three of them ruled by his former generals. Asia was ruled by Seleucus and his family, who founded the Seleucid Empire; Greece and Macedonia were ruled by Antigonus, and Egypt was ruled by the most famous of these generals, Ptolemy. The fourth unit, Asia Minor (Turkey), became independent.

### Antigonids Rule Greece for 113 Years

Antigonus and his successors ruled most of the Greek mainland from 281–168 BC, when they were finally defeated by the Romans. The conflict with Rome had escalated slowly and then come to a head when the Antigonid kings, notably Philip V, had provided help to the famous general, Hannibal of Carthage, in his campaigns against Rome. This led to three wars with Rome and the eventual defeat of the Macedonians in 168 BC. The Romans removed the Antigonids from power, but a pro-Macedonian revolt in 147 BC led directly to the Roman occupation of mainland Greece.

### Ptolemaic Egypt—World's First Museums

Alexander's General Ptolemy established the Ptolemaic reign in Egypt, which lasted from 323–30 BC. By far the best known Ptolemaic Egyptian queen was Cleopatra VII, a white woman who won fame due

## THE PTOLEMIES: MACEDONIANS WHO
## RULED EGYPT FOR THREE HUNDRED YEARS

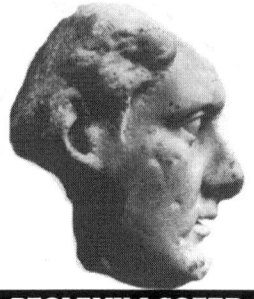  

**PTOLEMY I SOTER** | **ARSINOE II** | **CLEOPATRA VII**

Left: *Ptolemy I Soter, the first Macedonian ruler of Egypt. Ptolemy was one of Alexander the Great's generals who, upon the latter's death, took the land of Egypt as his kingdom in 323 BC. He set up a white ruling class over the large mass of mixed race inhabitants. The Ptolemies kept themselves separate from the mass of nonwhite Egyptians, most never even bothering to learn their language, but taking on the ways and customs of ancient Egypt.* Center: *Arsinoe II Philadelphus, wife of Ptolemy II, one of the most powerful of the Macedonian Egyptian queens. The Ptolemy family were to rule Egypt until the famous Cleopatra VII,* right, *who was defeated in battle by the Roman emperor Octavian Augustus at the sea Battle of Actium in 31 BC. Cleopatra committed suicide in 30 BC and Egypt became a Roman province. All through this period, whites were a minority in Egypt.*

to her relationships with the Romans Julius Caesar and Mark Anthony. Although the Ptolemies in particular ensured that their line was always pure Macedonian, they did take on many of the dress and cultural aspects of the long past ancient Egypt, calling themselves pharaohs, and producing monuments and buildings in the style of the ancient white Egyptians. Embalming and mummification became common once again.

Ptolemy I established a center of learning and research known as the musea, today called a museum—the first in the world.

The Ptolemaic reign provided a new short lease of life to Egypt, but the largely Arabic/mixed race local population soon overwhelmed the heavily outnumbered white Macedonians, who also had to contend with the vigorous new white civilization of Rome.

Ptolemaic Egypt included modern day Israel, parts of Syria, and even a small part of southern Turkey. Most of these lands were lost to military attacks by the Seleucidians—descendants of yet another of Alexander's generals—around the year 220 BC.

The loss of Palestine marked the waning of the Ptolemaic power in Egypt, with tensions between the overwhelmingly nonwhite Egyptians and the white Greek immigrant rulers erupting into violence. Upper Egypt broke away and was ruled by its own nonwhite population between

205–185 BC.

In spite of these pressures, the ruling white Macedonian Ptolemies preserved their Greek culture, and only the very last Ptolemaic ruler, Cleopatra VII (the most famous one), ever bothered to learn the Egyptian language.

It was this Cleopatra who, after first becoming the lover of the great Roman, Julius Caesar, married his friend Mark Anthony after Caesar's murder. A Roman army subsequently defeated Cleopatra and Mark Anthony's combined forces (the battle of Actium) and after this Cleopatra and Mark Anthony committed suicide.

This event marked the end of Ptolemaic Egypt, which was the very last Hellenistic kingdom. After the battle of Actium, Ptolemaic Egypt was handed over to Rome as yet another province. As the racial balance in the other parts of the area occupied by Alexander shifted increasingly against the Macedonians, so the remains of Alexander's empire slowly crumbled away into oblivion.

By the time of the defeat of Cleopatra VII, Alexander's empire had long since ceased to exist. As there were too few pure Macedonians to colonize the entire empire, the Macedonian outposts were little more than islands in a sea of people who had long since lost any semblance of racial homogeneity. It was, therefore, only a matter of time before these islands were submerged.

### Seleucids Crumble from Racial Diversity

General Seleucus seized an enormous part of Alexander's empire, the area stretching from southern Turkey to the Sinai Desert and eastward to include Mesopotamia and parts of modern day Iraq and Iran. Despite repeated attempts to encourage Macedonian settlers into the region, the Seleucids never had enough manpower to control the vast area properly. Fairly soon their empire also began to crumble under the pressure of trying to contain large numbers of widely diverse racial and ethnic groups within the borders of one state.

In the northern parts of the Seleucid Empire, for example, descendants of Macedonian soldiers teamed up with scattered Indo-European tribes and local mixed race peoples to break away from the Seleucids to form the relatively short-lived states of Bactria and Parthia. Some of these Indo-Europeans were marauding Celts, who had also occupied a part of Northern Macedonia.

The eastern reaches of the Seleucid Empire at one stage reached to the borders of India, but this region also steadily drifted out of control. In 168 BC, King Perseus of Macedonia was defeated by the Romans at the battle of Pydna and the Macedonian monarchy was abolished.

In 146 BC, Macedonia and Greece became direct Roman provinces after a short-lived rebellion by the Macedonians, and in 64 BC, the Seleucid Empire was conquered by the Roman general, Pompey, and became a Roman province. The Romans did not realize it then, of course, but in occupying these regions they also took on the problem which had led to the dissolution of Alexander's empire—the huge number of nonwhites who would soon overwhelm them in these regions and eventually penetrate right to Rome.

## *Alexandrian Age—Cultural Achievements*

The period from 320–330 BC is known as the Alexandrian age, and it contributed a number of philosophic, cultural, and scientific advances to Western civilization. It was during this time that three well known philosophies were formulated: Epicureanism, stoicism, and skepticism.

Epicureanism was started by the philosopher Epicurus (342–270 BC) of Samos on the Ionian coast in Turkey. He did not believe in an afterlife and taught that the highest good was to obtain material benefits during one's lifetime. This philosophy was later misinterpreted to mean merely sensual pleasure.

In opposition to Epicurus was Zeno of Cyprus, who argued that there should be only one aim in life—freedom from the desires of life, where the ideal state was to be tranquil and indifferent to both pain and pleasure. This philosophy was called stoicism. Skepticism said that all opinions about pain or pleasure were subjective so there could not be one sensible truth or dogma—the skeptics questioned the very basis of all facts.

## *Circumference of Earth Measured 200 BC*

As a result of Alexander's conquests, Greek science merged with what had been found in Babylon and Egypt and produced a number of advances. The expansion of geographic knowledge allowed scientists to make maps and plot the size of the earth, which was already identified as a globe through the observation of its shadow during a lunar eclipse.

The keeper of the Library of Alexandria, Eratosthenes (276–195 BC), calculated the circumference of the earth to within some 200 miles (321 km) by measuring the difference in angles of shadows cast at midday by two identical poles set in the earth in the north and south of Egypt.

In the third century BC, Aristarchus of Samos first propagated the theory that the earth rotates on its own axis and revolves around a stationary sun.

*Seleucus I Nicator, one of Alexander the Great's generals who founded the kingdom of Syria. As in all other parts of the Macedonian Empire, a white ruling class was created. They were all, however, soon to be submerged amongst the largely mixed race inhabitants of those regions.*

Not until the 1500s AD were scientists to realize that Aristarchus was right. Another great man from Alexandria was Euclid the mathematician (circa 300 BC), who developed the forms and theorems of geometry as still used today.

Archimedes (287–212 BC) of Syracuse is most famous for his discovery of the laws of hydraulics, that a solid object displaces liquid to the same volume as the object itself (which he, probably apocryphally, is said to have discovered while in the bath and then run outside naked in the street shouting "Eureka"). Archimedes also calculated the exact ratio between the circumference of a circle and its diameter, known as Pi, and developed the famous Archimedes screw, a means of pumping water uphill through the use of a large screw in a tube.

The greatest contribution of the Alexandrian age was the transference of a large amount of classical knowledge to the new power in Europe—Rome. When Roman legions occupied mainland Greece, they were so amazed at the civilization that they took sculpture, architecture, and much else back to Rome.

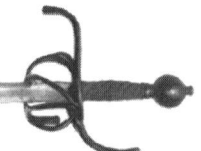

# CHAPTER ELEVEN

# The Age of the Caesars—Pre-Christian Rome

**The Italian peninsula had originally been settled by a Proto-Nordic/Alpine Mediterranean white racial mix during the Neolithic age, with the Alpine and Mediterranean elements being in the majority.**

From around 2000 BC, Indo-European migrants from central Europe (and originally from southern Russia) settled in northern Italy, crossing the Alps from present day Austria and Hungary. Amongst these people were Celtic tribesmen known as the Latini. Racially speaking, they were predominantly Nordic in nature. Another group of whites, known as the Etruscans, also settled in Italy by the year 800 BC.

## CELTS SACK ROME 387 BC

*The first sacking of Rome by the Celts. Gauls, from modern day France, attacked the city in 387 BC. The city held out for seven months before they capitulated and were forced to pay a weighty ransom in gold. The citizens of Rome were first alerted to the Celtic attackers by the honking of the sacred geese of the god Juno, who sounded the alarm as the Celts stormed the walls.*

## The Etruscans—Advanced Old Europeans

The Etruscans were a mixture of the original Old European white subgroups, but were culturally and militarily superior to the original inhabitants of Italy. As a result, they soon grew to dominate the major part of northern Italy. The Etruscans established an advanced society, building cities and settlements which were certainly far more advanced than anything else seen in the country till that time.

However, the Etruscans were not the only ones interested in Italy. By 800 BC, a number of the Greek city states had also established settlements in southern Italy and Sicily. These were not merely imperialist colonies; the outposts also served as a buffer from the increasing number of forays from the aggressive

## MEN WHO SHAPED THE HISTORY OF ROME

| | | | |
|---|---|---|---|
| *Marcus Agrippa (63–12 BC), Roman general who from 31 to 36 BC won a number of battles against the rivals of Octavian Augustus, which resulted in Octavian becoming the first Roman emperor.* | *Vespasianus, Roman emperor (69–79 AD), who led legions in Germany and Britain. Under his reign the suppression of the Jewish revolt was started. In 70 AD he had Rome's Coliseum built.* | *Marcus Nerva, Roman emperor (96–98 AD), who was the first to allow non-Romans—and thus ultimately nonwhites—to sit in the senate in Rome as regional representatives of the Roman provinces.* | *Hadrian, Roman emperor (117–138 AD), who realized that the empire was too big and halted its expansion. He built walls at the borders of the empire, the most famous of which bears his name in England.* |

and powerful city of Carthage, situated on the North African coast in the country known today as Tunisia.

### *Rome Founded By Etruscans 700 BC*

According to Roman legend, the city of Rome was founded around the year 753 BC by the orphaned twin brothers Romulus and Remus, who were saved from death in their infancy by a she-wolf who had sheltered and suckled them. Whatever the origins of the city, by the year 700 BC it had been firmly established on the seven hills around the Tiber River valley, and by the sixth century BC, the city and surrounding areas were ruled by the Etruscans.

Rome at this stage was ruled by kings elected by the people. The symbol of the elected king of Rome became known worldwide as a symbol of power: an ax head bound together in a bundle of reeds, called a fasces.

The rationale behind the symbol was that each tribe was represented by one reed—by themselves they could be easily broken, but bound together they could be a powerful force. The fasces symbol, which was used by the twentieth century Italian leader Benito Mussolini, can still be seen today reposing under the hands of Abraham Lincoln in the Lincoln Memorial in the capital of the United States of America, Washington D.C.; in the Oval Office; on the walls of the House of Representatives; and on the Supreme Court building, amongst many other places.

Advising the first Roman kings were the heads of all the leading families gathered together in a group called the senate. This body remained in place, with varying powers, until the fall of the Roman Empire some 1,500 years later. The senators and their families became the upper class of Rome, called the patricians, while the common people were known as the plebeians.

### The Early Republic (509–133 BC)

In the year 509 BC, a group of patricians led a rebellion against a particularly unpopular Etruscan king, threw him out, and set up a republic in Rome. This rebellion's most famous incident was a battle outside the gates of Rome when the legendary Roman soldier Horatio personally faced off against the Etruscan king's army while the bridge to the city was destroyed, preventing the Etruscans from regaining control of the capital.

The power held by the former king was now passed on to two annually elected rulers, called consuls. Other cities within central and northern Italy formed an alliance and challenged the power of the new republic of Rome, leading to a Roman defeat at the Battle of Lake Regillus in 496 BC.

Three years later, in 493 BC, the Roman Republic joined the alliance. It became known as the Latin League and it set about dislodging the last of the Etruscan strongholds.

Although originally not as advanced as the Etruscans, by 400 BC the Latini had adopted much of Etruscan culture and in all respects had surpassed their former masters, both militarily and culturally. The secret of their success—as indeed with the whole

*Roman lictors carrying fasces—reeds bundled together with an ax head. The symbol of authority in ancient Rome, it derived its meaning from the fact that singly, reeds can be broken and bent, but bound together, they are strong. The fasces became a worldwide symbol of authority, and can be found in much western architecture. Mussolini's Fascist Party took their name and party symbol from the fasces.*

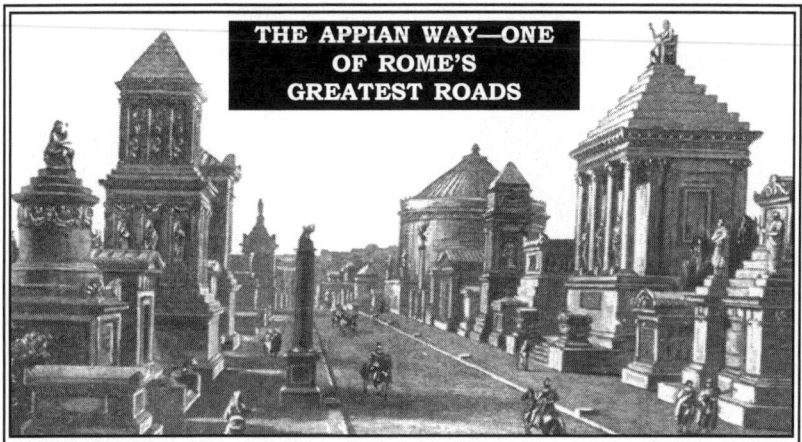

**THE APPIAN WAY—ONE OF ROME'S GREATEST ROADS**

*The Appian Way as it appeared at the height of Rome's prosperity. Originally built around 310 BC by Appius Claudius, this great highway ran from Rome to Capau, and was later extended to Brindisi. Extending from Rome, it was lined with lavish mansions and imposing tombs of noted Romans for nine miles. Today only a few ruins and the road remain.*

Roman Empire—was their astonishing ability to organize on a scale not seen since the days of the first Egyptians.

By 400 BC, the Latin League had successfully overthrown all the last vestiges of Etruscan rule, and from then on the Etruscan peoples were completely absorbed into the Latini, creating a Nordic/Alpine/Mediterranean mix which became characteristic of the early and middle Roman Empire, with Nordic elements tending to form the ruling class.

All the tribes making up the Latin League acknowledged Rome to be the leading city of the alliance, even though, as it later turned out, they were unhappy with the situation.

It was during this period of nation forming that the Romans wrote their first major legal code. In 450 BC, the Law of the Twelve Tables was laid down, which served as the basis for not only the entire Roman legal system, but also the basis of almost all modern legal systems in the world today. Mirroring the older Greek Spartan tradition, the Twelve Tables specifically called for the euthanasia death of any infant showing conspicuous deformities or retardation—an example of basic eugenics at work amongst these early Romans.

### Celtic Gauls Attack—The First Sacking of Rome 387 BC

The Romans faced another serious crisis. In 387 BC, Gauls, the descendants of Celtic tribesmen who had settled in France, launched an attack on Rome, and eventually sacked the city.

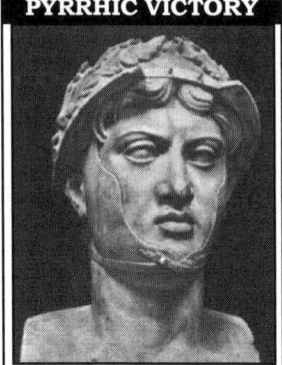

**PYRRHIC VICTORY**

*An original bust of Pyrrhus, king of Epirus in Greece, who came to Italy and Sicily with his army and elephants to help the Greek cities in those territories against the expanding Romans. Although gaining an initial victory, it was at such a cost to his forces that he was ultimately defeated. Ever since, any hollow victory which ultimately leads to defeat is known as a pyrrhic victory.*

They were only finally persuaded to leave by the Romans bribing them with gold. The Gaulish invasion showed a serious weakness in the ranks of the Latin League—the other components of the alliance had refused to help Rome against the Gauls.

This was not forgotten by the Romans, who, by 380 BC had not only rebuilt their city and erected huge defensive walls around it, but had also started preparing a new and more powerful army.

In 338 BC, after entering into an alliance with certain smaller tribes around Rome, the Romans turned on their former allies in the Latin League and decisively defeated them, becoming by 280 BC, the dominant force in Italy.

## Greek Wars and the Origin of the Pyrrhic Victory

As Roman power and influence grew, a clash with the Greek settlements in southern Italy became inevitable. War broke out as the Romans started occupying the southernmost points of Italy.

A Grecian king named Pyrrhus, from the city of Epirus in northern Greece, was hired by one of the Grecian cities in southern Italy, Tarentum, to help ward off the Romans. Pyrrhus managed to inflict a defeat upon the Romans which temporarily stayed the latter's excursions.

However, the cost of the victory—in terms of men and materials—was so great, that it exhausted the Greek expeditionary force, and by 270 BC, all of Italy had fallen to Rome, with the Greeks unable to maintain the war. Ever since then, any empty victory—which ultimately leads to a long-term defeat—has been called a Pyrrhic victory.

## Carthage—A Threat to Rome

With the elimination of Greek bases in Italy, only the city of Carthage on the North African coast seriously threatened further Roman expansion. Carthage had been founded around the year 800 BC by the

166

## CARTHAGE HARBOR—FOREMOST PORT OF THE ANCIENT WORLD

*The city of Carthage, situated on the present day Tunisian coast, was for many years Rome's greatest enemy. Originally established by the Phoenicians, who were an Old European/Mediterranean people who had mixed with a small number of Semites, the city's population received a massive infusion of Nordic blood when it fell under the control of the Macedonian Alexandrian empire.*

*Its ruling classes became almost exclusively Nordic, and the city was built up on a scale which rivaled Rome.*

Top: *A reconstruction of what the harbor looked like in its prime, based on archaeological diggings and Carthaginian and Roman descriptions of the great city.* Lower: *The remains of the harbor of Carthage, as it was captured in a photograph in the early 1920s. When Rome finally overwhelmed Carthage, its soldiers razed the city to the ground and built a Roman city next to the ruins.*

mixed Mediterranean/Semitic Phoenicians, and had become an independent and powerful force in its own right. A large Nordic infusion had taken place in the region after the occupation by Alexander the Great, and by the time of the wars with Rome, Carthage was at its peak.

The Latin word for Phoenician was Punicus—from which the word Punic was derived, hence the Roman wars against Carthage are called the Punic Wars.

### *First Punic War Fought Over Sicily*

In 264 BC, war broke out between Rome and Carthage over possession of the island of Sicily. After suffering initial reverses, the Romans defeated the Carthaginians, who were forced to sue for peace in 241 BC. In terms of the peace treaty, Rome administered Sicily, Sardinia, and Corsica, adding to the growing territorial possessions of the city republic.

## Second Punic War—Hannibal Invades Italy

The Second Punic War is also known as Hannibal's war, named after the great Carthaginian general who, after a long epic campaign, very nearly routed the power of Rome. After having lost control of Sicily and other Mediterranean islands, Carthage sent an army to invade and occupy Spain between 237–219 BC. The original whites and Celtic settlers in the region were no match for the battle experienced Carthaginians, and were overrun relatively quickly.

Then, starting in 218 BC, Hannibal led an army of about fifty thousand men and a troop of thirty-seven African elephants across southern France and through the Alps in northern Italy (only one of his elephants survived the incredible journey). For the next fifteen years he attacked the Romans up and down the length and breadth of Italy.

Hannibal had many victories, with the greatest being the Battle of Cannae where he defeated a numerically superior Roman force. For a while it appeared as if the Romans had finally met their match, but a Roman general, Scipio, hit upon the idea of repaying Carthage in kind. He invaded North Africa, using the logic that if Hannibal could invade Italy and threaten Rome, the Romans could invade North Africa and threaten Carthage. The tactic worked, and Hannibal was forced to return to defend Carthage, leaving behind much of his army on the European mainland.

Rome was then able to invade Spain and drive out the Carthaginian armies. Hannibal was finally defeated by the Romans at the Battle of Zama in 202 BC, and another peace treaty followed. According to the terms of this treaty, Carthage agreed to disarm, pay an indemnity to Rome, and hand over its Spanish colonies to Roman rule. Hannibal was never forgiven by the Romans, who pursued him right into Asia Minor (Turkey) where he committed suicide in 182 BC.

## Roman Occupation of Greece 146 BC

The defeat of Carthage left the Romans free to assert their authority in the east. The Macedonians, who had helped Hannibal, were the first to be punished for this deed by the Romans. The legions of Rome invaded Macedonia in 200 BC, defeating the Macedonian army in 197 BC. The Greek mainland then came under Roman protection, although many city states were allowed self rule.

However, continuous turmoil and infighting between many of these cities eventually compelled Rome to directly occupy the whole

## THE WAR THAT GAVE AFRICA ITS NAME

Right: *The Nordic face of Hannibal, that city's greatest warrior, from a silver coin struck at Carthage around 220 BC. Founded by the Phoenicians, the city of Carthage had received a major Nordic subracial input when it was occupied and colonized by Nordic Macedonians under Alexander the Great. It was from a long line of Nordic Carthaginian nobles that Hannibal was born.* Left: *A bronze bust of the Roman general, Publius Scipio, who finally*

PUBLIUS SCIPIO

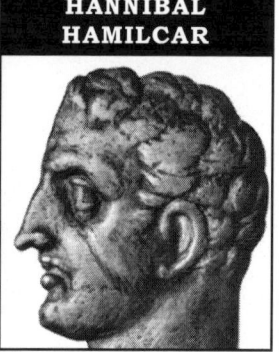
HANNIBAL HAMILCAR

*defeated Hannibal at the Battle of Zama in 202 BC. The Romans called their new colony "Africa"—and in this way the white Romans gave Africa (and Africans) the name by which that continent and its people are known today.*

Below: *Hannibal's troops crossing the Rhone River on their way to attack northern Italy. Only one elephant actually survived the crossing of the Alps.*

region, an operation which was completed by 146 BC (in that year Roman legions destroyed the Greek city of Corinth). For the next sixty years, Greece was almost completely administered by Rome, although some cities, such as Athens and Sparta, retained their free status. In 88 BC, Roman territories were invaded from the east by the king of Pontus, Mithridates. Many Greek cities supported the invading king in the belief that they would regain their independence.

A Roman army forced Mithridates out of Greece and crushed the rebellion, sacking Athens in 86 BC and Thebes a year later. Roman punishment of all the rebellious cities was heavy, and the campaigns fought on Greek soil left central Greece in ruins. In 22 BC, the Greek city states were separated from Macedonia and the Romans made these city states into one province called Achaea.

During the reign of the Roman emperor, Hadrian (117–138 AD), many of Athens' famous buildings were restored out of the ruins. The continuing Roman restoration work was interrupted by an invasion of Goths, who in 267 and 268 AD overran Greece, captured Athens, and laid waste the cities of Argos, Corinth, and Sparta. From the sixth to the eighth centuries, Slavonic tribes from the north migrated into the peninsula, occupying Illyria and Thrace.

After the Goths left, the Grecian peninsula, thoroughly ravaged by centuries of warfare and racial mixing, settled down to a period of relative obscurity as a province under the Eastern Roman Empire of Byzantium.

### Macedonian Egypt Allies with Rome

Rome had by this time succeeded in establishing itself as the dominant new power in the Mediterranean, and in 168 BC, Egypt (then still under Macedonian Ptolemaic rule) formally allied itself to Rome.

This meant that by 168 BC most of the Mediterranean—from Spain right around the Mediterranean coast through Greece, parts of Turkey, Egypt, and the North African coast up to Tunisia, was either under direct Roman rule or allied to Rome.

### Third Punic War—Carthaginians Exterminated

The enmity between Carthage and Rome was so deep that it could not be buried with a mere treaty, and in 146 BC, war between the two powers broke out once again. By this time, however, Roman power was vast, and Carthage was besieged and destroyed.

This time Rome wrote no treaty. To ensure that the Carthaginians never threatened them again, the Romans killed or enslaved the population, physically destroyed the city, and plowed over the ruins, putting salt into the earth so that nothing would grow there again.

At the end of the Third Punic War, the Romans physically occupied what is today known as Tunisia and refounded a new city of Carthage—a Roman one. They called it the province of "Africa," a name which later was used to refer to the entire continent. In this same manner, Roman conquests in the east led to the creation of the Roman

## BLOND ROMANS CONQUER NORTH AFRICA

*Above: A Roman mosaic from Carthage on display at the Bardo Museum in modern Tunis, Tunisia. The scene shows Romans pouring what appears to be wine from an amphora. The original color shows all the subjects with blond hair, an indication of the racial makeup of the Roman conquerors of North Africa. Note also the swastika motif framing the figures, a common pattern in Roman art.*

*Below: The remains of the Roman coliseum in the town of El Jem, south of Tunis. This well-preserved building is second in size only to the more famous Coliseum in Rome and is better preserved.*

province of "Asia"—once again a Roman name became the name of an entire continent.

## Civil Strife—The Late Republic 133–30 BC

In 133 BC, the ruler of an independent state in central Asia Minor (Turkey), one Pergamum, died. When his will was read, he had left his country to Rome. This somewhat bizarre wish—which was duly carried out—served as a springboard for the later Roman occupation of the rest of Asia Minor and the Middle East. The period from 133 to 30 BC is known as the Late Republic, during which Rome was to experience civil strife not seen since the days of the Latini insurrection against the Etruscans. In addition to this, Rome also engaged in a number of foreign wars.

## Slaves—The Seeds of Rome's Decline

From the earliest times the Romans had been importing slaves into their homeland. This ultimately led to Rome being filled with all manner of people who bore no resemblance to the Romans. Slaves from the Far East, Africa, and the Semitic speaking world filled the slave houses of Rome in their hundreds of thousands.

Eventually such large numbers created the possibility of open rebellion, with the most famous being the slave uprising led by Spartacus in 73 BC, which had to be suppressed by force of arms with a full Roman army.

**ROMAN CRAFTSMANSHIP AND SOPHISTICATION**

*The sophistication and technical skill of Roman civilization is revealed in this beautifully fashioned first century AD Roman silverware plate which was found in Hildesheim, Germany.*

### Civil War between Plebeians and Patricians

Internally, Rome had become increasingly divided between the patricians and the plebeians, especially with regard to land distribution. Some patricians realized the need for reform. The most famous of these was Tiberius Gracchus, who

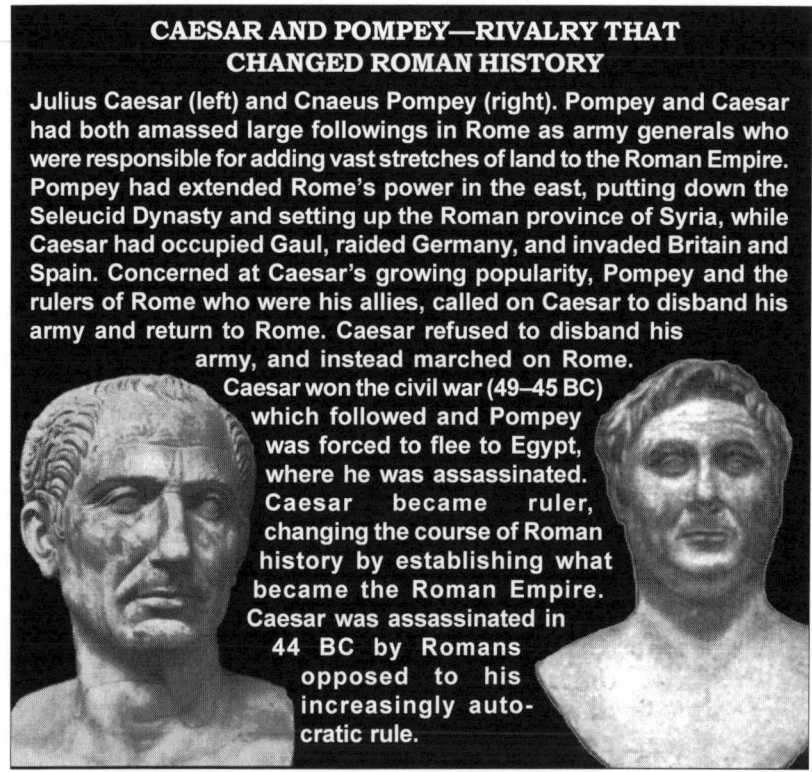

**CAESAR AND POMPEY—RIVALRY THAT CHANGED ROMAN HISTORY**

Julius Caesar (left) and Cnaeus Pompey (right). Pompey and Caesar had both amassed large followings in Rome as army generals who were responsible for adding vast stretches of land to the Roman Empire. Pompey had extended Rome's power in the east, putting down the Seleucid Dynasty and setting up the Roman province of Syria, while Caesar had occupied Gaul, raided Germany, and invaded Britain and Spain. Concerned at Caesar's growing popularity, Pompey and the rulers of Rome who were his allies, called on Caesar to disband his army and return to Rome. Caesar refused to disband his army, and instead marched on Rome. Caesar won the civil war (49–45 BC) which followed and Pompey was forced to flee to Egypt, where he was assassinated. Caesar became ruler, changing the course of Roman history by establishing what became the Roman Empire. Caesar was assassinated in 44 BC by Romans opposed to his increasingly auto-cratic rule.

was elected to the post of tribune (a modern equivalent would be prime minister) in 133 BC.

The reforms Gracchus implemented earned him the hatred of the wealthy classes, and in 134 BC he was assassinated. His work was then taken up by his brother, Gaius Gracchus, who was elected tribune in 123 BC. Also initiating far-reaching social reforms, Gaius succeeded in establishing a form of social welfare which did not work properly and almost bankrupted the state. It served only to stir up the hatred of the upper classes in a manner not seen even against Tiberius Gracchus.

In 121 BC, after a particularly severe outbreak of civil violence in which several thousand of his supporters were killed, Gaius Gracchus committed suicide. The deaths of the Gracchus brothers were to herald all-out civil war in Rome.

By the year 100 BC, a number of able Roman generals had risen to prominence. They subdued and held onto the numerous Roman colonies scattered around the Mediterranean coast. Each of these generals was in command of his own army, and although theoretically they were supposed to serve the Roman state, in reality they operated as private armies working in the interests of their generals.

After physically clashing with some of the other armies, General Cornelius Sulla emerged as the strongest leader and became the de facto ruler of Rome. Remarkably, after introducing a number of reforms (including extending the powers of the senate) Sulla resigned voluntarily from the affairs of state.

### Pompey and Caesar Clash—Caesar Crosses the Rubicon 49 BC

By this time two other generals had emerged, each with his own army: Pompey and Julius Caesar. Pompey had led Roman legions in Italy, Africa, Spain, Asia Minor, and even as far as the Euphrates River valley. He had also been instrumental in helping to suppress the famous slave uprising led by Spartacus in 73 BC.

Julius Caesar had conquered Gaul (France) and some of the Germanic tribes (descendants of the original Celts and far-off cousins of the original Latini) as far as the Rhone River. He had landed an invasion force in Britain between the years 58–51 BC.

As Caesar's name, fame, and influence spread, Pompey and others in Rome realized the threat and ordered him to disband his powerful army and return to Rome. He refused to do so, and instead marched to Rome from his base in France.

Caesar crossed the Rubicon River in 49 BC, irrevocably committing himself to war with Pompey (the Rubicon marked the official boundary of Rome, and hence once crossed, the declaration of war was taken for granted). Within a short while, Caesar crushed all opposition and formally established himself as ruler.

### Caesar the Man—Orator, Writer, and Conqueror of Gaul, Britain, Egypt, and Spain

Although the most famous of the Romans, Caesar only ruled for five years (49–44 BC). He was an outstanding writer and orator, and instituted far-reaching reforms, from altering the makeup of the senate to the institution of a public works program.

He also introduced the 365-day solar year calendar (based on Egyptian knowledge—in Rome it became known as the Julian calendar) which, with minor alterations, is the same one the Western world uses to this day. The month of July is named after him.

Caesar took as his mistress the Macedonian Ptolemaic queen, Cleopatra VII of Egypt, in what was most likely a strategic alliance on both their parts.

## GREAT RIVALS: OCTAVIAN AUGUSTUS AND MARK ANTHONY

*Octavian* (left) *was the grandnephew and heir of Julius Caesar. The first emperor of Rome (27 BC–AD 14), he brought to an end nearly a century of civil war and strife. He presided over an era of peace, prosperity, and cultural achievement known as the Augustan Age. When Caesar was assassinated in 44 BC, Octavian was serving in the Roman army in Illyria. Keen to avenge Caesar and secure his own position, he first made peace with his nearest adversary, Mark Anthony* (right), *Caesar's ambitious colleague. Along with a third potential rival, the general Marcus Aemilius Lepidus, the three men formed a triumvirate to rule Rome, after first dispatching all their combined enemies, including the famous orator Cicero. Octavian and Anthony then marched against the leaders of Caesar's assassins, Marcus Brutus and Gaius Cassius Longinus. Both were defeated and committed suicide in 42 BC. The triumvirate did not last. While Lepidus was in the east fighting Parthinians, Octavian removed him from office. Mark Anthony had in the interim married the Macedonian Ptolemy queen, Cleopatra of Egypt, and recognized Caesarion, her son by Caesar, as her coruler. This undercut Octavian's position as the only son of Caesar, and war was inevitable. Octavian and Mark Anthony clashed at the naval battle of Actium in 31 BC. Octavian won and both Mark Anthony and Cleopatra committed suicide the following year. Caesar's true son, Caesarion, was then murdered. In 29 BC, Octavian returned to Rome in triumph, at age thirty-four the sole master of the Roman world. In 27 BC the Roman senate gave Octavian the title "The August One" (Augustus), and from then on he was known as Octavian Augustus, eventually having a month of the year named after him. Despite being heaped with honors and titles—including the word "imperator" (from which the word "emperor" is derived)—Octavian never took on the formal trappings of a monarchy, always insisting that he had restored the republic. He nonetheless remained the real power in Rome for his lifetime. A patron of the arts, Augustus was a friend of the poets Ovid, Horace, and Virgil, as well as the historian Livy. His love for architectural splendor was summed up in his boast that he "had found Rome brick and left it marble." He also initiated moralistic legislation that included sumptuary (restrictions on private expenditure in the interest of the state) and marriage laws. He died peacefully in 14 AD, acknowledged as one of the greatest Roman rulers in all of that empire's history.*

In 44 BC, Caesar was assassinated on the steps of the senate in Rome by a group opposed to his almost royal control of the affairs of state. Caesar had considered his powers to be hereditary, and had left a will in which he named his eighteen-year-old nephew, Octavian, as his heir.

### Octavian Augustus—Caesar's Great Heir

After suppressing and exterminating much of the opposition (including the renowned orator and senator, Cicero), Octavian and one of Caesar's colleagues, Mark Anthony, ruled with complete autocratic powers for a decade.

Mark Anthony married Cleopatra, Caesar's former mistress, giving her Roman territories as wedding gifts. Octavian used this act as an opportunity to incite Rome against Mark Anthony and the long-standing partnership between the two degenerated into civil war.

Both Octavian and Mark Anthony had large fleets at their disposal, and they finally met in battle in 31 BC, at Actium in Greece. Mark Anthony was defeated and committed suicide, as did his wife the following year when the city of Alexandria was captured by Roman forces.

### Pax Romana—Rome Flourishes 30 BC–235 AD

At the end of a century of civil strife (133–30 BC), Rome was finally united under one ruler. Thereafter ensued what became known as the Pax Romana, the Peace of Rome, which lasted for well on two hundred years, from 30 BC to 235 AD.

This time also marked the racial undoing of the empire, caused by the long-term effects of the inclusion of foreign lands and peoples. This process was intensified through the bypassing of an ancient law

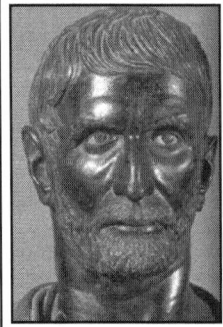

*"Et tu, Brutus" ("You as well, Brutus") are the words which Julius Caesar is reputed to have uttered when he saw that Marcus Brutus was one his assassins. During the civil war between Pompey and Julius Caesar, Brutus supported Pompey. After Caesar's victory, he was pardoned and became governor of Gaul in 46 BC and praetor of Rome two years later. During 44 BC he joined a conspiracy against Caesar, and took part in the assassination. Brutus then fled to Macedonia, raised an army, and joined battle with Caesar's successors, Mark Anthony and Octavian. His army was defeated, and Brutus committed suicide in 42 BC.*

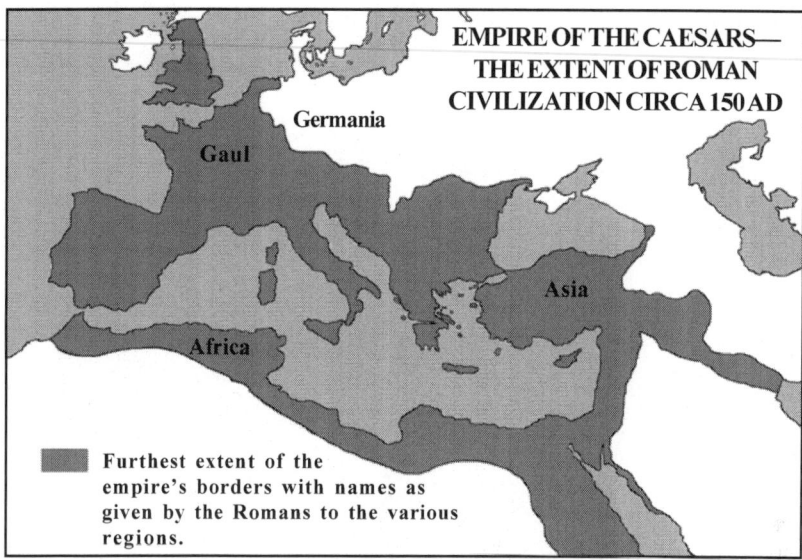

EMPIRE OF THE CAESARS—
THE EXTENT OF ROMAN
CIVILIZATION CIRCA 150 AD

Germania

Gaul

Asia

Africa

Furthest extent of the empire's borders with names as given by the Romans to the various regions.

created by that nation's founding fathers which prohibited marriages to non-Roman citizens.

Upon Octavian's victorious return to Rome in 29 BC, the senate conferred upon him the title of honorable or August (Augustus), a name by which he became known thereafter. Octavian Augustus held no official government position in Rome after 23 BC until his death in 14 AD. He was, however, de facto ruler of Rome through his position as supreme leader, or imperator, of the Roman army. It was from the word imperator that the word emperor was derived.

The time of the Pax Romana was also known as the "Principate" because political power was divided between the senate and the "principes." The princeps (singular) was the foremost person of Roman society, or the "first amongst equals," as Octavian described it. During his forty-four year reign Octavian Augustus established a stable and efficient public service, an equitable taxation policy, and consolidated the Roman Empire's borders.

Under his command the borders of the empire moved up the Danube River and into Germania as far as the Rhine, but he suffered a dramatic reverse when the Germans inflicted a massive defeat upon the Roman armies in 9 AD at the Battle of Detmold.

In the Middle East, Sulla's army had campaigned against the (by now racially mixed) Parthian Empire as early as 92 BC, but it was only the emperor Trajan who managed to finally subdue the Parthians—although he quickly handed their lands back to them in what was claimed to be an act of conciliation.

## The Julio-Claudian Dynasty Ends with Nero

After the death of Octavian Augustus, he was succeeded by four descendants of his family, called the Julio-Claudian family. The first two, Tiberius and Claudius, were just and efficient, and it was during the reign of Claudius that the occupation of Britain, begun by Julius Caesar approximately one hundred years earlier, was completed (in 43 AD).

The third Julio-Claudian emperor was the famous Caligula, who is reputed to have gone insane, once allegedly making a favorite horse into an ambassador.

The fourth Julio-Claudian emperor was the equally famous Nero, best known for his persecution of the Christians by throwing them to the lions. The Christians were at that stage still a tiny group, one amongst many flourishing under the Pax Romana. The Julio-Claudian line came to an end in 68 AD with Nero's suicide, with Rome suffering severe damage in a big fire in 64 AD.

## The Flavian Dynasty—Coliseum Built

A brief power struggle erupted upon Nero's death, and Flavius Vespasianus (also known as Vespasian) assumed power in 69 AD. He restarted orderly government and founded the Flavian dynasty, which lasted until 96 AD. The Coliseum in Rome (which still stands today) was built by the order of Vespasian, and was originally called Flavian's Amphitheater.

Vespasian's son, Titus, ruled from 79 to 81 AD. He is best remembered for his military exploit of capturing Jerusalem in AD 70, nine years before he became emperor. By the time of the last Flavian emperor, most Romans had accepted that the imperator, or emperor, was the real ruler of Rome.

## Nerva and the First Nonwhites in the Senate

Following the Flavian line came the Antonines—or the "five good emperors," who ruled from 96 to 180 AD. The first of these was the emperor Nerva, who ruled from 96–98 AD. Nerva is of importance because he established the rules of secession. Before he died he adopted a promising individual (who would thereafter be called a Caesar) who was then trained to take over the position of emperor when the time came. This system set the standard for many years to come.

## HEALTH AND FITNESS ROMAN STYLE—THE BATHS OF DIOCLETIAN

*A cross section of the greatest health and leisure complex in history, the magnificently decorated Baths of Diocletian, built during that emperor's reign (284–305 AD). Consisting of exercise halls, saunas, and swimming pools, the baths match any modern Western shopping and entertainment complex in size and grandeur, and covered an area greater than any modern sports stadium.*

Nerva was also the first emperor to allow members of the Roman senate to be chosen from all over the empire. This was a significant step, as the empire extended into territories such as North Africa and the Middle East, all of which had long since lost their significant white majority populations.

Nerva's rule marked the first appearance of non-Romans— and nonwhites—in the senate, and hence the government, of Imperial Rome. This process meant that by the end of the second century AD, senators of pure Roman descent were in the minority.

### *Dissolution of the Roman People*

The empire reached its peak in terms of territorial expansion under the next emperor, Trajan, who ruled from 98–117 AD. By this time huge numbers of racially foreign peoples were filling all of the noncontinental European Roman colonies, and were appearing in significant numbers in Rome.

The next emperor, Hadrian (117–138 AD), built the famous Hadrian's Wall of stone across the north of England to keep the remnants of the Scottish Celts out of Roman England. This was part of an attempt by Hadrian to reduce the size of the empire. Possibly he saw the process of disintegration at work, and he ordered many territories in the eastern parts of the empire to be given up. Under his rule, large slices of the eastern territories, except for Dracia (modern Romania) were effectively abandoned by the Roman Empire. If this was an attempt to stem the flood of foreigners pouring into the southern parts of the empire, it was a futile one.

### *Octavian's Attempts to Increase the White Roman Population Fail*

An overt attempt to preserve the Roman bloodline had been made by Octavian Augustus. He issued several decrees prescribing heavy penalties for celibacy or for marriage with slaves or the descendants of slaves. Another Octavian law was that all Romans between the ages of twenty-five and sixty must be married—and hopefully produce children.

Finally in the year 9 AD, Octavian announced tax concessions for Roman families with three or more children. Unmarried persons were barred from public games and could not receive inheritances, while childless married people could only receive half of any inheritance due to them. All these measures failed during Octavian's own lifetime.

As early as 131 BC, the Roman censor, Metellus, had called for a law compelling Roman citizens to marry. Julius Caesar, Augustus, Nero, and Trajan all offered prizes for Roman citizens having more than four children.

### *Roman Imperial Policy Encouraged the Growth of Non-Roman Peoples*

In continental Europe, the Pax Romana saw the benefits of Roman society bear fruit. The population increased and the Roman penchant for organization was swiftly taken up by the European peasantry in their regions. This process was enhanced by the Roman system of government, which relied on a few Roman administrators arriving in a region, and then getting locals to help with the administration and running of the territory in return for offices of state.

In this way the Romans "Romanized" many of their subject territories. While this did not affect the racial balance in Gaul and other parts of western and eastern Europe (central Europe or Germania remained forever out of Rome's reach), it had dramatic effects in the regions to the east and south which were majority occupied by nonwhite

**ROMAN APARTMENT BLOCK CIRCA 200 AD**

*A reconstruction of a block of apartments from the seaport of Ostia, the main port of the city of Rome, situated some sixteen miles downstream on the Tiber River. Mastering building techniques and styles that have remained essentially unchanged to this day, the Romans were able to create architectural wonders second to none, but only for as long as they themselves existed. As soon as enough non-Romans entered Italy—as slaves, immigrants, or labourers—the Romans became a minority in their own land and eventually disappeared completely, absorbed into the waves of newcomers. Once the Romans had disappeared, so did their civilization.*

peoples. This policy was also applied in the other reaches of the Roman Empire—with disastrous consequences for Rome in the Mediterranean territories of North Africa, Egypt, and the Middle East.

In these latter territories huge numbers of the racially mixed populations (consisting of white, Semitic, Arabic, and Mongoloid mixtures) drew the benefits of Roman civilization for as long as the Romans themselves existed. This meant a dramatic increase in the population due to increased living standards, and so the Romans helped to engineer the nonwhite racial flood that would eventually overwhelm them from the south.

It is interesting to note that the original Indo-European descended Romans viewed anyone who was dark with suspicion. The Roman proverb *"hic niger es, hunc tu, Romane, caveato"* ("He is black, beware of him, Roman") is recorded by Horace as being a common saying amongst Romans of the time (*Satire,* i. 4, 85).

This is not to say that the Romans of the Late Republic or of the Pax Romana resisted the physical integration process. On the contrary, they seemed to have welcomed it as an essential part of empire building and as a means to keep subdued populations under control. It is unlikely that they could have foreseen the long-term consequences it would create. The original spark which created the Roman civilization was extinguished when the last of the true Romans was bred out within the vast reaches of that empire. Hence there are today Roman ruins in Africa, the Middle East, and indeed even in Rome today—silent monuments to a people long gone.

### German Resistance Halts Roman Expansion

The Romans never managed to penetrate into central Europe past the Rhine River, with their last attempt to seize modern day Germany halted in the year 9 AD. This created a physical division in the white peoples of northwestern Europe. At that time one section (Gaul and Britain) fell completely under the sway of Rome, and the other section (the German tribes) remained Rome's implacable enemies, fighting the empire at every opportunity.

Ironically, these Germanic tribes (or barbarians as the Romans liked to call them) were originally far-off Celtic cousins of the Latini. It was these barbarians who finally overran Rome after it had bred its true Romans down to an insignificant minority, causing the great imperial flame to flicker and die.

### Extent of Empire Proves Its Undoing

At its height the Roman Empire stretched from England to the Rhine, from Spain to Asia Minor, and from North Africa to the Tigris/Euphrates Rivers. The vast number of peoples and races drawn into the empire's influence does not need to be exaggerated. Roman coins found in India and Scandinavia indicate the extent to which Romans traveled as traders or soldiers.

The Romans may have believed that the integration of foreigners into Rome and its system of government was the way to create an empire. The reality is, however, that nonhomogeneous societies are the least cohesive, while homogeneous societies are the most cohesive. So it was that the ever increasing number of foreigners within the empire made it all the more difficult to hold together. Internal dissension, political problems, and social ills were often compounded by brutal or incompetent emperors.

Finally, by 192 AD, the throne was actually auctioned by the emperor's own private guard (the Praetorian Guard, founded by Octavian Augustus) after a particularly ineffectual emperor had been murdered after just three months in office. The winner of the auction did not last very long, being in turn deposed by an emperor effectively chosen by the largest part of the army: one Septimus Servus.

### Rome's Fate Sealed—Caracalla and His Citizenship Edict of 212 AD

Servus himself was unremarkable, but his son, Caracalla, who ruled from 211–217 AD, was the Roman emperor who finally opened the racial floodgates on the Roman Empire and sealed its fate. In 212 AD, in an apparent attempt to broaden the Roman tax base, Caracalla passed an edict giving all free males within the empire citizenship of Rome. This proclamation, which effectively turned centuries of Roman law on its head, had effects far greater than just broadening the tax base.

Early Roman law had made provision for the maintenance of racial homogeneity by stipulating that persons could only be citizens if both their parents were Roman citizens. Those who married non-Roman citizens could not claim Roman citizenship for their children. This was a direct way of biologically excluding all foreign nationals from Roman citizenship.

As the Roman Empire expanded, so the definition of citizenship became broader and broader, till finally with Caracalla's edict, all free men, no matter what their racial or national origin, qualified for Roman citizenship.

The last hold preventing the dilution of Roman blood had been abandoned.

### Caracalla's Edict Gives Legal Support to Integration

While the early Romans placed great

**CARACALLA—EXTENDS ROMAN CITIZENSHIP TO NONWHITES 212 AD**

*The Emperor Caracalla (who ruled from 211–217 AD) extended Roman citizenship to all free peoples within the boundaries of the Roman Empire in 212 AD, and thereby gave legal sanction to the final dissolution of the Roman people. Previously, only persons born of Roman citizens qualified for citizenship.*

*Born in Gaul of a Roman father and a Syrian mother, his own dubious ancestry, as evidenced by his official portrait, must have played a role in his decision to extend Roman citizenship.*

emphasis on maintaining their racial homogeneity, by the first century AD the idea of universality had become an undercurrent and it was to become the main train of thought by the second century AD.

By the time of Caracalla's edict, a large amount of racial mixing had already occurred due to the sheer size of the empire and the fact that it included so many racially alien elements within its borders. This process was now given legal support.

Interracial marriages and mixed race children became more and more common after this, and slowly but surely, Rome and the Roman Empire in the Mediterranean lost its white leadership core.

Thus the fate which had befallen all the other great civilizations, namely the disappearance of the founding population through physical integration, crept up on Rome. Although this change in racial demographics was not as marked in Rome as in the easternmost outreaches of the empire, it was dramatic enough to change the very

## ROME: FROM BLOND TO PEPPERCORN HAIR

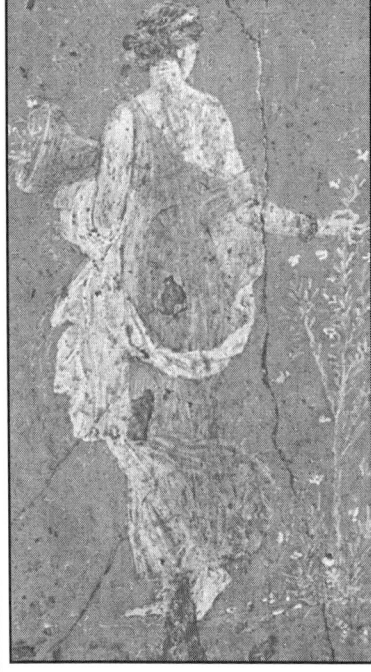

*The fall of Rome is encapsulated in these two images. Left: A painting of a blonde Roman woman in southern Italy: "Primavera," a wall painting from Stabiae, first century AD, National Museum, Naples. Compare this to the official bust of the emperor, Philip (244–249 AD), above. Born in the Roman province of Arabia, in what today is the village of Shahba, roughly fifty-five miles (eighty-eight kilometers) southeast of Damascus, Philip's father was a prominent local man, Julius Marinus, who had been awarded Roman citizenship and was thus not a native born Roman. Nothing is known of Philip's mother. Known as "Philip the Arabian," he was an emperor who was clearly not of pure European descent. This bust accurately captures his short "peppercorn" hair, an obvious sign of nonwhite ancestry, Vatican Museum, Rome.*

nature of the civilization. Foreigners from all over the mixed race Middle East poured into Rome, attracted by its wealth and status. Being granted citizenship, these foreigners were steadily absorbed into the Roman population, to the point where today very few Italians can still claim pure Roman descent.

The result is that certain population elements in the south of Italy and in Sicily are today clearly of mixed racial origin, mainly a mixture of Arabic and white. However, there are still flashes of the original population with light skin, light eyes and/or light hair.

The path followed by Rome mirrored that followed by Sumeria, the Middle East, Egypt, and Greece. All of these civilizations remained intact as long as the society which created them remained homogeneous. As soon as these societies lost their homogeneity and became multiracial, the very nature of the societies changed and the original civilizations disappeared. Rome would prove to be no exception to this rule.

# CHAPTER TWELVE

# Power and Purpose—The Glory of Rome

The fact that the Roman Empire dissolved into a multiracial polyglot does not detract from the very many fine cultural and engineering achievements of the original Romans.

It is, however, very noticeable that the greatest Roman achievements date from before the time of the racial dissolution of the empire—once again mirroring earlier civilizations.

## Roman Social Life—Sports and Athletics

Roman social life concentrated on great athletic and sporting events. The tradition of blood sports—gladiators killing each other for the amusement of spectators, was not a sport associated with the original Romans.

It only became common once Rome had started to fill up with foreigners, although there was certainly no active resistance amongst the original Romans to the rise of the bloody spectacles. The attraction to blood sports was also used as a political tool.

Very often prisoners who had been found guilty of some particularly heinous crime would be fed to the lions, as often happened with the early Christians under the emperor Nero.

Wrestling and chariot racing were both popular amusements. The largest sports stadium in Rome was the Circus Maximus, which could easily seat approximately 300,000 people and could be filled with water to reenact sea battles between regular sized ships.

The Circus Maximus stood for centuries, but its stone was eventually broken

*The might of Rome was founded on the superb discipline, training, and weaponry of legionnaires such as this.*

186

## CIRCUS MAXIMUS—LARGEST STADIUM COMPLEX IN HISTORY

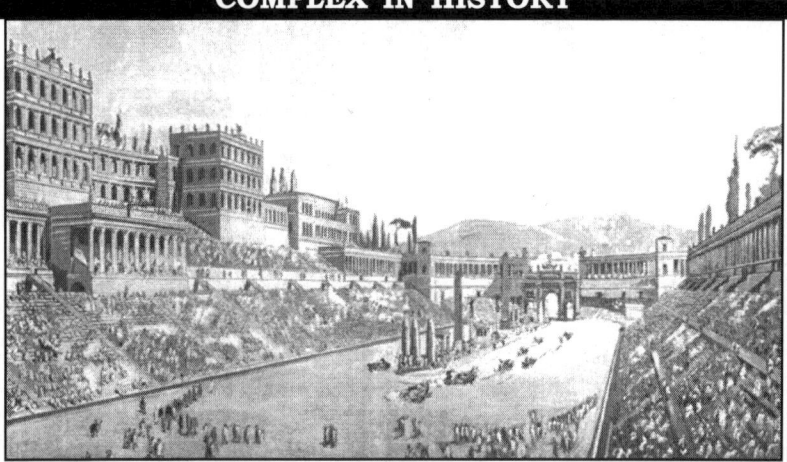

*The huge Circus Maximus in Rome. This was the greatest Roman entertainment complex of all time, able to seat 300,000 spectators. The first parts of the Circus Maximus were built around 600 BC, and substantially enlarged by Julius Caesar, who also added canals which could flood the theater floor so ships could be sailed to reenact sea battles. The Circus Maximus, which was far larger than the famous Coliseum, did not survive. It was broken up and much of its stone was used to build the many Christian churches in Rome today after that religion came to dominate Europe.*

up for use in Christian buildings during the Middle Ages. Almost every major Roman town, from North Africa right through to the Near East, boasted a theater or amphitheater—some are still in use to this day.

### *Roman Religion—A Mixture of Beliefs*

One distinguishing feature of Roman religion before the advent of Christianity was that there was no single faith or belief. In many ways the religious world of Rome reflected the empire. It was a mix of different cults and beliefs, with influences from Greece, Egypt, and the Middle East.

Many of the oldest Roman gods reflected the nature of the first Romans—representing the practical needs of daily life and military prowess.

### *Roman Gods' Names Still in Use Today*

Janus and Vesta guarded the door and hearth; Lares protected the field and house, Pales the pasture, Saturn the sowing, Ceres the growth of the grain, Pomona the fruit, and Consus and Ops the harvest. Jupiter, the ruler of the gods, was not only credited with bringing rain, but was also known for his weapon, lightning (as was the Greek chief god, Zeus) and was the protector of the Romans in their military activities beyond the borders of their own community.

Mars was a god of young men and war and along with Jupiter, Quirinus, Janus, and Vesta, formed the first Roman pantheon of gods.

As part of their policy of absorption, native gods from conquered surrounding lands were usually granted the same honor with which the Roman gods were held.

Formal invitations were often issued to the religions' leaders to take up residence in Rome. There they were entitled to build temples to their gods and bring with them whatever precious artifacts were associated with their beliefs. This growth in the number of foreign religions had another serious consequence—foreigners were attracted to the city in ever increasing numbers.

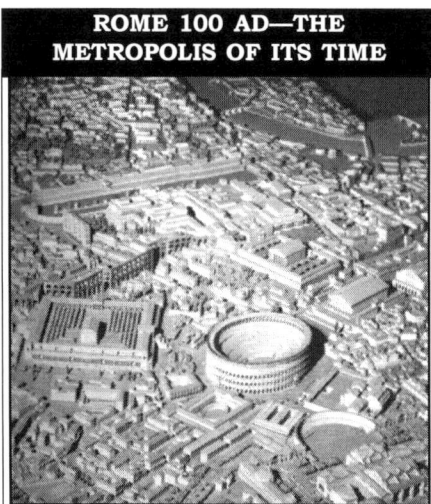

**ROME 100 AD—THE METROPOLIS OF ITS TIME**

*Matching any modern city in size and complexity, this model of the ancient city of Rome shows the Circus Maximus in the background and the Coliseum in the foreground. With running water, ordered streets, blocks of apartments, and huge educational and entertainment facilities, the citizens lacked for nothing.*

Deities from neighboring tribes in Italy which became Roman gods included Diana, Minerva, Hercules, and Venus. The Roman religious calendar also reflected Rome's willingness to absorb foreign cults.

The oldest Roman festivals lasted till the very end of the pagan Roman era, and marked the original Indo-European festivals of spring and winter. One of the most important festivals was the Saturnalia which was celebrated for seven days, from December 17 to 23, during the original winter solstice time. All business was suspended, slaves were given temporary freedom, and gifts were exchanged.

Another important festival was the Lupercalia, which celebrated Lupercus, a pastoral god. The festival was celebrated on February 15 at the cave of the Lupercal on the Palatine Hill, where the legendary

*Virgil (70–19 BC) is known as the greatest of all Roman poets, mainly because of his epic poem the* Aeneid, *which told the story of Aeneas, who moved from Troy to Italy.*

*The great Roman historian Tacitus (55–117 AD), who, along with Pliny, was one of Rome's greatest historians and social commentators.*

founders of Rome, Romulus and Remus, were supposed to have been nursed by a she-wolf.

The Equiria, a festival in honor of Mars, was celebrated on February 27 and March 14, traditionally the time of year when new military campaigns were prepared.

The growth in the number of temples in Rome also indicated how willing the Romans were to allow all manner of cults to flourish under their rule.

Roman society adopted the fairly liberal approach that each person could conduct his own particular religion as he wished as long as it did not disturb the public order. This, combined with the huge areas which fell under Roman domination, saw any number of cults and beliefs stream into Rome from all parts of the known world: Mithraism from Iran, Judaism from Palestine—even the worship of the Isis cult from Egypt became popular after Cleopatra VII visited Rome for a year as the guest of Caesar. Influences from far and wide all competed for converts in Rome.

All the non-Christian religions were prohibited in AD 392 by an edict of Emperor Theodosius after Christianity had become dominant.

### *Roman Literature—Massive Heritage*

Culturally, the early Romans left a massive heritage, contributing to Western Civilization some of the most famous writers and thinkers outside of classical Greece. All educated Romans were bilingual, speaking Latin and Greek.

• Marcus Tullus Cicero (106–43 BC) was one of the most famous Latin writers, producing texts on a wide number of topics, including analyses and discussions of Greek thought, especially that of Plato and the Stoics.

• Virgil (70–19 BC), the greatest of all Roman poets, mainly because of his epic poem the *Aeneid,* which told the story of Aeneas, who moved from Troy to Italy and helped establish the Latini people.

**WORLD'S FIRST GEODESIC MAP 200 AD**

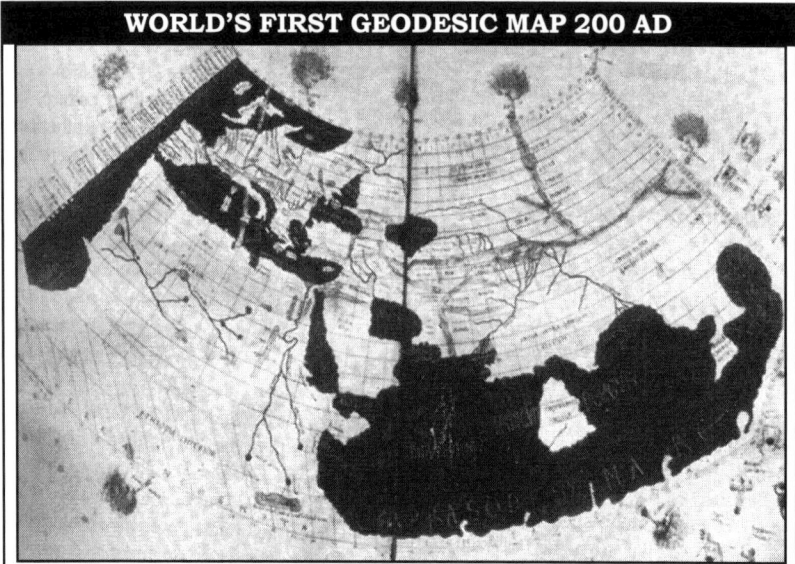

*The first map to represent the earth on a curved surface (and hence part of a globe)—devised by the Roman-Greek scientist Ptolemy, working during the second century AD.*

• Ovid (43 BC–17 AD) is most famous for his poem *Metamorphoses,* which contains stories from classical mythology. He also won renown as a poet of pleasure and love, and after one particularly bad sexual scandal involving a member of an imperial family, was exiled to an outpost on the Black Sea.

• Livy (59–17 BC) wrote an immense history of Rome, the first comprehensive history of that type undertaken.

• Tacitus (55–117 AD) wrote several pieces including *Germania* and *The Annals,* which were critical of Roman society and the emperor system of rule.

• Plutarch (46–120 AD) is most famous for his biographical work of forty-six famous Romans and Greeks, called the *Parallel Lives.* This work was used some 1,600 years later by the English playwright William Shakespeare to obtain details for two of his tragic dramas, *Anthony and Cleopatra,* and *Julius Caesar.*

• The historian Pliny the Elder (23–79 AD) assembled what can be called the first encyclopedia, the *Natural History.*

The Macedonian remnant in Egypt kept up the scientific research work started under the Ptolemies.

Alexandria was once again built up into a huge city, spawning the famous geographer Ptolemy (circa 200 AD) who was the first to draw a map of the world onto a curved surface, working off the original

Greek plans drawn up by Eratosthenes.

Galen (139–200 AD) was another Romanized Greek, who established the principles of medicine used in Europe until the early Renaissance period.

### *Roman Art—Set World Standards*

As with many things architectural, early Roman art copied Grecian forms. This was readily apparent in the style of sculpture, and many statues of Greeks which have survived to the present day are Roman copies of Greek originals.

**SPECTACULAR AND ENDURING ENGINEERING**

*A tribute to Roman engineering—the Roman built aqueduct at Segovia in Spain, still supplies that town's water, nearly 1,800 years later.*

Roman art has set the standard against which all other art is measured—even to the point where an object or style is known as "classical" or not. This is an indication that, even two thousand years later, little improvement has been made upon Roman design.

### *Architecture—Invention of Concrete*

The Romans unashamedly took many building designs from the Greeks, including various column types and the now famous Greco-Roman building style of a triangular roof set atop rows of columns. The Romans perfected and added to these designs, creating structures which are still awe inspiring today and unequaled in sheer aesthetics.

Many of the buildings in Rome date from the height of the empire. Some Roman structures, such as the famous water aqueduct in Segovia, Spain, are still working today, nineteen centuries after they were built. Roman roads were the autobahns of their day, and the road system set up by the Romans was not equaled until the twentieth century.

The workmanship which went into many of the constructions of the time would be hard to match even in the modern era—and this in spite of the advantage of modern tools. The Romans started town planning as a skill: laying out new cities on a grid pattern for ease of commuting. Their inventions of concrete and the vaulted dome made possible the huge buildings later to become known as cathedrals.

However, this frenzied building activity had its price. Masses of slaves provided the cheap labor to build these edifices, and the influx of slaves combined with natural immigration to the Roman center provided the demographic shift which brought about the empire's downfall.

### Slaves—The Racial Time Bomb

Slavery was an institutionalized part of Roman society. Due to the sheer size of the empire, many slaves were foreign. Greek slaves were held to be the best type to own (they were the whitest slave, after Gauls or Germans, who were less common as slaves). Arabs, blacks, and others of mixed race from the Middle East also made up a huge number of the slave population.

The importation of these racially alien slaves had an impact upon the demographics of Rome over a period of time. The number of slaves in Rome and Italy was tremendous: in 45 AD, it has been estimated that a third of the entire population were slaves. There were enough of them to form their own seventy thousand strong army, as happened in 73 BC, when the slave leader Spartacus led the famous slave uprising.

It took an entire Roman army to suppress that uprising, yet the practice of slavery continued, and ultimately cost the Romans their very existence.

**SUBSTANTIAL ENGINEERING TO SECURE THE EMPIRE**

*A reconstruction of the Roman castle at Deutz, near Cologne, one of the oldest frontier towns guarding the Rhine River border of the empire against the Germans.*

# CHAPTER THIRTEEN

# Opponents and Allies—Rome and the Celts

**By 600 BC, the Celts had firmly established themselves in France, having thoroughly absorbed most of the original Old European population in that region. These Celtic tribes lived in relative stability in small villages and the occasional larger town.**

They had a strongly developed sense of social status, with the aristocracy being warriors and the middle and lower classes the tradesmen and laborers. Almost all the descriptions of their lifestyles come from Roman writers, including Julius Caesar, who was head of the Roman army which occupied Gaul in 54 BC.

Roman historians reported that the Celtic warriors had long hair and often engaged in battle naked, which was apparently used as a shock tactic. The absence of armor—although they did use shields—was a distinct disadvantage in battle, particularly against the well-prepared Roman legions.

### Gauls Found City of Milan and Attack Romans 400 BC

The enmity between Rome and the Celts (or Gauls, to give them the name that they had by the time of the Roman occupation of France) went back to 400 BC. In that year, Gaulish armies invaded northern Italy.

There, one of their early bases was later developed into the city of Milan. by 387 BC, the invading Gauls had occupied Rome, only

**GALLIC WARRIOR—FRIEND AND FOE OF THE ROMANS**

*A Gallic horseman. At first the Gauls fought the invading Romans bitterly, but once subdued, they became firm allies.*

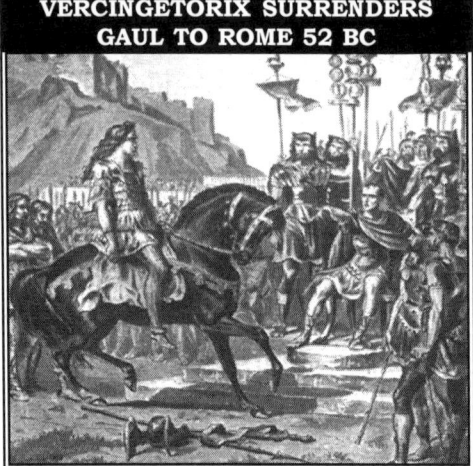

**VERCINGETORIX SURRENDERS GAUL TO ROME 52 BC**

*The Gaulish rebellion came to an end with the rebel leader, Vercingetorix surrendering to Caesar. After conquering modern day France and moving on to Britain, Caesar had to rush back to Gaul to face a full-scale rebellion in 52 BC, led by Vercingetorix. After being cornered and besieged at Alesia, the Gaulish chief surrendered to Caesar in an attempt to save his own people. Caesar had him sent to Rome in chains where he was kept prisoner for six years before being executed.*

leaving after the Romans paid them a ransom in gold.

### Roman Revenge 350 Years Later

The Romans never forgot nor forgave the Gaulish invasion of 400 BC. They bided their time, and after a series of minor clashes, Roman armies under General Caesar rolled into Gaul in 54 BC.

The swiftness of the invasion and the superb Roman army organization smashed the Gauls, enslaving almost the entire population which numbered three million by Roman count. The cruelty with which the Romans suppressed the Gauls triggered a great uprising in central France. This rebellion, led by Vercingetorix, king of the Arverni tribe, spread to other tribes around the country and was only suppressed after two years of war. Gaulish resistance intensified with each Roman counterattack. Caesar showed no mercy—when he occupied the rebel-supporting town of Avaricum, he ordered the execution of all forty thousand inhabitants.

Spurred on by these and other outrages, Vercingetorix and his Gaulish allies launched a renewed assault on the Roman army. For a while, the Roman expedition nearly foundered, but eventually superior Roman organization won the day.

Vercingetorix and eighty thousand of his men were cornered in the fortified town of Alesia on the Seine River. Caesar's army settled down to a siege, preparing their defenses well enough to ward off attacks by Gauls from outside. Finally, in an attempt to save his people from extermination, Vercingetorix personally surrendered to Caesar in 52 BC. Caesar had the Celtic king sent to Rome in chains, where he was kept prisoner for six years before being publicly strangled and beheaded. The Gaulish rebellion was at an end.

## *Celts from European Mainland Settle in Britain*

The island of Britain had in the interim also been settled by waves of Celts, producing the same mix of European types as had happened elsewhere in Europe.

Generally though, the Celtic Britons were not as Nordic as their Celtic cousins across the channel in France. This was due to the fact that a smaller number of Nordic Celts had crossed the English Channel to mix with the original Neolithic population of Britain. Nonetheless, the Celts had a significant cultural influence on the island, in both art and language.

**JULIUS CAESAR INVADES BRITAIN 55 BC**

*Caesar leads the assault on Britain. In 55 BC, Julius Caesar and a Roman army landed in Britain to strong resistance from the Celts and Britons. Great was Caesar's surprise when he found that the Celts had chariots. It was only after an inconclusive battle that a stalemate was reached which allowed Caesar to leave without conceding defeat. Caesar launched another invasion of Britain the following year, and this time managed to subdue a larger number of Celts. Most of the country remained independent for nearly another ninety years until 43 AD when a renewed Roman offensive subdued almost all of present day England.*

Yet more Celts moved to Ireland, taking the ancient Indo-European language with them. The very name Eire is, like Iran, derived from the word "Aryan." Eire was never conquered by the Romans (although they did have a fort outside Dublin, but this appears to have been an emissary party only) and thus remained known as a Celtic stronghold.

## *First Roman Invasion of Britain 55 BC*

In 55 BC, Caesar undertook the first Roman crossing of the channel to Britain. Upon landing, he sent an emissary, a Romanized Gaul named Commius, to the Celtic tribes of southeastern Britain to try and establish some sort of peaceful accord. This came to naught when Commius was captured by one of the Celtic tribes.

The Romans were surprised to find that the Britons had war chariots. This was bad news for the Romans, as bad weather had prevented Caesar from bringing his cavalry across the English Channel with the rest of the army. For a while it seemed as if Caesar's two legions would be driven out of Britain. Then Commius, who had been released as part of a diplomatic cat-and-mouse game, managed to lay his hands on some local horses with which the Romans whittled down the Celtic advantage. A stalemate was achieved after an inconclusive battle. It was the respite that Caesar needed, and shortly thereafter the bulk of the Roman legions withdrew to Gaul. Caesar was fêted in Rome for the expedition to Britain, although it was minor in comparison to the far more significant conquest of Gaul.

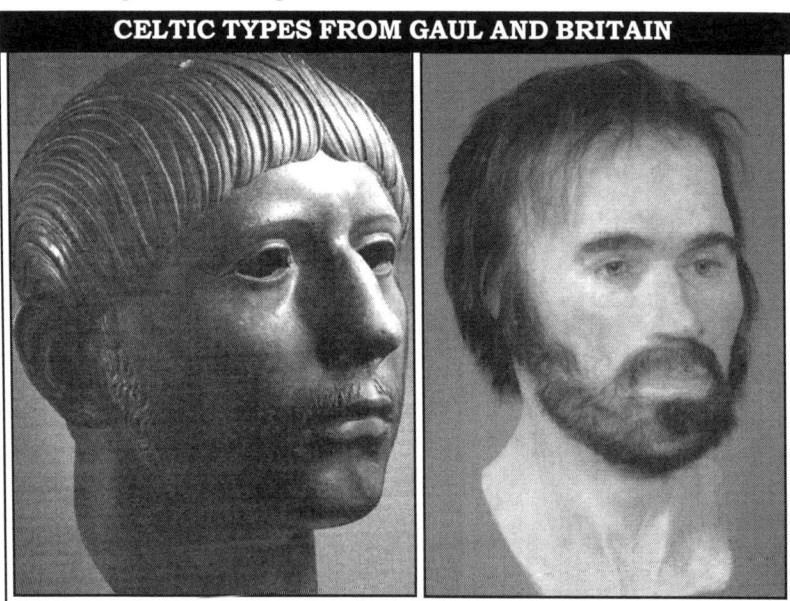

**CELTIC TYPES FROM GAUL AND BRITAIN**

*Celtic types, from Gaul and Britain. Left: A Roman bronze casting of a (French) Gaul chieftain—an excellent depiction of a Gaulish nobleman from the time of the Roman invasion. Right: A reconstruction of the head of Lindow man, the Iron Age (100 AD) body found in a Cheshire, England, peat bog in 1984. This would have been the typical Celt that the Romans encountered, fought against, and finally mixed with, in Britain.*

## Caesar Launches Second Invasion 54 BC

The following year, 54 BC, Caesar launched yet another invasion of Britain. This time he landed a force several times larger than used in his first expedition—and included a two thousand strong cavalry.

Caesar hoped to land his forces, march quickly into the heart of the Celtic territory, and inflict a defeat upon the scattered tribes before they could unite into one army. The plan nearly failed because the landing beaches were chosen poorly. To compound the problems, a storm forced the Romans to spend ten days dragging all the ships onto the dry land to prevent them from being sunk. This delay gave the Britons enough time to sound the alarm and to draw up their army, uniting under a chief named Cassivellaunus.

Nonetheless, the overwhelming force with which Caesar had invaded allowed him to defeat the united Celts. This caused the Celtic alliance to wither, and some significant tribes went over to the Roman side. The most important of these were the Trinovantes of Essex, who had reason to disapprove of Cassivellaunus because he had, in an earlier skirmish, slain their chief.

Cassivellaunus went on the offensive, attacking a major Roman camp in Kent, but was defeated. Caesar's victories were not, however, complete. The earlier loss of time meant that winter was now approaching, and the quick outright conquest he sought still evaded him. Even worse, rebellion was brewing in Gaul.

Caesar and Cassivellaunus then agreed to a peace treaty whereby the Celts would pay an annual tribute to Rome and would safeguard Roman interests in Britain. Thus concluded, Caesar hurriedly

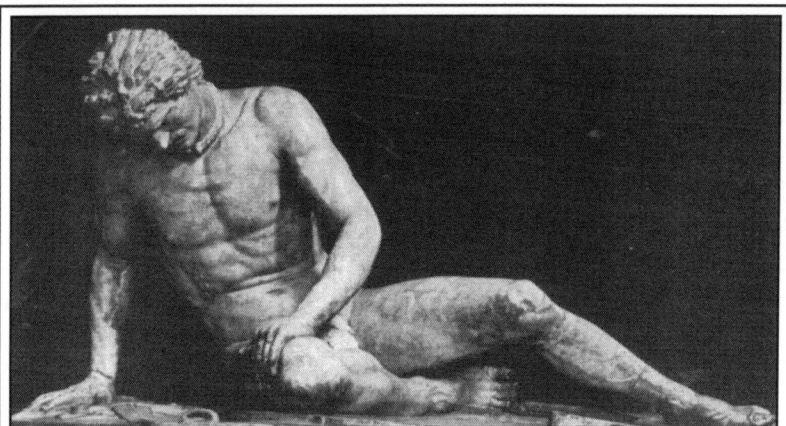

*Dying Gaul, Roman sculpture, circa 230 BC. An excellent portrayal of the racial characteristics of the Gauls with whom the Romans were to do battle.*

left Britain to return to Rome and then back to Gaul, where he had to face Vercingetorix's uprising.

Any thoughts Caesar may have had of a third invasion of Britain were shelved by subsequent events which saw him seize power in Rome in 50 BC.

*The apex of Celtic craftsmanship is exemplified by the famous torc from Snettisham in Norfolk, Britain, dating from approximately 60 BC. According to legend, the Celtic queen, Boadicea, wore precisely such a torc when she rode into battle. Worn as a necklace or as an armband, the torc was regarded by the Celts as a good luck symbol.*

## Caesar's Conquest of Spain in Six Weeks

Caesar did not limit his Celtic conquests to Gaul and Britain. In a six-week campaign in 49 BC, he conquered Spain as well, bringing the Celts in that country under Roman rule. Prior to this conquest, only a portion of southern Spain had been in Roman hands, seized from the Carthaginians during the Punic Wars. The process of Romanization of Spain also began in earnest after this date.

### Third Roman Invasion of Britain with Elephants 43 AD

Caesar's successor, Octavian Augustus, planned a number of invasions of Britain, but all were postponed due to distractions elsewhere in the empire. Britain, therefore, remained in a state of semi-independence for another one hundred years.

It was only in 43 AD that the emperor Claudius finally ordered a full conquest of Britain. An army of forty thousand men assembled under the command of Aulus Plautius duly invaded the island that year. The powerful Roman army swept inland, defeating determined Celtic resistance around present day London. The Roman forces spread out, employing powerful weapons such as bolt catapults against tribesmen armed with only bows, arrows, and slings. Nonetheless, the Celts defended to the death places such as the ancient hill fort of Maiden Castle in Dorset.

Claudius decided to be present at the final victory, and landed in Britain with additional forces and elephants, which must have seemed akin to dragons to the Britons.

The Celtic tribes then surrendered near what became the city of Colchester, and Claudius was able to leave after a stay of only sixteen days, finally having added the province of Britain to the empire.

### Celtic Rebellion under Boadicea 61 AD

The initial Roman occupation was not universally accepted. By 47 AD, open resistance had broken out. This discontent simmered on

**QUEEN BOADICEA ATTACKS ROMANS 61 AD**

*Queen Boadicea of the Iceni leading the Celtic rebellion against Roman rule in 61 AD. At first she won some great victories, overrunning the Roman towns of Colchester and London. Noted as having long blonde hair, the Celtic queen was finally defeated by superior Roman organization at the Battle of Loughton. Retreating to the great forest today known as Epping outside London, she took poison in order to avoid capture.*

until 61 AD, when it finally erupted into open revolt under the leadership of the Iceni tribe in Norfolk.

The spark came with the death of the Iceni king, which had caused a Roman unit to enter that territory. After engaging in looting, the Roman soldiers publicly whipped the king's widow, Boadicea, and raped her daughters. This public shaming was the last straw, and the Iceni, joined by many other tribes, broke out into open revolt. Led by Boadicea, they seized several Roman strongholds, including Colchester and London, both of which were sacked and burned. Some seventy thousand Roman and Romanized Celtic fatalities were inflicted in the destruction of these two centers.

Although shaken by the ferocity of the uprising, the Romans drew together their forces and met Boadicea's army in central Britain. There, through superior organizational ability and better training, the Romans were able to inflict a massive defeat upon their numerically superior enemy. Roman accounts of the battle say that some eighty thousand Britons were killed on the field that day, while the Romans only lost four hundred.

The Boadicean revolt was the last major native rebellion the Romans experienced in Britain for the next two hundred years. From then on, the military conquests of other parts of the island, reaching north into lower Scotland, continued without major interruption. By 80 AD, the Romans had pushed the most rebellious Celts up into the Scottish Highlands.

One of these rebellious tribes, the Caledonians, nearly defeated the Roman legions at the Battle of Mons Graupius in 83 AD. The Romans prevailed, however, and the Caledonians vanished into the Highlands. Nonetheless, the ferocity of the far northern Celtic defense meant that the Romans never pushed home the advantage, and slowly withdrew southward.

*Hadrian's Wall, northern England. Built by the Romans to ward off marauding Picts attacking from what is today Scotland.*

By 122 AD, the Roman Emperor, Hadrian, who had visited the province of Britain, ordered the building of a fortified wall across the north of England to keep out the northern barbarians. Many parts of this wall, named after Hadrian, can still be seen to this day.

By 212 AD, the Romans were firmly entrenched in England (as opposed to Britain) and the Romanization process was almost total, being sped up by the 212 AD Edict of Caracalla granting Roman citizenship to all free inhabitants of the empire. This led to the automatic legalization of the already de facto situation of soldiers taking wives from the local population.

This policy did not have the same racial effects on the Romans in Britain and France as what it had on the Romans in the Middle East. The mixing of Roman, Celtic, and original European subgroups did not disturb the racial homogeneity of either the conquerors or the conquered peoples, unlike in the southern and eastern reaches of the empire where the local nonwhite populations soon swallowed up the white Romans.

In 287 AD, a revolt once again broke out in Britain, even though by this stage many Romans had become Britons and vice versa. The rebellion was led by Romanized Britons and Romans who disliked the emperor of the time, Maximian, who had been appointed as coemperor by Diocletian. A specially dispatched Roman army subdued the rebellion in 296 AD.

According to the Roman records, the rebels employed a large number of German mercenaries. This was ironic, because many of the newly arrived Roman legionnaires were also German mercenaries. This rebellion was the last major armed action undertaken by the Romans in Britain.

### Roman Control Lost 410 AD

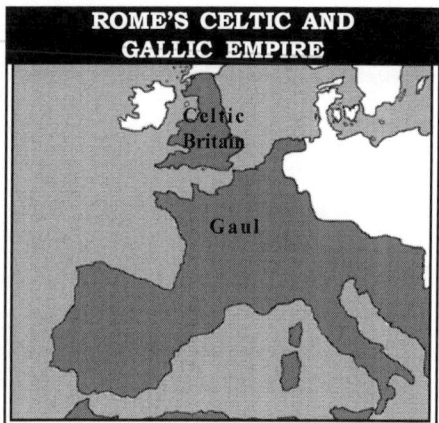

**ROME'S CELTIC AND GALLIC EMPIRE**

*The vast regions conquered by Julius Caesar and his successors in Gaulish France, Celtic Spain, and Celtic Britain.*

As the Roman Empire began to disintegrate due to its cosmopolitan nature, central control over the furthermost colonies began to be more difficult. Finally, around 410 AD, Emperor Honorius ordered the Roman legions to officially withdraw from Britain, telling the people of Britain that they no longer had a connection to Rome and that they should defend themselves. Within a very short period of time, Britain was subjected to a new wave of Germanic invaders in the form of the Saxons and other Teutonic peoples. The Roman period of influence was at an end.

# CHAPTER FOURTEEN

# The Useful Foe—Rome and the Germans

**The Germanic peoples had spread throughout the area now known as Germany for two millennia until they reached the Rhine River around the year 300 BC. Some adventurous tribes even crossed that river, penetrating what is today Belgium (the Romans called these tribes the Belgae, hence that country's name). These advances invariably brought the Germans into conflict with the Celts in France, and after the Romans occupied Gaul, with the Romans themselves.**

Germanic tribes had clashed in 113 BC with the Romans when an invading tribe had passed through northern Italy. Although the invading Germans had been defeated in battle and driven off by the Roman forces, other tribes still occasionally dared to launch raiding parties into Roman occupied Gaul. In 57 BC, for example, the German Saubian tribe seized present day Alsace-Lorraine in France.

Julius Caesar was forced to intervene to prevent further German incursions. He defeated the German invaders, and drove the few survivors back across the Rhine River, which became the border between Roman Gaul and Germania.

### First Roman Invasion 55 BC

In 55 BC, Caesar built a wooden bridge across the Rhine, near the present day city of Cologne. Over this first ever bridge on that river, the Romans took the war to the Germans in their own territory.

Having been beaten several times in a row by the Romans, the Germans withdrew eastward into the forests, leaving the Romans free to destroy the scattered remaining German settlements on the eastern

*German tribesmen, drawn from an original Roman illustration. Men such as these made up the German army under Hermann Cherusker, and were the only Europeans to stay the mighty hand of Rome itself. This illustration, from a German history published in 1861, shows the German in the center as having a Roman short sword—presumably a trophy from some unfortunate Roman.*

bank of the Rhine River. After just over two weeks of plundering, the Roman army withdrew back over the bridge, declaring the entire western bank of the Rhine to be officially Roman territory.

### Second Roman Invasion and the Use of German Mercenaries

Some two years later, in 53 BC, Caesar again crossed the Rhine River and broke the threat of German tribes in Westphalia. He even recruited some German mercenaries to fight with his army which he used to subdue Vercingetorix the Gaul in France.

After Caesar had finally subdued the Celts, he was challenged by Pompey back in Rome to disband his army. Caesar then famously marched on Rome, which ultimately led to his seizure of power. Some six thousand German mercenaries marched with Caesar's army to Rome, the forerunners of many thousands who would end up serving in the Roman army.

**GERMANS FORCED TO BEHEAD EACH OTHER**

*The Germans proved to be the only people subject to a Roman invasion who managed to fight off and defeat the Caesars. This relief is from the Antoine Column, and shows Romans forcing German prisoners to behead each other.*

This development—the use of German and Celtic mercenaries—would play a significant role in both keeping the Romans out of Germania and in keeping the Roman Empire alive long after the majority of the original Roman stock had vanished.

After taking power in Rome, Caesar tried to subdue the still rebellious Celts who lived in the Alps north of Italy. It took some thirty years for the Roman legions to finally quell these hardy mountain dwelling people, and afterward their lands were formally annexed to Rome.

### Third Roman Invasion—Elbe River Reached

By 15 BC, the Roman Empire's borders extended as far north as the Danube River and as far east as the Rhine, but over the latter river, hostile Germans still lurked. In 12 BC, the Romans under General

Drusus launched a new attempt to invade the German heartland. Although the Germans put up stiff resistance and inflicted several major defeats upon the Roman forces, Drusus defeated the major German tribes and in three years managed to reach the Elbe River in central Germania.

At the height of his victories, Drusus died after falling off his horse. He was replaced by General Tiberius (who was later to become emperor) and by 7 BC, most of the territory between the Rhine and Weser Rivers had been seized. The Roman military machine seemed unstoppable, and it even pushed on to some lands beyond the Weser River, inhabited by a tribe known as the Cherusci.

On all fronts, the Germans were forced to fall back toward the east over the Elbe River, or face subjugation by the Romans. It seemed that it was only a matter of time and the Germans would also suffer the fate of the Gauls in France. Many of the cruel tactics employed by Caesar in France were used against defeated German tribes under Roman control.

### Hermann Cherusci—Trained by the Roman Army

However, the Roman policy of drawing subjugated peoples into the administration of their own territories and Romanizing them was applied in Germania as well. In 1 AD, two young Cherusci princes, the sons of the king of that tribe, were selected to be sent to Rome and commissioned in the Roman army.

One of the brothers became completely Romanized and took on the name Flavius, while the other kept his German name, Hermann, although the Romans called him Arminius. Hermann served five years in a Roman legion, became a Roman citizen, and was employed on active service in two expeditions against other rebellious colonies. All the while, he retained his German roots, unlike his brother.

Hermann returned to his homeland in 8 AD as a senior soldier and administrator in the region under the Roman general, Varus. Never once did the Romans suspect Hermann's true intentions, which were to throw the Romans out of his homeland.

### Battle of Teutoburger Wald—Defeat Halts Roman Expansion

As soon as he was in a position to act, Hermann set about organizing a rebellion amongst the Germans. Using his position as a German prince to influence a large number of German tribes, Hermann

## ROMANIZATION OF GERMANY HALTED— TEUTOBURGER WALD 9 AD

*The 9 AD Battle of Teutoburger Wald marked a turning point for the Roman Empire in the West. Hermann Cherusker was a Romanized German who, once appointed to a senior post in the Roman army, used his position as a German prince to organize a rebellion against Roman rule in Germany. After creating a diversion and tricking the main occupying Roman army into penetrating a forest near the present day town of Detmold, Hermann's forces ambushed the Romans. After days of intense hit and run attacks, fifteen thousand Romans were killed and the few survivors fled over the Rhine River which henceforth became the German/Roman border.*

secretly began preparing his own great German army—no doubt using much of what he had learned during his training in the Roman army. He was able to recruit a large number of Germans in the area who were also serving in the Roman army, all of whom supported his dream of expelling the Romans from Germany.

In 9 AD, Varus's Roman army was encamped west of the Weser River in the modern day German state of North Rhine Westphalia. Hermann arranged to have a German tribe start a diversionary battle to the east. Always ready to respond to any sign of trouble, Varus and the Roman army set off in that direction.

Hermann put his plan into action. Gathering up his secretly recruited army, he set out in pursuit of Varus. The Germans caught up with the unsuspecting Roman column in the middle of the Teutoburg Forest, near the present day town of Detmold. In the forest, Hermann's forces ambushed the Romans.

For three days the battle raged, with Hermann employing unusual guerrilla tactics, repeatedly attacking and then suddenly withdrawing into the forest before the Romans could create their set battle formations. Hermann knew from his training in the Roman army that his enenies did not have an adequate defense against this tactic. After three days of continuous ambushes, they were exhausted. No sleep, constant attacks by German raiders, and unfamiliar territory took their toll and the Roman lines broke.

Only a handful of Roman soldiers escaped from the forest to tell the tale. Most were killed in combat. Those who were captured suffered the fate of many Germans and Celts who had earlier fallen into Roman hands—they were killed on the spot.

News of the victory spread throughout occupied Germania, sparking off a rebellion which forced the Romans to retreat all the way back to the western side of the Rhine River once again. The war with the German tribes dragged on for eight more years, but by 17 AD, the Romans had accepted the Rhine River as the formal border between Germania and Rome. Germany was never to be invaded again by the Romans.

Although Hermann had succeeded in uniting the German tribes against Rome, this unity was short-lived. Once the Romans had been driven from their land, the German tribes lost little time in lapsing back into intertribal warfare. Hermann was assassinated in 21 AD—by a German. Thus Germania once again became a land of fierce and warlike tribes, all battling with each other for territory as they had done before the advent of the Roman incursions.

## QUINCTILIUS VARUS AND THE THREE LOST LEGIONS OF GERMANIA

*Publius Quinctilius Varus (46 BC–9 AD), the Roman general who was defeated and killed by Hermann's forces at the Battle of the Teutoburger Wald. Varus had a distinguished career prior to his death, being appointed governor of the Roman province of Africa (from where this coin comes) and of Syria. He also helped suppress a Jewish rebellion in Palestine after the death of Rome's client king Herod the Great in 4 BC.*

*In 7 AD, Varus was appointed to govern the fledgling colony of Germania. In 9 AD, Varus had stationed his armies near the Weser River with his three legions, the Seventeenth, the Eighteenth, and the Nineteenth. Tricked into an ambush by the Germanics under Hermann, the legions were utterly defeated and Varus killed. The last of the eagle standards from the lost legions were only recovered in 42 AD. The Romans never again used those legion numbers due to the shame associated with the enormity of the defeat. According to the biographer Suetonius, the Roman emperor Augustus, upon hearing the news, tore his clothes, refused to cut his hair for months and, for years afterwards was heard to moan, "Quinctilius Varus, give me back my Legions!"*

### "A Pure and Unmixed Race"—Tacitus Describes the Germans

The Roman historian Tacitus, writing during the first century AD, made the following insightful remarks on the racial nature of the Germans: *"I concur in opinion with those who deem the Germans never to have intermarried with other nations but to be a pure and unmixed race, stamped with a distinct character. Hence, a family likeness pervades the whole, though their numbers are great. Their eyes are stern and blue, their hair ruddy, and their bodies large."*

In what became a major twist of irony, Rome

**MONUMENT TO HERMAN'S VICTORY**

*The Hermannsdenkmal (or Hermann monument), located in the Teutoburg Forest, North Rhine Westphalia. It was built near the site of the Battle of the Teutoburger Wald in which the Germanic tribes under Hermann defeated a Roman army in 9 AD, effectively halting Roman expansion into Germania.*

began to rely more and more on German and Celtic mercenaries to fill the ranks of its armies. This was caused by the demographic changes at work within Italy which saw declining numbers of Romans. Rome, with its status as capital of the empire, had acted as a magnet for slaves and immigrants from all over the known world, but particularly from the Middle East.

### Rome Increasingly Mixed—Blonds Decline

By the time of the Battle of Teutoburger Wald, the Roman nobility was already in terminal decline. Even though they had tried to maintain their original racial heritage, their numbers had been reduced. This was due in part to their declined fertility levels, which were a result of a combination of factors including the use of lead water pipes and the use of sapa (lead acetate) as a skin lightener (a valuable racial indicator in itself). High lead intake has the side effect of sterility, an

**GERMAN MERCENARIES FILL ROMAN ARMIES**

*A German cavalryman serving in the Roman army. The Roman army began to rely heavily on German mercenaries to fill its ranks as white Roman numbers declined. From Trajan's Column in Rome.*

issue which is noted as having plagued the Roman upper classes.

By the end of the second century AD, the lower classes of Roman society had reached the point where a significant number had been replaced by what were in effect mixed or nonwhite racial types gathered from the four corners of the empire.

In his book, *The Gallic War,* Caesar, who was himself a Nordic type, compared the Romans of that time with the Gauls, remarking how blond the Gauls were and, in comparison with the Romans, how tall they were. (Caesar went on to describe Celts in Britain as being blond, but not so much as their Celtic brethren in Gaul.) This is not to say that Rome of this time was a completely nonwhite city—there remained a large number of whites, but the demographic trend was most certainly against them.

This had implications for the recruitment of Romans for their army: with increasing numbers of foreigners in Rome, the number of volunteers for military service declined dramatically.

Although they had taken on the dress of Roman civilization, they either refused to serve in the army or were simply not up to the exacting physical demands, preferring mercantile pursuits to the rigors of a military life.

### German Mercenaries Fill the Roman Army—Average "Roman" Soldier's Height Increases

The Germans and Celts therefore ended up being the primary source of recruits for the Roman armies. This is not surprising, considering that in racial terms they were much closer to the original Romans than the majority of inhabitants of Rome from the second century AD onward.

By the time Caesar's conquests of the Celts had ended, Roman records show that the average height of the Roman soldier had been lowered to around five feet. As the number of German and Celtic mercenaries increased in the Roman army, the average height began to rise. By 300 AD, the average height had risen to around five feet five inches, an indication that the racial type of the average soldier had changed substantially.

So it was that the "Roman" armies began to fill up with non-Roman soldiers. Romanized Germans and Celts formed a significant number, possibly even a majority, of foot soldiers and commanding officers. These Romanized Germans and Celts were to play a significant role in the remaining years of the Western Roman Empire. It was they who, predictably, formed the backbone of the resistance to the last "barbarian" invasions which saw the final physical fall of Rome.

A Romanized German soldier was the last (self-declared) emperor in Rome. By that date (476 AD), the last true original Romans had for all practical purposes disappeared, having been swallowed up in a mass of immigrants from all regions of the empire.

## *New Germanic Invasions—Franks, Saxons, and the Goths*

In the second century AD, German tribes went on the offensive against Rome and crossed the Danube River. They were bloodily defeated by a Roman army, which contained a significant number of German and Celtic mercenaries. During the third and fourth centuries, German tribes called the Franks and the Saxons also raided Roman settlements in France and Britain respectively.

These smaller incursions continued until the final chapter in the saga of the German-Roman Wars was written by the Goths, who featured prominently in Rome's final military defeat.

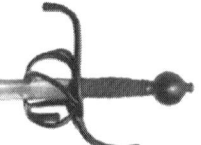

# CHAPTER FIFTEEN

# Racial Cauldron—Rome and the Middle East

**The story of Roman expansion to the east is as dramatic as the conquering of western Europe, but there was one critical difference with a hugely important consequence. It was the extension of the empire's borders to the east which ultimately led to its downfall, as this was the gateway for vast numbers of people to be drawn to Rome who shared a different genetic inheritance than the original founders.**

As had been the case with every great civilization before it, Rome fell because the original people who created the empire disappeared. They were submerged into a mass of foreigners, replaced by immigrants and the descendants of slaves brought in from all over North Africa, the wider Mediterranean, and the Middle East.

### Gradual Dissolution of the Indo-Europeans

Prior to the Roman expansion into the Middle East, the process of racial integration in that region had proceeded apace. Original Indo-European and Old European Mediterranean types had all but vanished in North Africa and the Middle East by the year 100 BC. In the space of a few hundred years, these white peoples had been submerged into the far faster breeding Semitic, Arabic, and Asian elements filling up the region.

### Blue Eyed Persians Visit India 600 BC

One example of how the whites were submerged in the Middle East can be seen with the Indo-European origin Persians, who reached present-day Azerbaijan around the year 900 BC. After mixing with another less

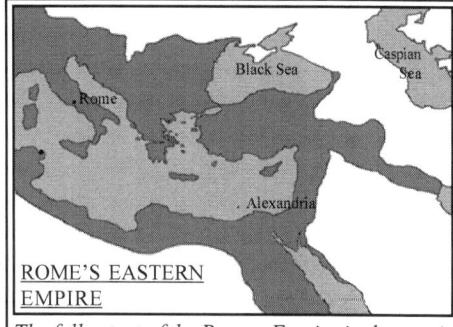

ROME'S EASTERN EMPIRE

*The full extent of the Roman Empire in the east is shown here: from the Tigris-Euphrates Rivers to the southern reaches of the Nile—masses of mixed race peoples from this region were given access to Rome.*

## ROMAN ENGINEERING GENIUS IN AFRICA

*The Roman aqueduct at Cherchel on the Algerian coast, North Africa. Serving the city of Caesarea, it was built in three superimposed tiers of arches and was the largest work of its kind to be constructed on the African continent. The deserted ruin stands as evidence of how, once the original white Roman genes had been dissipated into the local mixed race inhabitants, the drive to create and maintain such structures vanished with them.*

numerous Indo-European tribe, the Medes, the descendants of these peoples established their rule over a large territory including modern day Iran, a large part of Iraq, and other land extending as far as modern southern Turkey.

In 600 BC, Persian envoys visited India, and their visit was recorded in a series of paintings made by Indian artists in Bombay (and which are on view today in the Ajanta caves outside that city). The racial makeup of the envoys tells an interesting story. Of the three Persians depicted, one has blond hair and blue eyes, the second has dark hair and blue eyes, and the third has dark hair, dark eyes, and is obviously more Semitic in appearance. This is a good indicator of the racial demographics at work in Persia at this time. Today, a few widely dispersed examples of light colored eyes and hair amongst the overwhelmingly Arabic population of the Middle East are the only reminders of the ancient rulers of this territory.

This scenario was replicated across the entire region. The Indo-European tribes and the Old European Mediterranean peoples, who had together provided the impetus for the great ancient civilizations, had for all practical purposes, disappeared by the time that the Romans started pushing east. The end result of these racial changes was that by

**PETRA FLOURISHES UNDER ROMAN RULE**

*The famous "rock city" of Petra, in modern Jordan, flourished under Roman rule and many incredible building works were carried out—including this famous "rock temple" cut out of a cliff.*

the time of the Roman Empire, the native population of the Middle East was already racially very mixed.

## Mixed Race Pontus Threaten Rome 110 BC

The first Roman move east came about when the king of Pergamum, a state which existed to the east of the Roman borders, turned his nation over to Roman rule in terms of his will upon his death. Next to be occupied by the Romans was a part of western Turkey called western Cilicia, which was annexed as part of an anti-piracy campaign in 102 BC. Shortly thereafter, Ptolemaic Egypt and the states of central Anatolia (eastern Turkey) became formal vassals of Rome.

A belligerent mixed-race people, the Pontus, invaded the lands to the east of the Roman Empire in 110 BC. They swept through much of northern Turkey and occupied land around the Black Sea, including the Crimea. Eventually they penetrated part of Roman ruled Greece. The Roman emperor Sulla ordered an army east and the Pontus were defeated. The act of pursuing the invaders led to Roman rule being extended to northern Turkey and large parts of land around the Black Sea.

By 66 BC, relations between the Pontus and Rome had once again deteriorated and war broke out. This time the Roman general Pompey formally annexed the Pontus kingdom. This extended Rome's reach into the southern part of Crimea and into the Caucasus region between the Black and Caspian Seas.

## Syria and North Africa

To the south, Syria was made a Roman province, along with Palestine and even a slice of the Arabian peninsula extending nearly halfway down the Red Sea, including for the first time vast numbers of Arabic Semites in their original homeland in the Arabian peninsula.

In 50 BC, Caesar swept to power in Rome. General Pompey gathered together an army in Greece to try and dislodge him, but was defeated (with the help of six thousand German mercenaries) at the battle of Pharsus in 48 BC.

Caesar went on to march right through North Africa in 46 BC. This meant that with the exception of Spain and parts of Greece, all of the areas collected into Caesar's grasp by his astounding series of military campaigns had nonwhite majorities.

Caesar's successors also extended Roman control over other parts of the Middle East. Octavian Augustus reinforced Roman rule in Turkey and extended the empire's borders deep into the Caucasus. Roman vassal states extended as far as a few hundred miles from the Caspian Sea.

### Romanizing of Arabic Semites Implemented

The vast number of Arabic and mixed racial types present in the Middle East and North Africa were all put through the Romanizing process. Within the space of a few decades they were allowed to elect senators to the Roman senate in Rome, and their sheer weight of numbers

**TIMGAD, ALGERIA—ROME'S LOST AFRICAN CITY**

*The Roman city of Timgad, in modern day Algeria, stands today as a massive ruin, but when the Romans occupied the region it was one of their major centers on the North African coast. However, the province of Africa was the first step in the undoing of the Roman Empire. As it spread its borders ever more eastward, it started incorporating more and more nonwhite peoples into its borders. This infusion of non-Romans eventually caused the empire to lose its racial homogeneity and fall.*

meant that true Romans soon made up a minority of senators in the capital of the empire. Under these conditions, it takes no imagination to understand how the relatively small group of original Romans lost control of the racial makeup of Rome.

It was demographically impossible for the Romans alone to supply the manpower to run such a vast area. As a result, they were forced to Romanize the local population and recruit soldiers and tradesmen from them. Very often, only the most senior civil servants in the Roman provinces were actually originally from Rome—and in many cases, even they were replaced in the course of time by locals.

Eventually the logical step was taken by the emperor, Caracalla, in 212 AD, when he gave all free men in the empire Roman citizenship. The racial implications of this step were important and were discussed in a previous chapter. The most famous of these "new citizens" was Philip the Arab, who was a Syrian-born Roman citizen who became emperor.

### Palestine 4 AD—Jews Petition for Inclusion

The Jewish tribes in Palestine (who were originally a Semitic tribe, but had, like almost all the peoples in that region, been fairly heavily mixed with other racial groups over the course of time) had been independent since shaking off the declining Seleucid kingdom in 129 BC.

The Jews maintained their independence until 4 BC, when their king, Herod, died. Anarchy broke out in the territory, and eventually a group of Jews petitioned Rome to occupy Palestine and make it into a Roman province so that order could be restored. This duly happened, and from 4 AD onward, a large portion of Palestine, known as Judea, became part of the empire.

### Trajan Crushes the Parthian Revolt in Syria

In 66 BC, the mixed race Parthians (resident in Syria, Iran, and Iraq) broke out in open revolt against Roman rule. This rebellion sparked a similar uprising in Judea, where groups of nationalist Jews had decided to try and eject the Romans.

A Roman general in charge of one of the armies in Palestine, Vespian, suppressed the Jewish revolt, and then, instead of turning his attention to the Parthians, returned to Rome to suppress the anarchy and civil strife which had followed the suicide of Emperor Nero.

The Parthians took advantage of the chaos to declare themselves independent, and for a while all of modern Iraq and all of Iran became independent of Roman rule. The only consolation for the empire was that other Roman vassal kingdoms now extended as far as the Caspian Sea.

Parthian independence did not last long. The Roman emperor, Trajan (98–117 AD), finally launched a counterattack, using an army largely comprised of German and Gaulish mercenaries. Trajan's army defeated the Parthians, and marched as far east as the Tigris and Euphrates River basin, in what is today called Kuwait.

The very next emperor, Hadrian, realized that the Roman legions were overextending themselves. He embarked upon a deliberate program of withdrawal and consolidation, and the Roman armies were withdrawn to the easternmost point of the Euphrates River, near the present day Turkish border.

### Roman Control Disintegrates Circa 200 AD

After 200 AD, the enemies of Rome were battering at the gates. In the north, on the borders with Germania, one of the last of the great Indo-European invasions had created a new and powerful force in the form of the Goths. Spreading out across Germania, the Goths soon started raiding Roman outposts in Gaul and in the east, crossing the Danube River.

Some of their racial cousins created a Gothic power in southern Russia, which also beat upon the doors of the Roman provinces in the Black Sea basin. The Romans barely clung to their strong points under the new wave of attacks.

**"FAKE" PHARAOH— ROMANIZED EGYPT**

*Very often, confusion exists in the public mind over what exactly was ancient Egyptian and what was not. This is understandable if the scene below is studied. Appearing to be a relief from Egyptian antiquity, it is in fact a representation of Cleopatra and Julius Caesar, with their son, Caesarion. The relief was made during Caesar's lifetime. Cleopatra was the last of the Ptolemies, a dynasty set up by one of Alexander the Great's generals. The Ptolemies took on the ways and customs of the ancient Egyptians, even down to art and dress. This then is the reason why this image of Julius Caesar can be found at the Temple of Hathor in Dendra, Egypt.*

## DARK FACES FROM ROMAN EGYPT SIGNAL FATE OF THE EMPIRE

*Roman controlled Egypt became one of the prime examples of how nonwhites filled up the borders of the Roman Empire after that nation annexed the Middle East. Here are two examples—both portraits on coffins—dating from 200 AD in Roman Egypt. The faces of both men show the very clear effects of racial mixing—slowly but surely the nonwhite element of the lands in the Middle Eastern part of the Roman Empire grew and seeped toward Rome. Within a short period of time, the scattered Romans in the Middle East were racially disintegrated, spelling the doom of the empire.*

Meanwhile, in the east, the Parthians had been finally overthrown by the mixed race Persians, who began to make excursions into Roman territory. Around 258 AD, the Persians broke the power of many important Roman vassal states, overrunning Armenia and Syria. The Roman citadel of Antioch was sacked in 260 AD.

In Africa, Roman control fared no better. In 268 AD, the Syrians seceded from the empire and Roman forces in Egypt lost control over the southernmost parts of that land. The Eastern Empire seemed on the point of collapse under the pressure of continual native rebellions which were compounded by the inability of the locally recruited "Roman" armies to suppress the uprisings.

### *"Roman" Army in Mesopotamia Composed Mainly of German Mercenaries*

Raising new mercenary armies in Gaul and Germania, the Roman general, Caesar Galerius, pursued a successful war against Persia in 297 AD, occupying half of Mesopotamia.

This remained the eastern frontier of the empire until 626 AD, when the Persians once again forced a contraction of the Eastern Empire's borders.

By 626 AD, the Roman Empire had been divided into East and West. Like the Western Romans, the Romans in the Eastern Empire barely resembled the original Romans, and relied greatly on German and even Viking mercenaries (the Eastern Roman emperor's private guard was composed exclusively of Viking mercenaries) to hold their borders against their Persian enemies.

The Eastern Empire and the Persians were kept so busy in a long drawn out war that neither of them took any notice—until it was too late—of the rise of Islam in the south. This power would eventually overrun the last parts of the Eastern Roman Empire.

# CHAPTER SIXTEEN

# By Stealth and Steel—Christianity

**The rise of Christianity as the dominant religion of post-Roman Europe played a major role in shaping the course of history, not only on that continent but also in all parts of the world to which European people spread.**

**The story of the origins of this remarkable religion—and its influence on the course of civilization, therefore deserves a full examination.**

## Rome's Pontifex Maximus—An Important Position

**AUGUSTUS WEARING THE ROBES OF THE OFFICE OF PONTIFEX MAXIMUS**

*A statue from circa 20 BC shows Octavian Augustus wearing the robes of office of Pontifex Maximus ("Greatest Pontiff"), the high priest of the ancient Roman College of Pontiffs. A religious office under the early Roman Republic, it was later absorbed into the Imperial office. In an attempt to provide some sort of cultural unity, the emperor became chief priest of all the religions in Rome. The religion followed personally by the emperor came to be regarded as the most desirable amongst the citizens, and this played a major role in helping to popularize Christianity after the emperor Constantine converted to that faith.*

Religion in pre-Christian Roman times was marked by diversity. There was never really a single theme in the worship of any particular god or set of gods, and it remained very much a haphazard collection of local beliefs, varying greatly from region to region.

It was only after the time of the emperor Octavian Augustus that any formalization of religious beliefs came into being. After Octavian, all the Roman emperors were known by the title of *Pontifex Maximus* or "Greatest Pontiff."

The idea of this title was that the emperor would be the formal head of whatever particular cult happened to be the most popular at that time in the empire. This was not limited to a single religion—it could also be any number of beliefs which were in existence simultaneously. The Pontifex Maximus position was the Romans' attempt to try and create some sort of religious unity, although all cults were accorded equal status.

The position of the emperor as chief priest of what was deemed to be the unofficial state religion or religions was to have major consequences. Very often, a cult either gained or lost popularity solely because of the emperor's interest in it.

One of the more obvious examples occurred when the Macedonian queen of Egypt, Cleopatra, visited Rome. The presence of somebody thought to be an Egyptian queen (she was, of course, not of Egyptian stock but actually Macedonian) sparked off a major revival in the ancient Egyptian cult of Isis, which eventually died out once again.

### Christianity Originates in the Middle East

Before it came to dominance, Christianity was merely one more of these numerous cults, and, like many of its competitors, originated in the Middle Eastern reaches of the empire, in the Roman province of Judea (also known as Palestine).

Following the conquests of Alexander the Great, Palestine had been ruled intermittently by either the Ptolemies or the Seleucids, both descendants of Alexander's generals of the same name. It was while under the rule of the Seleucids that the great temple in Jerusalem was built as a center for the Jewish religion, a surviving wall of which is today known as the Wailing Wall.

The Semitic speaking peoples living in Palestine were known as Jews, a tribe which had been in existence for many centuries prior to this. What set the Jews apart from their neighbors was their religion, which, in contrast to their neighbors, was monotheistic. Its one god, Jahweh or Jehovah, was, and still is, central to the Jewish religion, although monotheism originated with the ancient Egyptian pharaoh Akhenaton. Other religions all had a pantheon of gods, each looking after a particular aspect of life on earth and in the beyond.

### The Jewish Rebellion against Seleucid Rule 168 BC

Seleucid rule in Palestine caused many Jews to take on the ways and even the Greek language of their rulers. This led them into conflict with the more nationalistic Jews, and a minor skirmish broke out between these two groups in 168 BC. The fighting provoked the ruling Seleucids into trying to stamp out the Jewish religion. Amongst their measures, they ordered the Jewish temple in Jerusalem to be stripped of its Judaic artifacts and dedicated to the worship of the Greek god Zeus.

The Jews rebelled at this order, and after a short military conflict, were able to exact partial independence from the Seleucids in 142 BC, and full independence in 129 BC. The leader of the Jewish rebels was one Judas Maccabeus, and he became the first Jewish king in Palestine, creating the Maccabean dynasty which lasted until 64 BC.

## Romans Invited into Palestine 64 BC

Independence in Judea did not bring stability, and the Jewish state was continually wracked by internal dissent and rebellion. In the midst of one of the civil wars, a group of Jews appealed for help from the Roman general Pompey, whose army was completing the conquest of Turkey and Syria at the time. He agreed to help, and Palestine was occupied as a Roman protectorate in 64 BC.

### CITY OF CAESAREA BUILT BY HEROD TO HONOR ROMANS

*The extent of Roman power in Palestine is illustrated in the ruins of the city of Caesarea Palaestina, situated in northern Israel on the Mediterranean coast. Built on the ruins of an earlier settlement by the Jewish King Herod to honor the Roman emperor around 25 BC, the city contained a deep sea harbor, markets, wide roads, baths, temples to Rome and Augustus, and imposing public buildings including an amphitheater. Every five years the city hosted major sports competitions, gladiator games, and theatrical productions. The theater was the first of its kind in Palestine, and was maintained throughout the Roman and much of the Byzantine eras. It had a seating capacity of around four thousand and is used to this day.*

True to their long established practice, the Romans immediately began Romanizing the Jews and recruiting locals to run the province. In this way, the Roman senate appointed the Jew Herod as king of Judea in 37 BC, who ruled until his death in 4 BC. After his death, Judea was divided up into smaller units, most of which were ruled by other Roman appointed governors.

### *Jews Move to Rome—First Expulsion 19 AD*

During this time some Jews immigrated to Rome, making use of the traditional lack of Roman control over entry into the city. However, their presence aroused a marked anti-Semitism even amongst the fairly easygoing Romans. In the year 19 AD, the Jews were to experience for the first time a situation with which they would later become familiar. In that year, the Roman emperor Tiberius formally barred all Jews from Rome and deported all those he could find in the city.

This ban on Jews only lasted a few years, for it was not long before they, along with ever increasing numbers of other foreigners from all parts of the empire, once again took up residence in Rome. By this time, Jews had started settling in other parts of the Middle East, Asia Minor, North Africa, and Egypt, in each of these places attracting the enmity of the local populations.

### *Jewish Revolt—"Horrid Cruelties"*

In Palestine itself, dissension was always brewing. In 66 AD, nationalist Jews rebelled against Roman rule and the Roman garrison in Jerusalem were slaughtered. The revolt spread quickly to all parts of the province, fanned by a marked hatred for Rome.

This Jewish hatred for the original Roman Empire was well documented to the point where the famous English historian Edward Gibbon, in his classic work, *The Decline and Fall of the Roman*

**EMPEROR TITUS—CRUSHES JEWS AND TRIGGERS DIASPORA**

*The emperor Titus—Roman conqueror of the Jews and destroyer of Jerusalem, an act accomplished in 70 AD. In 68 AD, the Jews rebelled against Roman rule, despite having originally asked the Romans to occupy that land to bring order and peace to it. Roman revenge for the Jewish vacillation was severe—the Jews were forbidden to enter Jerusalem upon pain of death and dispersed from Palestine into North Africa and the Middle East in a movement known as the Diaspora. This laid the basis for the great Jewish immigration into Europe.*

*Empire* (Lippincourt, Philadelphia, 1878, vol. 2, page 4), had the following to say: *"From the reign of Nero to that of Antoninus Pius, the Jews discovered a fierce impatience of the dominion of Rome, which repeatedly broke out in the most furious massacres and insurrections. Humanity is shocked at the recital of horrid cruelties which they committed in the cities of Egypt, of Cyria, and of Cyrene, where they dwelt in treacherous friendship with the unsuspecting natives; and we are tempted to applaud the severe retaliation which was exercised by the arms of the Legions against a race of fanatics whose dire and credulous superstition seemed to render them the implacable enemies not only of the Roman government, but of all human kind."*

### MASADA—JEWISH REBELLION ENDS

*The hilltop fort of Masada, Israel. During the course of the Jewish rebellion (which started in 68 AD), Roman legions occupied Jerusalem in 70 AD. They drove out or killed the Jews in the city, and about one thousand remaining Jewish rebels fled to the remote mountain fort. Undeterred, the Romans followed them and laid siege to the rebel stronghold. After a two year siege, during which the Romans built a massive earth ramp all the way up the one side of the mountain (which can still be seen in the foreground), all but seven of the Jews committed suicide rather than being taken alive, fully aware of the fate that awaited them should they be captured by the avenging Romans.*

It was, therefore, not surprising that the Romans sent an army to quell a new uprising in 68 AD. This successfully squashed the Jewish rebellion in 70 AD, and the last of the Jewish rebels were besieged at the mountaintop fort of Masada.

After a lengthy siege, Masada fell to the Romans in 73 AD. Palestine remained under nominal Roman control for some eight hundred years thereafter, first as part of the Western Roman Empire, and then as part of the Eastern Roman Empire.

## Titus Suppresses Jewish Revolt in Palestine—Triggers Diaspora 70 AD

The suppression of the 70 AD rebellion had another important consequence. The Romans, furious at the continued rebellions, renamed Jerusalem Ælia Capitolina and outlawed the practice of Judaism. Jews were forbidden entrance to the city under pain of death. As a result, the Jews were scattered throughout the world in a movement known as the Diaspora. A large number went north into southern Russia, mixing with local tribes

**ROMANS DISPLAY JEWISH TROPHIES ON ARCH OF TITUS FROM VICTORIOUS CAMPAIGN IN PALESTINE**

*The crushing of the Jewish revolt in 68 AD by a Roman army was commemorated as a great feat of arms. On the Arch of Titus, erected in Rome and still standing to this day, Roman soldiers are shown bringing Jewish trophies (note the menorah taken from the Jewish temple in Jerusalem) back to Rome.*

along the way and eventually penetrating into eastern and central Europe. A number of Jews went out along Turkey and settled in Rome, while a small number settled in Gaul. However, not all Jews went north—a significant portion went west along the North African coast, setting up Jewish communities all the way to Tunisia, and finally crossing into southern Spain.

### Origin of the Ashkenazim and Sephardim Division in Jewry

The Jews who went to Europe via the east absorbed a substantial amount of European blood, and became known as the Ashkenazim, or European Jews. Those who settled in North Africa became known as the Sephardim. This division in Jewry exists to this day, and is most marked in Israel where the two communities, the Ashkenazim or "light" Jews and the Sephardim or "dark" Jews (dark because they did not mix with the number of Europeans to the same extent that the Ashkenazim did) tend to vote for different Israeli political parties. Only their unique religion has kept them bound together after a fashion, although even this is divided into subsects.

### Judaism—Uniquely Racial Religion

Although Christianity sprang from Judaism, its Jewish adherents were at first fiercely persecuted by the Jewish religious leaders. This was linked to the fact that Judaism had one particularly unique trait in that it was the first specifically racial religion. While all other religions had no limitations on who could become adherents, Judaism was limited by blood inheritance.

The uniqueness of the Jewish god was that he was a god only for the Jews, not for anyone else. Biological laws of descent were built into Judaism as divinely inspired laws. To this day, there is a rule that only someone born of a Jewish mother can be a Jew.

While some less strict Jewish communities have relaxed this rule to allow conversions from other faiths, the orthodox Jewish community follows this law to the letter. It is still followed to this day in Israel as citizenship is based exclusively on Jewish descent and not national origin.

### *Essene Beliefs—Origins of Christianity*

While this racial religion unquestionably helped to preserve the Jewish identity, it irked some of them, who felt that their god was for all people, and not just the Jews. Around the year 100 BC, this dissenting group founded a new sect. It was loosely based on parts of the Talmud and introduced some new ideas to Judaism, most notably that their god was for all people.

This dissenting group of Jews became known as the Essenes. They developed a whole series of books relating to morals and lifestyles, including a monastic tradition, and pacifism. Most notably, they claimed to have a teacher, who they called the "Teacher of Righteousness," who, they said, had been murdered and then rose from the dead.

The universality of their version of Jahweh (that he was a god for all people, not just for the Jews) remained the biggest point of difference between the Essenes and mainstream

**ESSENE'S DEAD SEA SCROLLS— OLDEST BIBLICAL TEXTS**

*The Book of Isaiah, as laid out in the Dead Sea Scrolls, discovered in Palestine in 1947. They were the holy books of a subsect of Jews called the Essenes, who lived in the first century BC. The Essenes were persecuted by other Jews, who disagreed violently with the Essene belief that the Jewish god, Yahweh, was actually a god for all people, and not just the Jews. Many of the concepts which were later to become fundamental to Christianity were contained in the Essene religion. They even had an allegorical story about a wise prophet who was killed and then rose from the dead, known to them as the "Teacher of Righteousness."*

Judaism. This ideological clash eventually brought the Essenes into open conflict with their fellow Jews, and the rabbinical leaders urged the Jews to stamp out the new cult.

Although it is not recorded what happened to the Essenes in Judea (it is presumed that the Jewish suppression worked in that region), the Essene tradition lived on amongst a small group of Jews, most of whom eventually left Palestine for more receptive ears elsewhere in the Roman Empire.

In Judea, the Essenes all but vanished, leaving behind only some of their holy books which they hid in caves around the Dead Sea. It was these books, discovered by chance in 1947, which become known as the Dead Sea Scrolls.

The basic ideology and format which the Essenes created laid the basis for what later became Christianity. It combined three major elements: the base beliefs of Judaism (today the Bible's Old Testament), The Indo-Aryan Zoroastrian (Persian) belief of heaven and hell (which does not appear in the Old Testament), and the Essene story of a killed and resurrected leader. From these strands, the religion was reworked and reformulated until it finally became Christianity.

### *Jesus Christ—No Contemporary Evidence*

It is an important but little known fact that there is no contemporary (from his time) evidence showing that the biblical figure of Jesus Christ actually existed. The first source of information about the person who became known as Jesus Christ are the Gospels of the Bible's New Testament. As these works only appeared some 80 to 120 years after Christ's death, they are not contemporaneous.

It is therefore possible that the person who was deified by Christianity could be a composite character based on the stories surrounding several Essene leaders, particularly the one they called the "Teacher of Righteousness."

The first time that the name Jesus Christ appears in any Roman records (and they were generally meticulous in record keeping) is the book *The Jewish Wars,* by Josephus, a Romanized Jew, who was commissioned to write a history of the Jewish rebellion. Josephus's work was first published in 90 AD.

Other researchers have claimed that even this reference is a later addition to Josephus's work, citing irregularities in the actual passage. In the disputed passage, Josephus makes mention of a small sect of Jews who claim to follow a messiah figure called Jesus, but the mention is brief and in passing. In any event, by the time of Christ's alleged death (circa 33 AD) Christianity had very few followers, especially amongst the Jews themselves, who regarded the Christian philosophy as nothing but a reworking of the Essene cult, and did their best to silence it.

### Saul of Tarsus Launches Christianity and Is Beheaded by Nero

One of the most zealous of these Jewish persecutors of the Essene ideology was a man by the name of Saul of Tarsus. He is unique in that he is the one major character who features in the New Testament for whom contemporaneous evidence does exist.

At some stage, according to the Bible, Saul experienced a vision and was persuaded that the Christian religion which he had been suppressing was actually correct. Saul then changed his name to Paul and set off on long evangelistic tours of Asia Minor, Cyprus, and Greece, attracting small bands of followers and writing proselytizing pieces along the way.

Returning to preach in Jerusalem, he was violently attacked by his fellow Jews and was imprisoned for two years. Following an appeal to the Roman emperor, Paul was transferred to Rome in 60 AD. Placed under house arrest, he was eventually beheaded by the emperor Nero, who developed a particular hatred for the new religion. Paul did much to create and solidify the groundwork for Christianity, and many of his writings were taken up into the New Testament.

### Roman Persecution and Tolerance of Christianity

The official Roman attitude to religion was one of tolerance—except where they were openly subversive to Roman rule. Early Christians refused to take part in any Roman state ceremonies (viewing them as pagan) and would not serve in the army or hold public office, echoing the Essene beliefs of a century earlier.

This attitude prompted the Roman leadership to begin a program of persecution against the Christians. The first major campaign was launched by the emperor Decius in 250 AD and the last by Diocletian in 302 AD. Persecution had opposite the desired effect on a religion which thrived on martyrdom, and it steadily gained new adherents despite the state's attempts to stamp it out.

The Christian religion had to compete for supremacy with a number of other religions in the Middle East and the Roman Empire. It

## NERO—MALIGNED ENEMY OF CHRISTIANITY

*The Roman emperor Nero reigned from 37 AD to 68 AD, and was a great persecutor of Christianity, overseeing the throwing of Christians to the lions in the Coliseum amongst other things. As a result, later historical accounts of his life tend to be biased, leading to his portrayal as the personification of evil. In July 64 AD, two-thirds of Rome burned while Nero was at Antium. Biased versions of history have usually held that he either set the fire—something that was impossible, as he was not present—or that he played the fiddle while Rome burned (the fiddle was not invented until 1500 years after his death). Nero claimed to have proof that Christians had set the fire, and persecuted them even more vigorously after the event. In contrast to his image as an uncaring madman, he ordered that all the people made homeless as a result of the fire be housed and provided with grain, all at state expense. He then had the city rebuilt with fire precautions. Nero was also an accomplished artist and man of letters, and personally acted in several important plays of the time. He was emperor when the Jewish revolt in Palestine broke out. As a result of internal politics, in 68 AD the Gallic and Spanish legions, along with the Praetorian Guards rose against him, and he fled Rome. Declared a public enemy by the senate, he committed suicide on June 9, 68 AD.*

only grew large enough to be a serious contender after the emperor Galerius issued an Edict of Toleration in 311, making Christianity legal in the eastern part of the empire.

## *Constantine's Conversion 312 AD*

The breakthrough for Christianity in the Roman world came with the emperor Constantine's conversion to that religion in 312 AD. The background to his conversion—or, as many scholars have claimed, his alleged conversion—is shrouded in controversy.

It is commonly claimed that Constantine, while engaged in battle with a rival claimant to the throne, had a vision of a cross in the sky, above which were written the words *In Hoc Signo Vinces* ("In this sign you will conquer"). It is alleged that he took this as a sign from the Christian god that he would win the battle—if he converted to Christianity. Constantine went on to win the struggle for the throne, and then did convert to Christianity.

While many have questioned the veracity of the "vision" story, the reality is that Constantine issued the Edict of Milan in 313 AD, which legalized Christianity throughout the empire and placed it on a par with all other religions.

**CONSTANTINE CONVERTS TO CHRISTIANITY 312 AD**

*Constantine at the Battle of Milvian Bridge, 312 AD. The decisive battle of Constantine in his campaign against a rival claimant to the Eastern Roman Empire's throne marked a major turning point in history.*

*It was at this battle that he reputedly saw, written in the sky, the Latin phrase "In Hoc Signo Vinces" (In this sign you will conquer) and a cross.*

*By choosing Christianity and the cross as his emblem, Constantine caused the Christianization of the Roman Empire and ultimately all of Europe.*

With the conversion of the emperor of Rome to Christianity, the established pattern of following the emperor's lead in religious matters came into play. Very rapidly, Christianity became one of the most popular religions throughout the Roman Empire.

### *"Donation of Constantine"—A Fabrication Which Gave the Church Political Power*

Constantine's conversion to Christianity led directly to the most famous forgery in European history, known as the "Donation of Constantine."

This document purports to be a signed document by Constantine with its principal feature the granting of temporal authority over the city of Rome and the entire Roman Empire to the bishop of Rome (who was to become the pope). Although there are many glaring factual errors in the text of the document, which by themselves show the document to be a forgery, the Donation of Constantine was accepted as genuine until the fifteenth century. It was used by the Catholic Church to claim political power in not only the Roman Empire but ultimately in all nominally Christian lands. Eventually the Donation of Constantine was rejected as a forgery—but by then the Church had established itself in almost all of Europe, power founded on a forgery.

### *Julian the Apostate Tries to Stem Christianity*

One of Constantine's successors, the emperor Julian, attempted to reverse the Christianisztion process, earning him the name Julian the Apostate. He simply overturned Constantine's adoption of Christianity as the state religion, relegating it to just one of many competing religions once again. The manner in which Julian reversed the progress of Christianity served as an example of the arbitrary way in which the personal wishes of the emperor could influence the whole empire.

**EMPEROR JULIAN—
PAGANISM'S CHAMPION**

To underline the point, the next emperor after Julian converted the empire back into a formal Christian state. The end result of all this to-and-fro activity was that from the year 395 AD, Christianity became the legal, sole, and official religion of the Roman Empire.

*The emperor Julian, nephew of the Christianizer Constantine, was raised as a Christian, but always secretly abhorred that religion and favored the old Roman gods. When he became emperor in 361 he overturned his uncle's decision to favor Christianity, and very nearly halted the progress of that religion through the empire. His successors were Christians and they undid his reforms.*

Christianity became widely known in southern Europe some 1,700 years ago, and was only accepted in northern Europe many hundreds of years after that. The last northern European country to formally adopt Christianity was Iceland around the year 1,000 AD.

### *The Evolution of the Office of the Pope*

As Christianity became formalized throughout the empire, each major town was assigned a religious leader, called a bishop. Gradually the bishop of Rome came to be recognized as the most important and assumed the title of "Pope" (from the Greek word meaning father).

By the seventh century AD, the pope had become the spiritual leader of all Christendom and was in possession of great political power, aided by the forged Donation of Constantine. The pope even adopted the Roman emperors' color, purple, which to this day remains the most used color in the Catholic Church.

### *Disputes Almost Immediate*

Although there was initially only one Christian church—the Catholic Church—disputes over interpretations of the religion broke

## CODEX SINAITICUS—WORLD'S OLDEST "COMPLETE" BIBLE

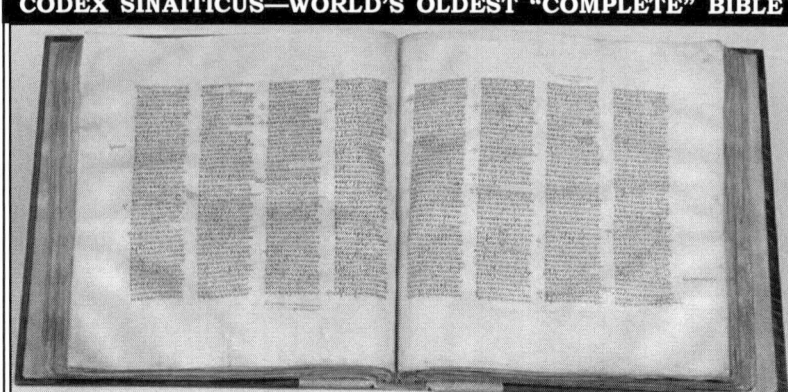

*The Codex Sinaiticus, a manuscript of the Bible written in the middle of the fourth century AD, contains the earliest existent copy of the New Testament and most of the Old Testament. The handwritten text is in Greek. The New Testament appears in the original vernacular language (koine). The Old Testament is the version known as the Septuagint which was adopted by early Greek-speaking Christians.*

*The Codex Sinaiticus was probably compiled after the First Council of Nicaea in 325 AD, at which disparate manuscripts used by Christian leaders all over the Roman world were compiled into one book to try and avoid disputes over interpretation. Modern Bibles differ in a number of places from the Codex Sinaiticus, which omits the following verses: Matthew 12:47, 16:2b–3, 17:21, 18:11; Mark 15:28, 16:8–20; Luke 22:43–44; John 5:4; Epistle to the Romans 16:24. Phrases which do not appear include: Mark 1:1 "the Son of God;" Matthew 6:13 "For thine is the kingdom, and the power, and the glory, for ever. Amen;" Luke 23:34, "Then said Jesus, Father, forgive them; for they know not what they do."*

*An interesting part of the Codex Sinaiticus which was omitted in later versions of the Bible can be found in its Matthew 27:49 verse which describes the piercing of Christ's side by a Roman solider with a spear while on the cross. According to the Codex version, the soldier "took a spear and pierced His side, and immediately came out water and blood" (on display at the British Library, London).*

out amongst its supporters. As Christianity spread, it became more and more disorganized, with serious disputes erupting amongst the various missionaries.

One of the earliest clashes was over the concept of what was called "Arianism" (named after Arius, a Christian leader in Alexandria), in regard to the three components of the Trinity: God, Christ, and the Holy Ghost. The belief that all three of these beings were one and the same was challenged by Arius who argued that the Christ figure could not be God as well. So seriously was this dispute taken, that Emperor Constantine called a special meeting of all the major leaders of the religion in 325 AD, to the now famous Council of Nicaea, to discuss the problem. At the Council of Nicaea it was decided that the Arian doctrine was incorrect, and it was declared a heresy.

## *The Bible Created—First Council of Nicaea 325 AD*

Several other disputes over doctrine made the religious leaders gathered at Nicaea realize that if some weighty final word on the outline of their belief was not forthcoming, the religion could splinter into factions. The problem was that there was no such outline or book in existence.

The council at Nicaea then took it upon themselves to create such a book, and turned to whatever texts they could find. To achieve this, they gathered up all the existing manuscripts being used by the Christian church in various parts of the empire, and compared and selected which ones to include in the final version.

This was not without its difficulties. The books now contained in the Old Testament were largely oral before 300 BC, although some had been written down by Jewish rabbis. King Ptolemy II of Philadelphus (285–246 BC) is credited with ordering the translation of the Jewish religious books into Greek. The Christian version of the Old Testament was only established as a comprehensive work by the scribe Origen around 250 AD, and up until that time only loose translations of the Ptolemaic Greek work formed the basis of that religion's teachings.

## *New Testament Collated 200 AD—Vague Origins of Biblical Writings*

The origins of the New Testament are very vague. By the end of the first century AD, the writings of Saul/Paul (called the Pauline Epistles) consisting of letters to the various Christian communities in Asia Minor and Rome had been established as a collection of inspired works. The Gospels which make up the first part of the New Testament only emerged after the writings of Paul had become well-known, and long after his death.

This is evidenced by the fact that in his writings there is no mention of any other New Testament book or gospel, and his account of what Jesus did on the night he was betrayed (1Corinthians 11:23) differs substantially from that recounted in the Gospels of Matthew, Mark, Luke, and John. It is clear that if the four gospels were in existence at the time when Paul wrote his epistles (around the year 55 AD), he would have at least mentioned them, or very likely quoted from them. The earliest existent gospel consists of fragments of the Gospel of John, dating from about 100 AD, and which is in Greek.

By 200 AD, the Church had developed the New Testament in its present form, although it was still written in various languages, including

Greek and Hebrew. The only book which did not yet feature in the collected works was the Book of Revelation. Where this last chapter came from no one knows for sure, but by the fourth century it had been included in the New Testament.

Not all of these various manuscripts were in accord with each other, and this presented a real problem for the Council of Nicaea. Finally, the decision was taken to simply leave out several early Christian manuscripts which did not fit in with the other books.

The most famous of these "left out" (or "apocryphal") books include The Book of Enoch, the Epistle of Jude, the Epistle of Barnabas, fragments of the Book of Jubilees, and the Gospel of St. Thomas. The latter was discarded because the events described therein are at serious variance with the events described in the four more well-known Gospels.

The Council of Nicaea went a long way toward formalizing the Bible as Christians know it today, in an attempt to prevent the church from splitting again as it nearly did over the Arian controversy. In this attempt they failed, and some of the most grievous conflicts in Europe were over different interpretations of the Bible.

### *The Spread of Christianity Is Resisted by Balts, Slavs, and Germans*

When the Roman Empire in the West collapsed, Christianity had been spread throughout its former dominions, with the exception of the Germans, the Balts, and a significant section of the Slavs. Nonetheless, the Germanic tribes who participated in the sacking of Rome at the formal end of that empire did not destroy the Roman Catholic Church along with the Roman state.

The leader of the church in Rome, the pope, survived the Germanic invasions, and went on to become an important political player in his own right. The Church also lost no time in sending Christian missionaries to the pagan tribes, the most famous of them being Wufilas (311–383 AD) who worked amongst the Visigoths.

Another famous missionary was Patrick, who although born in Britain, went to Ireland and became the Christianizer of that island, later being made a saint by the church for his efforts.

### *Saxon Invasion Causes Britain to Revert to Paganism*

The Roman Christianization of the British Isles was set back with the invasion of those lands by pagan Germans (the Angles and Saxons) following the collapse of the Western Roman Empire. As a

## ST. AUGUSTINE RE-INTRODUCES CHRISTIANITY TO BRITAIN 597 AD

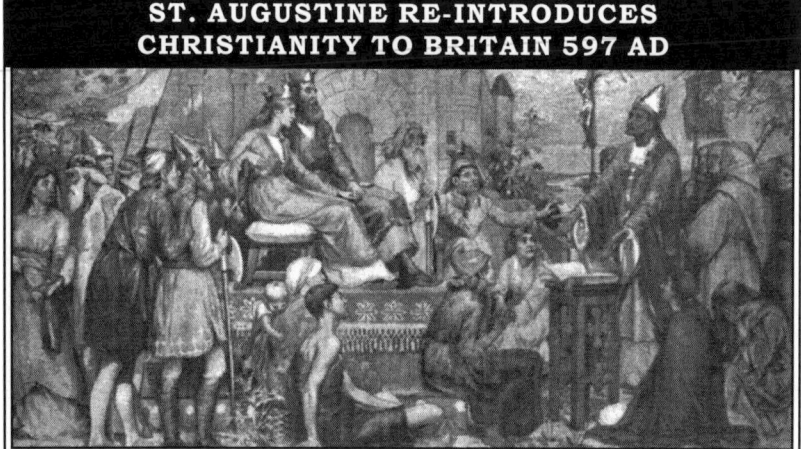

*The return of Christianity to Britain. That religion, introduced during late Roman rule, had been stamped out in England during the Angle and Saxon Germanic invasions following the fall of Rome. In 597 AD, the pope sent a missionary, St. Augustine, to try and Christianize the British population. He was fortunate in receiving the aid of King Ethelbert and his queen, Bertha, and managed to establish a significant Christian following in that land. Here Augustine is pictured preaching to a Saxon king.*

result, most of the British mainland became pagan once again, with Christianity only surviving in the Celtic fringes of Ireland and Wales.

To counteract this development, the Catholic Church sent a missionary, St. Augustine, to Britain from Rome in 597 AD. Augustine managed to convert an important Anglo-Saxon ruler to Christianity, and that religion began to spread once again in Britain.

Christian Britain in turn gave rise to the missionary, St. Boniface, who spent thirty-five years amongst the German tribes on the mainland of Europe before he was killed in 755 AD. Catholic missionaries were also active amongst the Germanic tribes living in Scandinavia, but met with much less success than in Britain or Central Europe.

### *The Conversion of the Frankish King Clovis I in 496 AD*

The Franks were a Germanic tribe who had emerged from northern Europe to occupy much of what is today Germany and France. With the fall of the Roman Empire, the Frankish tribes had set up small kingdoms scattered up and down the length and breadth of these two territories.

One of the most important conversions to Christianity on the mainland of Europe was the first king of the Franks, Clovis I, in 496 AD. He invaded the Visigoth Empire in 507 AD, causing them to abandon the part of France they had occupied since the fall of Rome and to retreat to Spain. The Frankish king, Pepin the Short, who reigned from 741 to 768 AD, was notable for being the first ruler of France to receive from the pope an official sanction to his kingship. Pepin was crowned by the English missionary, St. Boniface, acting on behalf of the pope, in 752 AD. This would be the first of many times that the pope would see fit to approve leaders of states in the name of God.

In 768, Pepin's son, Charlemagne (Charles the Great), inherited the Frankish kingdom. It was this king who was directly responsible for the introduction of Christianity to the Germans.

### Charlemagne Murders Tens of Thousands of Non-Christian Saxons

To destroy German paganism, Charlemagne proclaimed harsh laws applicable to those Germans under his control who refused to be baptized into Christianity. Eating meat during Lent, cremating the dead, and pretending to be baptized were all made punishable by death.

In 768 AD, Charlemagne started a thirty-two-year long campaign of what can only be described as genocidal evangelism against the Saxons under his control in western Germany. The campaign started with the cutting down of the Saxon's most sacred tree, their version of the World Tree or Yggdrasil (the symbol of the start of the earth and the source of all life in the ancient Indo-European religions), located in a sacred Saxon forest near present-day Marburg.

Charlemagne quickly turned to violence as a means of spreading Christianity. In 772, at Quierzy, he issued a proclamation that he would kill every Saxon who refused to accept Jesus Christ, and from that time on he kept a special detachment of Christian priests who doubled as executioners. In every Saxon village in which they stopped, these priests would execute anybody who refused to be baptized.

Then in 782, at Verden, Charlemagne carried out the act for which he is most notoriously associated. He ordered the beheading of 4,500 Saxons who had been caught practicing paganism after they had agreed to become Christians.

Charlemagne's constant companion and biographer, the monk Einhard, vividly captured the event in his biography of the Frankish king. In it is written that the king rounded up 4,500 Saxons who *"like dogs that return to their vomit"* had returned to the pagan religions they had been forced to give up upon pain of death. After having all these Saxons beheaded, *"the king went into winter camp, and there celebrated mass as usual."*

Twelve years later, in 794, Charlemagne introduced a law under which every third Saxon living in any pagan area was kidnapped and forced to resettle and be raised amongst Christian Franks.

### Coercive Christianity Takes Root

With the use of violent and bloody coercion, Saxon and German paganism was quite literally killed off. Most of the survivors became Christians more out of fear than out of genuine conviction. Christianity finally spread to the Goths, through a Christian slave named Wulfila, who translated the Bible into Gothic.

Before the end of the fourth century, Christianity had spread to the Vandals, the Burgundians, the Lombards, and other German tribes within the direct sphere of influence of the Western Roman Empire.

By the year 550 AD, the only non-Christian tribes were to be found in Bavaria and those parts of Germany north from there—including virtually all of the Danes, Scandinavians, Balts, and Slavs to the east.

### Pagan Origins of Christmas and Easter

Through sheer terror, Christianity then became the dominant religion of the previously pagan central Europe. Yet, because some pagan customs were far too entrenched to be rooted out, they were quietly incorporated into Christianity. In this way, Easter, for example, was absorbed to become a celebration of the resurrection of Christ—although its pagan origins are clearly shown in the symbolism of the egg and the rabbit. Both of these come directly from the pagan goddess of fertility, Eoster (from which Easter was derived), who used the egg and rabbit as fertility symbols. The date of Easter—at springtime,

**CHARLEMAGNE AND ENFORCED CHRISTIANITY**

*The sword and the cross: Charlemagne, and two of his armed priests. The Frankish king was directly responsible for the forced and violent introduction of Christianity to much of western Europe. This was at least partially achieved by killing pagans who did not want to convert to Christianity.*

235

## DESTROYING WHITE PAGANISM BY FORCE—BONIFACE CUTS DOWN THOR'S SACRED TREE

*The Christian missionary, St. Boniface, cutting down the sacred great oak tree of Geismar, Hesse, in 724 AD. The oak tree was sacred to the god Thor, and was one of many pagan sites which the Christians destroyed in their ultimately successful campaign to destroy the pagan religions. Similar acts of desecration were carried out against numerous non-Christian sites, with Roman temples singled out for destruction. Despite this, many of the original customs remained, such as the celebration of the spring and winter solstices. The Christians took the celebration of the pagan goddess of fertility, Eoster, and turned it into the Christian rite of Easter. The winter solstice, which marked the longest night of winter, was turned into the festival today known as Christmas.*

when new life emerged from winter, was linked to Eoster, and this was why it was celebrated at that time of year.

The same happened with the winter solstice, which was originally a pagan celebration to mark the turning point of winter. The pagans marked the longest night of the year with a fire, a pine tree, and gifts to mark the fact that they had survived yet another winter. Christianity combined the solstice celebration with the birth of Christ, in this way preserving much of the outer trappings of the pagan celebration which are still kept in modern times.

The church was uneasy with the pagan undertones of the celebration, particularly the "Christmas tree." This led to the Catholic Church officially banning the celebration of Christmas no less than three times, all of which were unsuccessful.

Christmas was also banned in Britain by Oliver Cromwell in 1647, and in 1659 by the Puritans in the American colony town of Boston in New England. The ban in Boston was so long lasting that Christmas only became fashionable again in that city in the 1800s.

## Teutonic Knights Exterminate the Last White Pagans in Eastern Europe

The only significant group of whites left in Europe who were not, nominally at least, Christians by the year 1000 AD, were found in eastern Europe and along the Baltic Sea coast. To destroy this last bastion of paganism, the Church employed the services of some of the most fanatic Christians of all—the Teutonic Knights. This organization was first established in Palestine in 1190 as a charitable religious military order, providing first aid during the Crusades. By 1198 they had taken on a military role and took an active part in the war against the Muslims, becoming known as the Teutonic Knights.

Membership in the order was strictly limited to Christian German noblemen. The Teutonic Knights received official recognition from Pope Innocent III in 1199, and adopted the official uniform of a white tunic with a black cross. Soon their deeds on behalf of Christendom became famous.

In 1210 they were invited to Hungary by the king of that country to participate in a war against the non-Christian pagan tribes in eastern Europe. The Teutonic Knights responded to the call, and through the use of violent tactics similar to those employed by Charlemagne, became the Christianizers of the people of that region. This task soon became the sole obsession of the Teutonic Knights and by 1226 the order had set up permanent settlements in northeastern Europe.

## Teutonic Knights Stamp out Paganism and Are Rewarded with Prussia

In 1226, the Holy Roman Emperor granted the Teutonic Knights control over what was then Prussia (today northern Poland) to rule as a fiefdom on condition that they converted all the locals to Christianity. In 1234, Pope Gregory IX granted the Knights control over any other territory that they might conquer from the pagans. The Teutonic Knights soon built a series of imposing castles to defend their new territory, some of which still stand today.

From the safety of these castles they waged their own brand of evangelicalism, which was limited to the Frankish king Charlemagne's recipe: once a number of pagans had been captured, they were offered the choice of either accepting Christianity and being baptized, or being killed on the spot. Unsurprisingly, almost all chose conversion. The price for being caught practicing paganism after being baptized was death.

**IMPRESSING THE PEASANTS**

*Impressing the peasants—cathedrals designed to project the Church's power. Siena Cathedral (1285 AD), Italy. The psychological effect of these cathedrals upon the surrounding peasants, who had never before seen a building higher than two or three floors, would have been considerable. Many peasants certainly believed it when they were told that God lived in these stunningly beautiful cathedrals.*

As was the case with the genocidal evangelicalism of Charlemagne, the first one or two generations of converts were in all likelihood not genuine. Usually they would pay lip service to Christianity in order not to be killed (there is evidence for this in the numerous recorded instances of the tribes reverting to their pagan ways once the Teutonic Knights had moved on to a new area).

However, by the third generation or so, the young children knew no other religion, and in this way Christianity replaced the original Indo-European religions.

### German Settlement in Prussia

The Teutonic Knights realized that the easiest way to change the nature of a society was to change its inhabitants, and actively encouraged already Christianized Germans to settle in Prussia. By 1300, the Teutonic Knights were one of the most powerful organizations in Germany, controlling territory which stretched from the Baltic Sea into central Germany, a private empire which saw them engaging in, on average, eight major wars every year.

### Battle of Tannenburg Sees Knights Defeated 1410

It was only a matter of time before the Teutonic Knights ran out of pagans to convert. By 1386, the last of the major non-Christian tribes in the north, the Lithuanians, had all more or less been converted, and the order started to lose the reason for its existence.

In addition to this, the methods employed by the order had not endeared it to the local populations, even though they were all now Christians. This enmity flared up into a new war in 1409, when the king of Poland invited all enemies of the Teutonic Knights to participate in a campaign against the order. This led to the Battle of Tannenburg in

1410, which saw the Teutonic Knights defeated. In 1525, the order's grand master, Albrecht of Hohenzollern, became a Protestant and dissolved the order in Prussia. Scattered elements of the order lived on but the last were finally expelled in 1591 from the Baltic.

Christianity came to be the dominant religion of Europe for four reasons. Firstly, paganism was swept aside because it was less organized and formalized; secondly, those hardcore pagans who refused to convert were either threatened with death or in some cases just executed; thirdly, Christianity was used as a political excuse by kings and popes to expand their own territories; and fourthly, through the use of syncretism (the merging of many aspects of European paganism with Christian belief).

# CHAPTER SEVENTEEN

# The First Great Race War:
# Attila the Hun 372–454 AD

**Amongst the assortment of tribes on the eastern borders of the Roman Empire, one group in particular held sway: the Goths. This tribe, in the form of its various subdivisions, such as Ostrogoths, Visigoths, and others, was to play a significant role in the final overrunning of the Western Roman Empire.**

When the Romans and the Goths first came into contact, however, Roman force of arms held them at bay beyond the eastern European continental borders of the empire. The Goths and their racial cousins, the Germanic tribes, kept up a continuous localized war with the Romans for many years, and would have doubtless continued to do so for even longer had a powerful racial foe not emerged which threatened to destroy them all. Into the midst of the struggles between the Germans, the Goths, and the Romans was to come the very first open race war in Europe—the invasion of the Asiatic tribe of the Huns.

### Asiatic Nomads of Mixed Race

The Huns, described by Roman sources as "short, brown skinned and slant eyed," were a Mongoloid-based racial group who originated from the Asiatic Steppes. They were a wild aggressive group who lived by force of arms. Although they shared some genetic commonality with the Chinese, they waged war on those people as well.

The Huns were continuously marching outward seeking new victims to plunder, and in a feat remarkable for the times, headed out west from the Steppes in a series of waves beginning from around 100 AD. They reached the Caspian Sea by around 158 AD, and by 360 AD had crossed the Volga River into modern day Russia.

Soon they were all over the Black Sea basin, the original Indo-European homeland, and it was there that they first came into contact with a European tribe—the Alans.

### Alans Become the First Victims 372 AD

The unsuspecting Alans were attacked by the Huns in 372 BC. Using their finely developed cavalry skills, the Huns easily crushed the

*The Asiatic terror swept across Europe, resulting in the death of countless thousands of whites. The most important legacy left by the Huns was not, as this nineteenth century woodcut suggests, the huge toll in white lives lost as a result of their invasion, but rather in the admixture of their genes into a minority of the far eastern Slavic peoples, helping to create what is today incorrectly regarded as the "Slavic" look. In fact, huge numbers of Slavs have retained their European gene pool intact, and it is a common error to attribute the so-called "Slavic look" to the entire population in the region occupied by the Huns.*

Alans in a short series of encounters. Remnants of the Alans fled south and west, seeking refuge with the Gothic tribes, bringing with them the first news of the Asiatic terror.

### Ostrogoths Fall before the Hun Invasion

If the Ostrogoths wondered what had befallen the Alans, they did not have to wait long to find out. The Huns swept further west and invaded the Ostrogothic lands (in modern day western Russia). The Ostrogothic king, Hermanric, committed suicide when the scale of the invasion and defeat became apparent. His successor, Vitimer, was killed in a follow-up battle against another Hunnish attack. The Ostrogothic kingdom in western Russia disintegrated, and its survivors streamed further westward, into the lands of the Visigoths and Slavs.

### Visigoths Bargain with the Romans

Athanaric, king of the Visigoths, engaged the Huns at the Dniester River in modern day Bulgaria, but was defeated. After this setback, the Visigoths were forced to fall back and beg the Romans for permission to settle inside the empire's territory, which would in theory be safer from the ravages of the Asiatic army.

This appeal was made all the more remarkable when it is borne in mind that the Romans and Visigoths had been at war almost constantly for nearly two centuries. As a result, when the Romans finally gave permission to the Visigoths to move into their territory, it was at a terrible price. The Visigoths had to surrender all their weapons and hand over large numbers of their women and children as hostages.

The Visigoths crossed the Danube River into Roman territory in 376 BC and settled in modern day Bulgaria. There they managed to gain a temporary reprieve from the ravages of the Huns, but the conditions under which the Romans forced them to stay were such that it was not long before Visigothic resentment boiled over into open rebellion.

### Visigoth Rebellion—Battle of Adrianople

The Visigoths secretly rearmed themselves and launched a campaign against the Roman strongholds of Thrace and Macedonia in northern Greece. After an extended conflict, a Visigothic army defeated the Romans at the Battle of Adrianople in 378 AD. The Roman army was under the personal command of the emperor Valen, who had imposed the harsh conditions of refuge upon the Visigoths. Valen himself was killed in this battle. The defeat was all the more ironic as a large number of the Roman army's soldiers were Gothic mercenaries.

**ATTILA—THE SCOURGE OF EUROPE**

*Attila the Hun after a Roman depiction. Leader of an Asiatic terror which swept across Europe with such fury and cruelty that his name has remained to this day a byword for tyranny. Defeated in central France in 451 AD, the Huns attacked Italy in 452, the invasion being held up by an appeal from the pope. The Hunnish threat only faded after Attila died in 453 AD.*

The political result of the defeat was that the Eastern Roman Empire then accepted the presence of the Visigoths in central Europe, and many of the restrictions placed upon them by Valen were lifted.

While the Goths and the Romans were grappling with one another, the former Visigothic lands were being seized by the Huns. By the time of the Battle of Adrianople, the Huns had occupied most of Dacia, the land originally seized by the Visigoths from the Romans (and which corresponds to the present day country of Romania).

### Europe Invaded

At this stage the racial balance of Europe could have swung decisively in favor of the Asiatic Mongoloids. All the original Indo-European ancestral homelands in the Black Sea basin had been either destroyed or occupied by the Huns. In addition, the Huns also occupied large parts of western Russia and portions of central and eastern Europe. Parts of modern central Germany, Hungary, and Romania were also occupied.

Not content with these conquests, the Asiatic Huns pushed further westward, moving entire nations and destroying everything in their path. In this way the remnants of the Alans, and many other minor tribes were forced westward, in turn displacing other already settled peoples.

It was this displacement which led to further migrations of assorted Germanic tribes into Spain and even across the Mediterranean Sea into North Africa.

By 432 AD, during the reign of Roman Emperor Theodosius I, the Huns had increased their stranglehold on eastern Europe and parts of central Europe to the point where they collected a large annual tribute from Rome.

### Attila the Hun—Brutal Leader

In 433 AD, the Huns gained a new king, whose name would become a byword for the Asiatic terror: Attila. The new king established his headquarters at the village of Buda on the Danube River in 445 AD. Buda would later combine with another village on the other side of the river, Pest, to become Budapest, the modern capital of Hungary.

By this time, the Hunnish Empire stretched from the Caspian Sea in the east right up to the North Sea. In all of the area the Huns carried out a vicious racial war of extermination against the whites who were generally too weak to resist. Countless white settlements were wiped out, with the women routinely being carried off into captivity. In 452 AD, Attila began moving west again, with the intention of seizing France and finishing off all of Europe.

### Hunnish Blood Enters Eastern Europe

By this stage a small number of Huns had physically integrated with some of the peoples they had conquered, an inevitable result of such migratory warfare. Traces of the Mongoloid influence can still be seen amongst some peoples in eastern Europe. This has given rise to what the ill-informed have falsely claimed is the "Slavic look." This is not "Slavic" at all (true Slavs are very European), but is a reference to the minority of people who show a slight Mongoloid/Slavic ancestry.

As a result of this limited integration process, the Huns managed to recruit some locals into their army. This was the cause of some unscrupulous soldiers from various eastern European tribes being present in the Hunnish army which finally invaded France. If captured, these whites were dealt with in an extremely harsh manner by their racial cousins.

The Hunnish armies penetrated right into western Europe, and stood poised to push through to the Atlantic Ocean. Europe stood on the very brink of extermination.

### Battle of Troyes—United Whites Defeat Huns

The threat posed by the Hunnish army forced the ever squabbling Romans and Visigoths into a united front. A Roman army,

## HUNS SACK AND PILLAGE ROMAN VILLA 440 AD

*Asiatics, known as Huns, attacked the easternmost white tribes, the Alans, in 372 AD. Quickly annihilating them, they marched east, forcing the squabbling Romans, Germans, and Goths to unite and face the communal racial threat. An overt race war, fought across Europe, then followed, with the Huns being defeated at Troyes in central France and at Nedao in central Europe. White Europe was nearly extinguished by this threat. Above is a depiction of a scene which befell hundreds of thousands of whites—a non-white raiding party attacking a Roman villa and carrying off booty.*

under the last of the Western Empire's properly Roman generals, Aetius, joined up with a Visigoth army under their king, Theodoric I. Together they met the Hunnish army in central France near the present day city of Troyes in 451 AD.

In a daylong battle, both sides inflicted heavy casualties on the other. The Visigoth king, Theodoric, was killed in the fighting, but by nightfall the combined white army had gained the upper hand over the invading Asians. They were driven from the battlefield, their first major defeat in all of Europe. Attila was forced to retreat all the way from France to his base in Hungary. The Huns exacted a terrible revenge by slaughtering and looting those Europeans unfortunate enough to be in the path of their retreat.

### *Attila Slaughters Whites in Northern Italy*

Defeated in western Europe, Attila launched one more invasion, this time turning south. In 452, his armies penetrated northern Italy and razed the city of Aquileia to the ground, massacring the inhabitants. The survivors fled into the nearby marshes, where it is traditionally claimed they founded the city that became Venice.

**POPE LEO I MEETS ATTILA 452 AD**

*Pope Leo I meets Attila personally to try and halt the Mongol's attack on Rome. Having devastated Padua, Milan, Verona, and many other towns, Attila's army faltered after the famous meeting with the pope, mainly due to exhaustion and lack of provisions. Attila died the next year, in 453 AD.*

The next year, 453 AD, the sixty-year-old Attila died allegedly of a burst blood vessel incurred during his wedding night exertions following his marriage to a local German princess. It is a matter of debate as to how much of that story is true but what is certain is that Attila suddenly died, and that he did indeed take a blonde German girl, named Hildico, as his wife. In this he followed the example set by many of his fellow Mongoloid warriors, whose genetic footprint can be seen on some faces in eastern Europe and Russia to this day.

## Germanics Crush Huns and Save White Europe—Battle of Nedao 454 AD

Attila's death was the signal for revolt by the Europeans who had been subjugated by the Huns. In 454 AD, the Goths, Slavs, and others who had managed to survive the nearly seventy years of cruel Asiatic rule, rose up. At the Battle of Nedao in that year, the combined Germanics finally defeated the Huns, destroying their power forever.

The Battle of Nedao became one of the most significant battles in white history. Without it, Europe would most likely have been completely overrun by Asiatics before 500 AD. The Germans, as victors over the Huns, became famous amongst their racial cousins, with the Icelandic word for German to this day still translating literally as "peoples' defender."

### The Huns Flee to Sea of Azov

Suffering total defeat at the hands of the Germans, the surviving Huns then fled back into the Far East. They only stopped when they reached the Sea of Azov in southern Russia, possibly because they felt that was far enough from Europe to avoid retribution for their invasions.

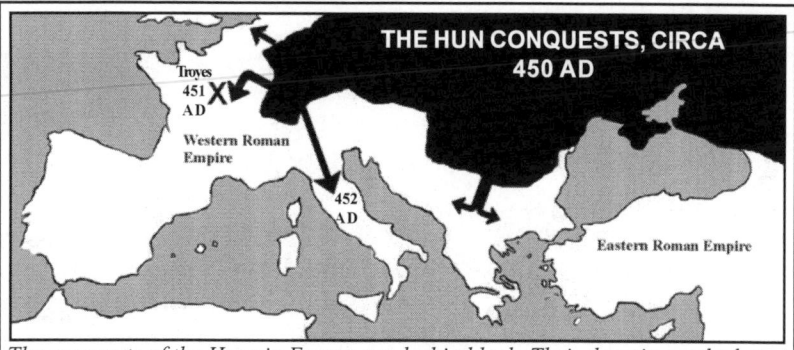

*The conquests of the Huns in Europe marked in black. Their domain reached west over the Rhine River into central France, and included central Germany and almost all of the modern day southeastern European countries. X marks the spot in France where the Huns were defeated at the Battle of Troyes by a united Roman and Gothic army in 451 AD. The Huns also raided northern Italy and struck at Constantinople. For over twenty years Attila had his headquarters in Budapest, the capital of modern Hungary.*

### The Hunnish Legacy

Although they had been driven out of Europe, the Huns left two significant legacies. Firstly, they gave their name to the territory which had served as their European base, the land today called Hungary; and secondly, some admixture of Mongoloid genes occurred amongst the Slavic tribes which had been under the Asiatic Hunnish occupation for nearly eighty years.

For their part, the Slavs expanded eastward into the regions of Russia which had previously been overrun by the Huns, once again mixing with scattered remnants of the partly Hunnish, partly Slavic peoples in those areas. This continual back-and-forth genetic movement further added to the racial mix of what became the southernmost reaches of Russia. Today this region is divided between Russia proper and the independent Islamic states which emerged after the breakup of the Soviet Union.

### Invasion Route Established into Europe

For the next thousand years, the territory between the Black and Caspian Seas became an invasion route for waves of nonwhite hordes from Asia: The Avars, then the Turks (who were finally driven from the European mainland after the First World War in 1918), the Magyars (who occupied Hungary), and other Asiatics, some descendants of whom eventually became the Gypsies still found in Eastern Europe.

# CHAPTER EIGHTEEN

## The Triumph of the Slaves—The Fall of Rome

**For centuries, scholars have debated how the Roman Empire, once so mighty and powerful, could have come to an end. Explanations have included a lack of morals, economic overexertion, or that the empire became too unwieldy to administer.**

All of these explanations have ignored the real cause of the dissolution of Roman power, namely that the Romans themselves disappeared, submerged amongst a mass of foreigners. The driver for this submersion was the reality that Rome was a slave driven economy and society. At the time of Augustus, for example, fully one-third of the population of Rome and Italy were of slave extraction, some two million people out of a total population of six million. Simple demographics was the cause of the collapse of Rome.

### Twenty-five out of Twenty-six Emperors Die Unnaturally

From 193 AD, Roman emperors made no attempt to disguise the fact that they were absolute rulers. The Senate, previously the supreme power, served in an advisory capacity only, leading to this period of Roman history being called the "Dominate" for the obvious reason.

By now, the empire had encompassed much of the known world, and the stress and strains of trying to run a polyglot nation began to take its toll. For the fifty year period between 235 and 285 AD, there were twenty-six different emperors. Only one of them died a natural death. During this period of anarchy, Rome was wracked by civil war, intrigue, and foreign invasion.

### Diocletian Divides Empire

The emperor Diocletian took the throne in 285 AD. His reign, which lasted until 305 AD, was marked by a period of relative stability because he took the important decision to divide the empire into two parts. The division into Eastern and Western Empires took place in 286 AD.

The Western Empire retained Rome as its capital, while the Eastern Empire received the city of Nicomedia in Asia Minor (modern day Turkey) as its capital. There was an implicit racial implication to the division of the empire, although there is no evidence that this was Diocletian's intention.

Diocletian created a post of coemperor to rule the Western Empire, as he chose to rule the Eastern Empire. Each emperor was called an "Augustus" and each had an assistant, called a "Caesar." The Caesar was supposed to succeed the Augustus, thus attempting to solve the continual problem of secession.

### Constantinople—Eastern Empire's Capital

The emperor Constantine's conversion to Christianity gave the Christians the upper hand in their battle against other religions in the empire. Constantine decided that what was needed was a new Christian capital, and in 326 AD he selected the site of the ancient city of Byzantium, situated on the Bosporus Strait connecting the Mediterranean with the Black Seas.

**DIOCLETIAN—STABILIZED EMPIRE**

*The emperor Diocletian was a military genius who became one of Rome's greatest later rulers. The increasing size of the empire and the inclusion of all sorts of nationalities was reflected in this man. Born of obscure origins in the Balkans, Diocletian became emperor in 285 AD. The fact that people born outside of Rome could settle in Rome and even become emperor meant that the original Romans themselves soon became outnumbered—by either non-Roman whites like Diocletian, or by non-Roman nonwhites from the Middle East, which made up half the empire.*

Constantine called the city New Rome, but it soon became known as Constantinople and is today known as Istanbul (so named after it was conquered by invading Muslim armies one thousand years later). The city took six years to build, and was consecrated in 330 AD.

### Byzantium Slows Nonwhite Influx to Rome

The establishment of Constantinople and the Eastern Roman Empire, also called Byzantium, had an important by-product in that it contributed toward slowing down the masses of immigrants from the mixed race Middle Eastern territories to Rome. Constantinople served as a destination for many who otherwise would have settled in Rome, although by this time, the latter city had already been almost completely overrun with foreigners.

### The Goths Attack Rome

Even at the height of her power, Rome had never been able to penetrate north, and the appearance of the Goths saw even more ferocious raids take place from Germania and the eastern borders.

The huge geographical distance between the various Gothic tribes led to a division into two main sections: the Visigoths, or West Goths, who settled the territory from the Danube River to the Dniester River, and the Ostrogoths, or East Goths, who settled in the region eastward from the Dniester River to the Volga River in present day Russia.

The Visigoths pressed westwards, encountering the Romans around 250 AD, when they invaded the Roman province of Dacia in southern central Europe near the Danube River. Roman reports mention the Goths to be the tallest of the German tribes, with their hair ranging from red to almost white.

After several initially inconclusive skirmishes, the Visigoths inflicted a massive defeat upon the Romans in 251 AD, wiping out an entire Roman army and killing the emperor, Decius. Soon thereafter, the Romans abandoned Dacia, a province which they had conquered and held for 150 years. From then on, the Danube River once again formed the border between the Germanics and Rome.

The Visigoths also captured and plundered Athens in 267 AD, a Roman outpost since the time of the Punic Wars. For another century, bands of Goths would wage incessant and uncoordinated warfare in the Balkans with the Romans.

### Forty Thousand Visigothic Mercenaries Recruited

As was by now usual for the Roman Empire, their enemies could also be their mercenaries. For approximately 150 years after the defeat of the Roman army in Dacia, an uneasy coexistence was established between the Romans and Goths. Short on their own soldiers, the Romans started recruiting individual Goths as mercenaries.

In this way, the Roman records show that during the reign of Constantine, some forty thousand Goths were recruited into the Eastern

## GOTHS AMBUSH ROMAN COLUMN ALONG THE DANUBE CIRCA 400 AD

*A Roman army unit is ambushed along the Danube River by a ferocious Gothic assault in this painting which accurately captures the dress, weapons, and racial types of the two armies. Many of the Roman soldiers were, in fact, German mercenaries.*

Empire's army. Indeed, they formed the bulwark of the Eastern Roman Empire against the huge masses of mixed race invaders pushing against the eastern reaches of the empire.

### *Visigoths Break Open Western Roman Empire at Battle of Adrianople*

As detailed in the previous chapter, the unstable but fairly static border between the Goths and the Roman Empire along the Danube River was broken after the Hunnish invasion from the east.

The Visigoth leaders, fearing that they were going to be destroyed, petitioned Rome for help and permission to enter Roman territory to seek safety inside the official borders of the empire. This permission was granted in 376 AD and the Visigoths formally crossed the Danube River south into Roman territory.

The arrangement did not last long. The long-standing enmity between the Romans and their Germanic foes soon broke out into war. A Roman army sent to subdue the Visigoths was defeated at the battle of Adrianople in 378 AD.

This Gothic victory was important psychologically, for it shattered the belief in Western Roman invincibility. Soon, other Gothic tribes began to penetrate the empire's frontiers at will.

### Roman Armies Leave Britain 407 AD

As the military pressures increased on the remnants of the Western Empire, the decision was made to withdraw all Roman armies from Britain in 407 AD. Only those who had already assimilated into the local population were left behind, and the Britons were formally advised that they now had to look to themselves for protection against the Germanics.

It took less than fifty years after the Roman withdrawal for the first Germanic tribes to invade that island. Amongst the invaders were the Angles and Saxons, from whom the modern term Anglo-Saxon originated. The Angles and the Saxons dominated the Britons by force, although some British tribes, notably the Bretons, fled across the channel to France, where their name still exists as a geographical term (Brittany) and people from this region are still called Bretons.

The invasions of Gaul and Britain demonstrate how the Western Roman Empire was broken up, piece by piece, under waves of invading Germanics. The Roman failure to occupy and suppress Germania came back to haunt the empire, weakened as it was by demographic replacement.

### Roman Upper Classes Buy Blond Wigs

By 400 AD—around four hundred years after the time of Julius Caesar—the inhabitants of Rome were a pale shadow of the race who originally created the empire. Immigrants from all over the Middle East and North Africa had turned it into a melting pot made up of a mixture of Middle Easterners (Semites, mixed race Egyptians, Syrians, and Africans) and original remnant Romans, with no national sense of identity or common purpose.

This integration process had reached such levels that the Roman writer Juvenal recorded the habit of many wealthy Romans buying blond wigs to cover their dark hair. The blond hair was purchased from Germany and transported south to Rome to be made into wigs.

The following extract from Juvenal's Satire 6, exc. L, Book 4 of his *De Rerum Natura,* vi. 120, tells how the emperor's wife, Messalina, put on a blonde wig to disguise herself to visit houses of ill repute: *"Do you care about a private citizen's house, about Eppia's doings? Turn your eyes to the gods' rivals. Hear what the emperor Claudius had to put up with. As soon as his wife thought that he was asleep, this imperial whore put on the hood she wore at night, determined to prefer a cheap pad to the royal bed, and left the house with one female slave only. No, hiding her black hair in a yellow wig she entered the brothel, warm with its old patchwork quilts and her empty cell, her very own."*

The 1911 Encyclopedia Britannica adds the following: *"The fashionable ladies of Rome were much addicted to false hair, and we learn from Ovid, Amores, i. 14. 45) and Martial (v. 68) that the golden hair imported from Germany was most favoured. Juvenal (vi. 120) shows us Messalina assuming a yellow wig for her visits to places of ill-fame, and the scholiast on the passage says that the yellow wig was characteristic of courtesans."*

Ovid also mentions the custom of blond wigs and Pliny went so far as to give details of the different methods of dying hair blond.

The inhabitants of Rome also used sapa, or lead acetate, as a skin lightener to make their complexions

**ROMAN EMPRESS WHO USED BLONDE WIGS**

*Valeria Messalina was a Roman empress as the third wife of Emperor Claudius. She was famous for her sexual appetite and her blonde wig, which, according to many records, allowed her to work in a brothel in secret. The Roman use of blond wigs, derived from the inhabitants of Germania, became very widespread. Many emperors, including Caracalla, were famous for the habit.*

pale and paid a heavy price by unwittingly poisoning themselves at the same time. The emperor Caracalla, whose father was a Roman official stationed in Africa and whose mother was a Persian, was famous for wearing a blond wig.

### Roman Army Relies on Foreign Mercenaries to Ward off Foes

In what is fairly typical for such mixed societies, Rome at this time was divided into two economic classes: a very wealthy minority and a desperately poor majority. The wealthy minority, many of whom had made their money out of the flourishing slave trade, lived in relative luxury, while the masses lived in frightful urban squalor.

From this population the Roman army was unable to raise the enthusiasm or quality needed to man the frontiers, so the wealthy ruling classes of Rome paid huge amounts in bribes and mercenary fees to keep the armies up to strength.

Rome precariously survived on money rather than physical strength. Germanics threatened Rome's borders, and also made up the armies defending those same borders. This tactic was employed by both Western and Eastern Roman Empires, with the Western Empire using Germans, and the Eastern Empire using Goths. In what was ironic but nonetheless predictable, the last battles in Italy fought under Roman banners were between armies of Germanic-manned "Roman" armies and Germanic foes.

### Eastern Roman Empire Sends Army to Defeat Frankish Puppet Emperor

The replacement of the original Roman armies with non-Roman mercenaries came to a head with the invasion of the Western Roman Empire by an army sent by the Eastern Roman emperor in 394 AD.

The background to this astonishing event lay in the fact that a Frankish Roman army general, Arbogast, had, with the support of the Roman Senate, ensured that Eugenius was elected Western emperor in 394 AD. Arbogast's power base lay in his Frankish army which he brought with him into Italy, and it was obvious that Eugenius was little more than Arbogast's puppet.

The Eastern Roman emperor, Theodosius, unhappy with the blatant manipulation of the Western emperor by Arbogast, sent an army (ironically comprised of Germanic Goths and Vandals and under the leadership of two non-Romans, the Gothic prince, Alaric, and the Vandal, Stilicho) to remove Arbogast from power.

So it was that the bizarre situation was reached that competing "Roman" armies clashed with each other for power in Rome—when in reality, none of the combatants were actually Roman. The two armies met at the Battle of the Frigidus in September 394 AD. After two days of fighting, Arbogast's army was

**GERMAN STILICHO DEFENDS ROME**

*Stilicho, last general of the Western Empire, was actually a German. In this way the "Roman" army was, by the year 400 AD, composed of anything but Romans.*

defeated, and he committed suicide. Eugenius was killed the same day, effectively ending hostilities. (A by-product of this clash was that it ended the last pagan Roman senatorial opposition to the Christianization of the Roman Empire.)

After the battle, in accordance with Theodosius's instructions, Stilicho became effective master of the Western Empire. Alaric was in the interim chosen king of the Visigoths by his tribe.

### Massacre of the German Women and Children—The Revenge of 408 AD

The inhabitants of Rome resented both Visigoths and Vandals alike, and in 408 AD, Stilicho was assassinated.

This was immediately followed by a massacre of thousands of the wives and children of the German soldiers in Italy (it was easy to pick out the Germans, as their light coloring and hair stood in marked contrast to the vast majority of the inhabitants of most of Italy). This foolish act drove the Germanic tribes into reprisals.

For two years, Alaric led an embittered army consisting of his men, Stilicho's soldiers, and remnants of the defeated Frankish army, up and down the Italian peninsula, exacting a terrible revenge for the massacre of the Germanic women and children. During this time the marauding Germans took a heavy toll of the local population. Countless numbers were killed, considerably thinning out the largely mixed race population.

## GOTHS CONQUER ROME IN 410 AD BY SEVERING WATER SUPPLY

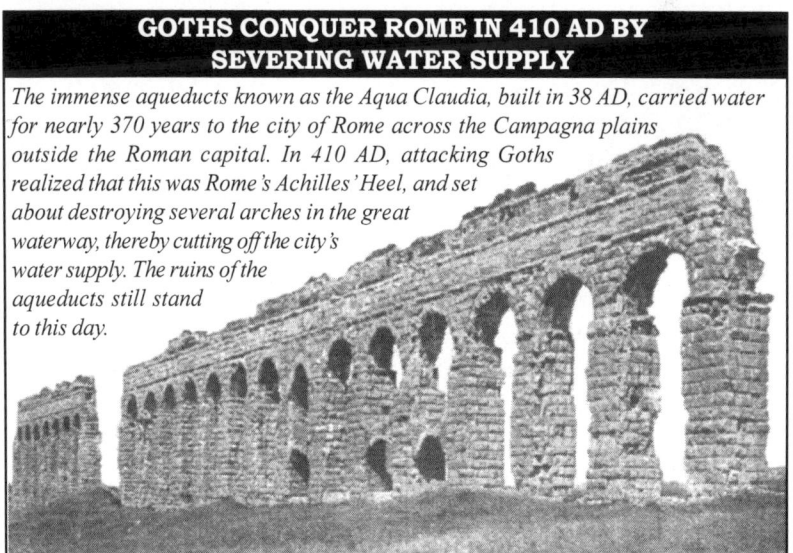

*The immense aqueducts known as the Aqua Claudia, built in 38 AD, carried water for nearly 370 years to the city of Rome across the Campagna plains outside the Roman capital. In 410 AD, attacking Goths realized that this was Rome's Achilles' Heel, and set about destroying several arches in the great waterway, thereby cutting off the city's water supply. The ruins of the aqueducts still stand to this day.*

**ALARIC'S GOTHS SACK ROME IN REVENGE 410 AD**

*The sacking of Rome by Alaric's Goths, 410 AD. The attack on the city followed a 408 AD massacre of the Germanic women and children by the largely mixed race Roman remnant population. Historians date the fall of Rome from 410, but the Romans themselves had long since vanished, submerged amongst the peoples and races they had conquered.*

In addition, Alaric demanded a huge ransom from the inhabitants of Rome and forced their slave traders to release some forty thousand German slaves from captivity.

### Goths Sack Rome—Official End of Western Empire 410 AD

Alaric's avenging army finally sacked the city of Rome on August 24, 410 AD. That date is marked as the official end of the Roman Empire in the West, although, of course, the last true Romans had long since vanished.

After this last great sacking of Rome, a semblance of an imperial line of rulers was reinstituted in the city. They were nothing more than a series of puppets for the invading Germanics. Finally in 475 AD, all pretenses were dropped. In that year, the first formal Germanic emperor was elected, when a German-born general, Orestes, forced the Roman Senate to elect his son. The next year, another German general Odovacar killed Orestes and, seeing no reason to continue the appearance of an imperial secession, simply declared himself head of state.

This first Germanic emperor of Rome who was not elected by the Senate is regarded by some historians as another formal end date of the Roman Empire in the West. As shown above, this is incorrect, as by that time the Western Empire had long before ceased to exist.

### The Vandals Sack Rome from the Sea—455 AD

One of the invading Germanic tribes, called the Vandals, marched right through Gaul into Spain in 409 AD. They were followed by Visigoths about ten years later, sparking off disputes between these two tribes over territory. The Vandals then sailed across the Straits of Gibraltar and conquered the Western Roman Empire's provinces in North Africa.

Under their able leader, Gaiseric, the Vandals established themselves as a major power. In June 455 AD, a naval-borne Vandal army invaded Italy and sacked

**BLACK SLAVES—ROME 400 AD**

*Black slaves in Rome picking grapes, a mosaic in the Church of Santa Costanza, Rome, fourth century AD. Millions of nonwhites were imported into Italy as slaves. Eventually they mixed with large numbers of the Romans, producing the mixed race types as illustrated in the fresco from Pompeii (see page 259).*

Rome. The ease with which this was accomplished serves as an excellent indicator of how the power of Rome had declined along with its original population.

The city, populated by large numbers of mixed race and Middle Eastern types thrown in amongst the remnants of the original Roman people, was either unwilling or simply unable to put up a defense in the tradition of the past glories of Rome. The city of Caesar became a stamping ground for anyone who wanted to loot whatever remained.

Gaiseric and the Vandals managed to repulse a few attempts by the Eastern Roman Empire to exact revenge for the raid on Rome, and ensured that their kingdom lasted until 534 AD. In that year, a surprise attack by an Eastern Empire army defeated the Vandals, and thereafter they collapsed into obscurity in North Africa. Having settled in what is today Algeria, the Vandals were quick to mirror Rome's decline. Within two hundred years, the Vandals were absorbed into the already mixed race inhabitants of North Africa, once again contributing to the maelstrom of genes which today makes up the North African Mediterranean basin.

### The Burgundians and the Franks Enter France

Yet another Germanic tribe, the Burgundians, moved across the Rhine River into France and settled in the Rhone River valley. They were followed by the Franks, who fanned out across northern Gaul, assimilating the local population as they went.

## *The Germanic Lombards Invade Italy*

In 568 AD, the third most significant population shift in Italian history occurred. Another Germanic tribe, the Lombards, poured over the Alps into Italy, and established a new kingdom, which largely replenished the Nordic racial stock in northern and central Italy. It was the Lombards who provided the impetus for the later north Italian-based Renaissance.

Thus, in less than a century after the Germanic tribes had first crossed the Roman Empire's borders in 406 AD, the mixed race remnants of the Western Roman Empire in northern Italy had largely been swept south by new Germanic blood. One thousand years of Roman multiculturalism was at an end.

## *Fewer than Five Percent of Rome's Population Were Romans in 50 AD*

The reality behind the collapse of the Roman Empire is apparent from the historical sequence of events. The people who created the empire, the original Romans, vanished. They were absorbed into the peoples they conquered, and whom they freely allowed to enter Rome.

Once the founding Roman population had been diluted through the mass importation of slaves and uncontrolled immigration, the nature of Roman society changed to reflect the changed population.

In the West, the Romans were absorbed by the racially similar and numerically superior Celts, Gauls, and Germans. In the East the Romans were absorbed by the racially dissimilar nonwhite mixed race Middle Easterners and North Africans, who also immigrated in massive numbers to Rome.

The noted British historian, Edward Gibbon, in his monumental work *The Decline and Fall of the Roman Empire,* estimated the number of people within the borders of the empire during the time of the emperor Claudius (43 AD) as some 120 million people. Of this amount, Gibbon says, only some 6,945,000 were proper Roman citizens.

The effect of the opening of citizenship to all in the empire and the toleration of unrestricted immigration into the city of Rome meant that the less than seven million original Romans were quickly overrun by the 113 million non-Romans, both white and nonwhite alike.

The Roman Empire collapsed because the Romans disappeared. The final explanation is as simple as that.

## THE REAL CAUSE OF THE FALL OF THE ROMAN EMPIRE—THE RACIAL CHANGE IN THE POPULATION MAKEUP

*The pictures on this page show how the racial makeup of Rome changed in less than four hundred years.* Top right: *From defeated foe to citizen. Roman soldiers carry Jewish treasures seized during the Roman-Jewish War of 68–73 AD. The scene is from the Arch of Titus, erected by the emperor of the same name to commemorate his victory over the Jews.*

Center: *A sarcophagus from 300 AD in the city of Rome showing the very same symbol—the Jewish menorah—combined with classical Roman scenes. This illustrates well the extent of how assimilated the various peoples of the world became in that city. Within 350 years the Jews had moved from a defeated and hated enemy of Rome, into being wealthy citizens.*

Below: *The absorption of nonwhites into the Roman population and the effects of racial mixing are evident in the face of this baker* (left) *from Pompeii, Italy. The fashion at the time was to have one's portrait painted on the walls of one's house. The eruption of the volcano Vesuvius preserved a great number of the houses in Pompeii, including both these portraits which date from circa 50 AD.*

*Compare the clearly mixed race features of this baker to one of his neighbors, a Nordic woman* (right) *whose house portrait was similarly saved. Eventually, the "baker" types were to dominate Roman society. This change in racial makeup of Roman society was the reason why the Roman Empire vanished—the original Romans were submerged.*

## RUINS OF ROME'S GREATNESS—HOW A CHANGE IN THE RACIAL COMPOSITION CHANGES THE PHYSICAL APPEARANCE OF A CIVILIZATION

*How the racial makeup of a population changes the outer manifestations of a civilization is illustrated in these sets of pictures.* Above left: *A reconstruction of the Palatine Hill, one of the centers of ancient Rome, as it appeared in the heyday of the Roman Empire. Alongside is the exact same view, only this time how the modern visitor may view the Palatine Hill: a few crumbling ruins. Once the original Romans had vanished, so did their civilization, even down to their buildings which lie scattered in the far corners of the Roman Empire, silent witnesses to the passing of a great people, submerged amongst the myriad of people and races in the Roman borders.* Right: *The Roman Forum, as reconstructed to what it looked like in its prime, and* Below: *A photograph of how the modern visitor may see the site. The crumbling ruins of what was once the greatest power on earth carry a message for modern society.*

*Civilizations can and do fall, and the mightiest of buildings can and do crumble in a few short centuries. This happens when the people who originally made a civilization become a minority by either foreign invasion or immigration, or are assimilated into new racial elements. This, then, is the great lesson of history: the disappearance of a people, or race, leads to the disappearance of all aspects of their civilization, even its physical manifestations.*

# APPENDICES

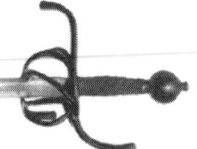

## Appendix 1: Genetic Evidence for the Aryan Invasion of India

*"Analyses of the male Y chromosome, plus genes hidden in small cellular bodies called mitochondria, show that today's genetic patterns agree with accounts of ancient Indo-European warriors' conquering the Indian subcontinent. The invaders apparently shoved the local men aside, took their women and set up the rigid caste system that exists today. Their descendants are still the elite within Hindu society. Thus today's genetic patterns, the researchers explained, vividly reflect a historic event, or events, that occurred 3,000 or 4,000 years ago. The gene patterns 'are consistent with a historical scenario in which invading Caucasoids—primarily males—established the caste system and occupied the highest positions, placing the indigenous population, who were more similar to Asians, in lower caste positions.' The data implies then 'that there was a group of males with European affinities who were largely responsible for this invasion 3,000 or 4,000 years ago,' said geneticist Lynn Jorde of the University of Utah. Further, 'when we look at the different components within the upper caste, the group with the greatest European similarity of all is the warrior class, the Kshatriya, who are still at the top of the Hindu castes, with the Brahmins,' Jorde said."*
— "History of Ancient Indian Conquest Told in Modern Genes, Experts Say," *San Francisco Chronicle*, May 26, 1999.

## Appendix 2: Genetic Evidence of Europeans in Ancient China

*"After years of controversy and political intrigue, archaeologists using genetic testing have proven that Caucasians roamed China's Tarim Basin 1,000 years before East Asian people arrived. The research, which the Chinese government has appeared to have delayed making public out of concerns of fueling Uighur Muslim separatism in its western-most Xinjiang region, is based on a cache of ancient dried-out corpses that have been found around the Tarim Basin in recent decades."* — "Genetic testing reveals awkward truth about Xinjiang's famous mummies" (Agence France-Presse), April 19, 2005.

*"(T)he 2,500-year-old Linzi population showed greater genetic similarity to present-day European populations than to present-day east Asian populations. The 2,000-year-old Linzi population had features that were intermediate between the present-day European/2,500-year-old Linzi populations and the present-day east Asian populations. These relationships suggest the occurrence of drastic spatiotemporal changes in the genetic structure of Chinese people during the past 2,500 years."* — "Genetic Structure of a 2,500-Year-Old Human Population in China and Its Spatiotemporal Changes," *Molecular Biology and Evolution* 17:1396–1400 (2000).

## Appendix 3: Western European Genetic Remnants in Egypt

*"We analyzed Y-chromosome haplotypes in the Nile River Valley in Egypt in 274 unrelated males, using the p49a,f TaqI polymorphism. These individuals were born in three regions along the river: in Alexandria (the Delta and Lower Egypt), in Upper Egypt, and in Lower Nubia. Fifteen different p49a,f TaqI haplotypes are present in Egypt, the three most common being haplotype V (39.4%), haplotype XI (18.9%), and haplotype IV (13.9%).*

*It is interesting to relate this peculiar north/south differentiation, a pattern of genetic variation deriving from the two uniparentally inherited genetic systems (mtDNA and Y chromosome), to specific historic events. Since the beginning of Egyptian history (3200–3100 BC), the legendary king Menes united Upper and Lower Egypt. Migration from north to south may coincide with the Pharaonic colonization of Nubia, which occurred initially during the Middle Kingdom (12th Dynasty, 1991–1785 BC), and more permanently during the New Kingdom, from the reign of Thotmosis III (1490–1437 BC).*

*The main migration from south to north may coincide with the 25th Dynasty (730–655 BC), when kings from Napata (in Nubia) conquered Egypt. Concerning less frequent Y-haplotypes in Egypt, haplotype VII distinguishes itself by increased preponderance north of the Mediterranean and in Eastern Europe (Lucotte et al., [1996]). Haplotype XV is the most widespread Y-haplotype in Western Europe (Lucotte and Hazout, [1996]), where its frequency decreases from west to east (Semino et al., [1996]; Lucotte and Loirat, [1999])."* — "Y-chromosome haplotypes in Egypt," *American Journal of Physical Anthropology,* Volume 121, Issue 1, Pages 63–66.

## Appendix 4: Genetic Evidence of Racial Mixing in Greece

*"Greeks are found to have a substantial relatedness to sub-Saharan (Ethiopian) people, which separate them from other Mediterranean groups. Both Greeks and Ethiopians share quasi-specific DRB1 alleles, such as *0305, *0307, *0411, *0413, *0416, *0417, *0420, *1110, *1112, *1304 and *1310. Genetic distances are closer between Greeks and Ethiopian/sub-Saharan groups than to any other Mediterranean group and finally Greeks cluster with Ethiopians/sub-Saharans in both neighbor joining dendrograms and correspondence analyses. The conclusion is that part of the Greek genetic pool may be sub-Saharan and that the admixture has occurred at an uncertain but ancient time."* — "HLA genes in Macedonians and the sub-Saharan origin of the Greeks," *Tissue Antigens,* February 2001, vol. 57, no. 2, pp. 118–127.

A study of mtDNA in Greece revealed the presence of the HpaI morph 1 sequence, which is a Mongoloid marker, introduced either through slavery or the mixed race Ottoman occupation. — "Mitochondrial DNA polymorphism in northern Greece," *National Library of Medicine,* PubMed, 1: Hum Biol. 1994 Aug. 66(4):601–11.

African Blood Groups in Greece: *"As usual in the Mediterranean area CDe is high, and cDe, presumably from African admixture, reaches about 6 percent." (p73) Cyprus: ". . . the presence of over 5 percent cDe suggests African immigration."* (p73) — Mourant AE, Kopéc AC, Domaniewska-Sobczak K. *The distribution of the human blood groups and other polymorphisms,* London, Oxford University Press, 1976.

According to a study conducted by Lluís Quintana-Murci et al and published in *The American Journal of Human Genetics,* (Volume 68, 2001, pages 537–542), the Middle Eastern Haplogroup HG9 runs at 28% in Greece. — "Y-Chromosome Lineages Trace Diffusion of People and Languages in Southwestern Asia," *The American Journal of Human Genetics,* 68:537–542, 2001.

Less than 50% of Greek Y-Chromosomes are of European origin, with the majority being 25% sub-Saharan/North African; 25% Middle Eastern; a small portion Asiatic. — "The Human Y Chromosome: An Evolutionary Marker Comes of Age," *Nature Reviews Genetics* 4, 598–612 (2003), August 2003 Vol 4 No 8.

## Appendix 5: Classical Literature References to Race

References to race abound in the works of Homer, the blind poet to whom credit is given for the two classic epics, *The Iliad,* and *The Odyssey.* Some selected quotes:

*"While he was thus in two minds, and was drawing his mighty sword from its scabbard, Minerva came down from heaven and seized the son of Peleus by his yellow hair."* — *The Iliad,* Book I.

*"As a cow stands lowing over her first calf, even so did yellow-haired Menelaus bestride Patroclus."* — *The Iliad,* Book XVII.

*"There fair-haired Rhadamanthus reigns, and men lead an easier life than anywhere else in the world."* — *The Odyssey,* Book 4.

*"Trust me for that,"* said she (Minerva, talking to Odysseus), *"I will begin by disguising you so that no human being shall know you; I will cover your body with wrinkles; you shall lose all your yellow hair."* — *The Odyssey,* Book 13.

*"On this Minerva came close up to him and said, "Son of Arceisius— best friend I have in the world—pray to the blue-eyed damsel, and to Jove her father."* — *The Odyssey,* Book 24.

The following quote is from Euripides, the ancient playwright: *"Ye gods! What joy to hark them on, to grasp the barbed dart, to poise Thessalian hunting-spears close to my golden hair, then let them fly."* — *Hippolytus.*

## Appendix 6: The Negro Presence in Ancient Greece

The classical Greeks most commonly described Negroes as "Ethiopians." In the works of Diodorus Siculus (Book 3.8.2), Ethiops, for example, are associated with black skin, woolly hair, and a flat nose. Arrian's *Indica* 6.9 states that the natives of southern India, though blacks, are not so flat-nosed or so woolly-haired as the Ethiopians.

Aristotle, in his *Physiognomia* 6.812A, said that those with "woolly hair" and those who were too swarthy (*Phgn.* 6.812B.) were cowardly. He meant this about Ethiopians. Xenophanes (*Fragments* 16, Diels) in a similar contrast recounts that the Negroes represent their gods as black faced and flat nosed, while the Thracians show their gods to be blue eyed and red haired.

Aristotle mentions a woman of Elis whose daughter by a Negro, was not Negroid but whose grandson was (*Generation of Animals,* 1.18.722A; *History of Animals,* 7.6.586A). This passage would be meaningless unless it referred to the offspring of a black-white union.

Plutarch (*De Sera Numinis Vindicta,* 21) relates a similar story about a Greek woman whose black baby caused her to be accused of adultery, although an investigation of her lineage revealed that she was the great granddaughter of an Ethiopian. Reference was made to a mulatto priest of Isis: his racial appearance is described as follows: *"... this man, whose cranium belongs to the type of Asia Minor and whose lower face and neck are those of a Negro, is obviously of a mixed race; we are dealing with a mulatto ..."* — Poulsen P, 1913 *Tête de Prêtre d'Isis Trouvée a Athènes* (Mélanges Holleaux, pp. 217–223. A. Picard, Paris, p. 218 and pl. VI).

Mixture between blacks and whites in the Greek world is confirmed by the evidence of sculpture. A vase of a temple boy from Olynthus is described by Robinson as a boy with *"almost negroid features"* (Robinson D. Y., 1931 *Excavations at Olynthus, Part IV, The Terra-cottas of Olynthus Found in 1928,* The Johns Hopkins University Press, Baltimore, p. 78, no. 384 and pl. 42).

Another Olynthus head whose features Robinson also regards as "almost negroid" is another obvious product of racial mixing (ibid p. 87, no. 405 and pl. 45). Both Aristotle and Plutarch discuss the racial characteristics of second and third generation black-white racial mixes in their works: *"Further, children are like their more remote ancestors from whom nothing has come, for the resemblances recur at an interval of many generations, as in the case of the woman in Elis who had intercourse with the Aethiop; her daughter was not an Aethiop but the son of the daughter was."* — Aristotle, *Gen. An.* 1.18.722A.

*"But parents may pass on resemblance after several generations, as in the case of the woman in Elis, who committed adultery with a negro; in this case it was not the woman's own daughter, but the daughter's child that was a blackamoor"* — Aristotle, *Hist. An.,* 7.6.586A.

Further references to racially mixed types stretching over generations can be found in Plutarch's *De Sera Numinis Vindicta,* 21.

## Appendix 7: Genetic Evidence of Racial Mixing in Italy

*"Each of the subregions analysed (NW Africa and SW Europe) shows sequences that originated on the opposite shore of the Mediterranean. This is particularly clear in the case of U6 and L in SW Europe. L sequences are found at frequencies 3% in Iberia and 2.4% in Italy. Three Italian L sequences have been described throughout Africa, and the remaining five are not found in >1,000 sub-Saharan individuals. Thus, the presence of L sequences cannot be attributed to migration from NW Africa, and may instead represent gene flow from other sources, such as the Neolithic expansion or the Roman slave trade."* — "Joining the Pillars of Hercules: mtDNA Sequences Show Multidirectional Gene Flow in the Western Mediterranean," *Annals of Human Genetics,* Vol. 67 Issue 4 Page 312, July 2003.

*"Among 64 individuals from 21 families with at least one known hemoglobin S carrier, African blood group markers were detected in 7 (11%). These findings indicate that hemoglobin S is only one of multiple African genes present in contemporary Sicilian populations."* — "Blood group phenotypes and the origin of sickle cell hemoglobin in Sicilians," *Acta Haematol,* 1978, 60(6):350–7.

*"Sicilian Hb S was identical to that found in USA black patients in electrophoretic mobility on both starch and citrate agar media, solubility, mechanical precipitation rate of oxyhaemoglobins, and minimum gelling concentration, as well as by peptide mapping and amino-acid analysis of all beta-chain peptides. Taken together with the presence in Sicily of African blood group markers and certain historical considerations, it seems clear that the source of Hb S in Sicily is Africa."* — "Sickle cell disease in Sicily," *National Library of Medicine,* PubMed, 1: J Med Genet. 1980 Feb. 17(1):34–8.

According to a study conducted by Lluís Quintana-Murci et al, the Middle Eastern Haplogroup HG9 runs at 20% in Italy. — "Y-Chromosome Lineages Trace Diffusion of People and Languages in Southwestern Asia," *American Journal of Human Genetics,* 68:537–542, 2001.

## Appendix 8: Classical Roman Writers on Race Mixing in Rome

Interracial unions were common enough in the time of the Roman satirist Juvenal (55–27 AD) for him to make specific mention of them. In his *Satire VI,* Juvenal, while discussing the advisability or otherwise of abortions, warns husbands that their wives may bear mulatto children: *"Rejoice, poor wretch; give her the stuff to drink whatever it be, with your own hand: for were she willing to get big and trouble her womb with bouncing babes, you might perhaps find yourself the father of an Ethiopian; and someday a coloured heir, whom you would rather not meet by daylight, would fill all the places in your will."* — Juvenal, *Satire VI,* lines 596–600.

The Roman writer Martial (38–104 AD), in attacking misconduct by Roman wives, mentions a Roman woman who bore her husband seven children, none of whom was of his *"race."* Martial says: *"One of them, with woolly hair, like a Moor, seems to be the son of Santra, the cook. The second, with a flat nose and thick lips, is the image of Pannicus, the wrestler . . . of the two daughters, one is black . . . and belongs to Crotus, the flute player."* — *Epigrams* VI, 39.

Roman women who had mulatto children were often charged with adultery in Roman courts, with the accusation being that the mixed race nature of their children was evidence of their adultery with slaves or nonwhite males other than their husbands. A common defense used in Roman courts was that of "maternal impression" which claimed that babies in the womb could be affected by the mother merely viewing, or being close to, nonwhites. As ridiculous as this defense was, it was used by the famous orator Quintilian (35–96 AD) to successfully defend a Roman woman on an adultery charge (St Jerome, *Liber de Nominibus Hebraicis (de Genesi)*, ed. J. P. Migne, p. 985).

Another famous Roman orator, Calpurnius Flaccus, (circa second century AD) also discussed the issue of *"maternal impression"* as an explanation for mulatto children, writing in a work entitled *De Natus Aethiops* ('Of Ethiopian Birth') he makes the white mother of a mulatto child say: *"Tell me then, did I love a Negro?"* She did not, and asserts that *"the element of chance may effect a great deal within the womb."* Of the child's color she says: *"You see there the skin scorched by an imperfection of the blood."* — *Bibloteca Latina*, Vol. 80.

Plutarch (*De Sera Numinis Vindicta*, 21 [563]) tells the story of a woman who gave birth to a black child and was accused of adultery, but subsequent investigation revealed that her great grandfather was an Ethiopian.

The Roman scholar Pliny (23–79 AD) mentioned yet another example of mulatto children: *"One certain example is that of the renowned boxer Nicaeus, born at Byzantium, whose mother was the daughter of adultery with a Negro. Her complexion was no different from that of the others [other white women], but her son Nicaeus appeared like his Negro grandfather."* — *Naturalis Historia* VII.12.51.

Racial mixing also took place in the Roman colonies, and specifically the colony they called "Africa." Claudian (365–408 AD) raged against the racial mixing taking place under the "Moor" ('Maur') Gildo, who had been appointed ruler of the colony of Africa by the emperor Valentian. Claudian wrote: *"When tired of each noblest matron, (Gildo) hands her over to the Moors. These Sidonian mothers, married in Carthage City, must needs be mate with barbarians. He thrusts upon me an Ethiopian son-in-law. This hideous hybrid affects the cradle."* — *De Bello Gildonico* I, 189.

### Appendix 9: Famous Historians on the Racial Decline of the Roman Empire

Although many historians have ignored the racial factor in the fall of the Roman Empire (and some have never even thought about it), there have been many who recognized race as the critical element. Amongst the more famous of these was Professor Tenney Frank, from Johns Hopkins University. Professor Frank, a recognized authority on the history of ancient Rome, is most famous for his work *An Economic History of Rome,* but his other works included the important *Race mixture in the Roman Empire,* published in the *American Historical Review* (July 1916, vol. 21, no. 4: 689–708).

Along with Frank, many other well-known and respected historians dealt with the issue of the Roman population change. Amongst these were Professor A.M. Duff, Charles Merivale, George La Piana, Theodor Mommsen, and the multiple authors of the *Cambridge Ancient History* and the Encyclopedia Britannica's *Historians History of the World.* Below follows a selection of quotations from these sources, discussing the change in the racial makeup of classical Roman society.

In his work, *Race Mixture in the Roman Empire,* Frank outlined how he first realized that race mixture was the cause of the change in Roman society. By studying the names of graves on the Appian Way in Rome, he found that huge numbers of late Roman Republic inhabitants had names which originated in the Levant, or Middle East, in strong contrast to the early inhabitants of Rome, who had Latin names. *"Unfortunately, most of the sociological and political data of the empire are provided by satirists. When Tacitus informs us that in Nero's day a great many of Rome's senators and knights were descendants of slaves and that the native stock had dwindled to surprisingly small proportions, we are not sure whether we are not to take it as an exaggerated thrust by an indignant Roman of the old stock"* (ibid).

*"It is probable that when these men wrote a very small percentage of the free plebians on the streets of Rome could prove unmixed Italian descent. By far the larger part—perhaps ninety percent—had Oriental blood in their veins"* (ibid).

Frank made a determined study of the tombs and monuments in Rome and the surrounding area, drawing up a database of over 13,900 different names. His analysis of those names concluded that about 70 percent were Greek, not Latin, in origin. These "Greek" names for the greatest part belonged not to true Greeks, but to Middle Easterners who had adopted Greek names, particularly after the conquest of their region by Alexander the Great.

The writer Juvenal, speaking of the Roman population, pointed out the Levantine origin of many of these people in his writings, referring to the Syrian River, the Orontes: *"These dregs call themselves Greeks but how small a portion is from Greece; the River Orontes has long flowed into the Tiber."* — Juvenal, *Satires III,* 62.

Frank went on to describe where these people with Greek names had come from: *"Therefore, when the urban inscriptions show that seventy percent of the city slaves and freedmen bear Greek names and that a larger portion of the children who have Latin names have parents of Greek names, this at once implies that the East was the source of most of them . . . by far the larger portion came from the Orient, especially from Syria and the provinces of Asia Minor, with some from Egypt and Africa (which for racial classification may be taken with the Orient). Some are from Spain and Gaul, but a considerable portion of these came originally from the East. Very few slaves are recorded from the Alpine and Danube provinces, while Germans rarely appear, except among the imperial bodyguard"* (Frank, ibid).

Frank explained the push and pull effect that led to the racial makeup change in Rome. He pointed out how native Romans were drawn away from Rome by colonization and military service, and of how their places were taken by slaves, in serfdom and as freedmen. *"During the early empire, twenty to thirty legions, drawn of course from the best free stock, spent their twenty years of vigor in garrison duty while the slaves, exempt from such services, lived at home and increased in numbers. In other words, the native stock was supported by less than a normal birthrate, whereas the stock of foreign extraction had not only a fairly normal birthrate but a liberal quota of manumissions to its advantage"* (Frank, ibid).

It is estimated that the slave population of Rome and its immediate surrounding area at the time of Augustus (circa 30 BC) was some 300,000–350,000 out of a population of about 900,000–950,000 (Hopkins, K. *Conquerors and Slaves, Sociological Studies in Roman History,* Vol. 1 Cambridge, 1978). For all of Italy, the figure was approximately the same. A figure of around two million slaves out of a population of about six million at the time of Augustus is accurate—this means that at this early stage one in every three persons in Rome and Italy was a slave (John Madden, *Slavery in the Roman Empire—Numbers and Origins,* University College, Galway, Classics Ireland, 1996 Vol. 3, University College, Dublin, Ireland).

The historian George La Piana said the following about how native Romans were drawn away from Rome by colonization and of how "new races" took their place in Rome: *"To this increase in the population the native stock seems not to have contributed much. Decimated by long wars, fought by citizen crimes, which secured to Rome a Mediterranean empire, its ranks were thinned still further by the withdrawal of colonies of citizens to the provinces beyond the sea and by a heavy decline in the birthrate even among the poorer classes. The native Roman and Italian population steadily dwindled and the gaps were filled by a new race"* (George La Piana, "Foreign Groups in Rome During the First Centuries of the Empire," *The Harvard Theological Review,* vol. XX, pp. 188, 189).

Far thinking Roman leaders saw the decline in native Roman numbers and the threat it posed. Professor A.M. Duff remarked, *"One of the most serious evils with which the imperial government was called upon to contend was the decline in population. Not only had the Italian stock almost disappeared from the towns, but the descendants of freedmen had not been born in sufficient numbers to take its place. Accordingly, while the Lex Papia Poppaea offered privileges to freeborn citizens for the possession of three children, it used the whole question of inheritances of freedmen and freedwomen for the encouragement of procreation"* (A. M. Duff, *Freedmen in the Early Roman Empire,* Oxford University Press, 1928, p. 191).

Charles Merivale, another renowned expert on Roman history, continued the story: *"The centre of the empire had been more exhausted by the civil wars than any of the provinces. The rapid disappearance of the free population had been remarked with astonishment and dismay, at least from the time of the Gracchi. If the numbers actually maintained on the soil of the Peninsula had not diminished, it was abundantly certain that the independent native races had given way almost throughout its extent to a constant importation of slaves"* (Charles Merivale, *The Romans Under the Empire*, vol. 2. pp. 395–397).

*"The remedies to which Caesar resorted would appear as frivolous as they were arbitrary . . . He prohibited all citizens between the age of twenty and forty from remaining abroad more than three years together, while, as a matter of state policy, he placed more special restrictions upon the movements of the youths of senatorial families"* (ibid).

Merivale also points out how Julius Caesar saw the danger of slave labor flooding Rome, and actually passed a law forbidding certain types of labor-intensive work from using only slaves: *"He (Caesar) required also that the owners of herds and flocks, to the maintenance of which large tracts of Italy were exclusively devoted, should employ free labor to the extent of at least one-third of the whole. Such laws could only be executed constantly under the vigilant superintendence of a sovereign ruler. They fell in fact into immediate disuse, or rather were never acted upon at all. They served no other purpose at the time but to evince Caesar's perception of one of the fatal tendencies of the age (i.e. race deterioration in Italy), to which the eyes of most statesmen of the day were already open"* (ibid).

Duff pointed out that by the time of Octavian Augustus, there were significant numbers of "Orientals" in Rome: *"Even in Augustus' day the process of Orientalization had gone too far. The great emperor saw the clouds, but he did not know they had actually burst. His legislation would have been prudent and not a whit excessive a century earlier; but in his time Rome was a cosmopolitan city, and the doom of the Empire was already sealed"* (Duff, ibid).

Frank's study of the Roman family lines revealed exactly how native Romans vanished. He wrote: *"The race went under. The legislation of Augustus and his successors, while aiming at preserving the native stock, was of the myopic kind so usual in social lawmaking, and failing to reckon with the real nature of the problem involved, it utterly missed the mark"* (Frank, ibid).

*"We know, for instance, in Caesar's day of forty-five patricians, only one of whom is represented by posterity when Hadrian came to power. Of the families of nearly four hundred senators recorded in 65 AD under Nero, all trace of a half is lost by Nerva's day, a generation later"* (ibid).

*"At the same time many were tempted to emigrate to the colonies across the sea which Julius Caesar and Augustus founded. Many went away to Romanize the provinces, while society was becoming Orientalized at home. Because slave labor had taken over almost all jobs, the free born could not*

*compete with them. They had to sell their small farms or businesses and move to the cities. Here they were placed on the dole because of unemployment. They were, at first, encouraged to emigrate to the more prosperous areas of the empire—to Gaul, North Africa, and Spain. Hundreds of thousands left Italy and settled in the newly-acquired land"* (Duff, ibid).

*"Such a vast number left Italy—leaving it to the Orientals—that finally restrictions had to be passed to prevent the complete depopulation of the Latin stock, but as we have seen, the laws were never effectively put into force. The migrations increased and Italy was being left to another race. The Roman thus gave away to the Easterner in Italy, while he made a place for himself in the provinces"* (Duff, ibid).

The *Cambridge Ancient History* adds: *"Augustus, recognizing the serious infiltration of alien blood into the body politic, introduced restrictions on manumission"* (*Cambridge Ancient History*, vol. VI, pp. 755, 756). *"Yet this proved but a slight check, and Tacitus records a significant remark that 'if freedmen were marked off as a separate grade, then the scanty number of free-born would be evident.' This shows how very few native free-born were left in Italy by our era. This freemen were now freedmen—ex-slaves or their descendants. They were taking over the complete population"* (ibid).

Freed slaves, mostly of Syrian or eastern extraction, became numerically strong in Rome. The emperor Philip was born in Syria, and became known as "Philip the Arabian" as a result. *"It seems unquestionable that the slaves from the eastern provinces were numerically preponderant in Rome, and—what is still more important—that they played a more important part in Roman life. Rome's policy of manumitting slaves was very liberal and the grant of freedom and citizenship made it possible for them to become merged in the citizen body of Rome. Former slaves and sons of slaves spread into trades and crafts that required civil standing, and in Cicero's day it was these people who already constituted the larger element of the plebian classes"* (La Piana, ibid).

*"One thing which must, most of all, have shocked the aristocracy, even though of recent date, was the large number of Orientals, especially freedmen, who—had been given some of the highest posts in the empire"* (*Cambridge Ancient History*, ibid).

Tacitus complained that in Nero's day, most of the senators and members of the aristocracy were now men of ex-slave status—and most of these were of eastern origin. By the third century AD, many of the emperors were actually descendants of the slaves of earlier centuries. La Piana stated it this way: *"The denationalized capital of the great empire came to be ruled by the offspring of races which originally had come to the city only to serve"* (La Piana, ibid).

*"This Orientalization of Rome's populace has a more important bearing than is usually accorded it upon the larger question of why the spirit and acts of imperial Rome are totally different from those of the republic. There was a complete change in the temperament!"* wrote Frank. *"There is*

*today a healthy activity in the study of the economic factors that contributed to Rome's decline. But what lay behind and constantly reacted upon all such causes of Rome's disintegration was, after all, to a considerable extent, the fact that the people who had built Rome had given way to a different race"* (ibid).

*"The profuse intermixture of race, containing without interruption from 200 BC far into the history of the Empire, produced a type utterly different from that which characterized the heroes of the early republic"* (ibid).

The replacement of the original Roman people by immigrants was marked first at the lowest levels of society, but then gradually made its way up through all levels. Septimus Severus was the first Roman emperor who was not of Roman extraction, born in North Africa. His wife was Julia Domna, a Syrian. Severus was succeeded by his two sons, who reigned for a while together, and then successively. The throne later came to two grandsons. In all, the Syro-Phoenicians dominated the Roman Empire from 193 AD to 235 AD.

The *Historian's History of the World* describes this period so: *"The Syrian emperors, as far as political traditions are concerned, inasmuch as they were not Romans and had none of the Roman prejudices, often give proof of an openness of mind which would have been impossible to the great emperors of the second century, all of whom were intensely conservative. They flung the doors of the empire wide open"* (*The Historians' History of the World, A Comprehensive Narrative of the Rise and Development of Nations from the Earliest Times as recorded by over Two Thousand of the Great Writers of All Ages,* edited by Henry Smith William,s et al, Encyclopedia Britannica, 1904 [5th ed., 1926] vol. 6, p. 404).

# INDEX

1443968R0

Printed in Great Britain by
Amazon.co.uk, Ltd.,
Marston Gate.